MYSTERIES AND SECRETS OF THE MASONS

LIONEL AND PATRICIA FANTHORPE

MYSTERIES AND SECRETS OF THE MASONS

THE STORY BEHIND THE MASONIC ORDER

THE DUNDURN GROUP
TORONTO

Copy-Editor: Michael Carroll
Illustrations: Theo Fanthorpe
Design: Andrew Roberts
Printer: Webcom

Library and Archives Canada Cataloguing in Publication

Fanthorpe, R. Lionel
    Mysteries and secrets of the Masons : the story behind the Masonic Order / Lionel and Patricia Fanthorpe.

Includes bibliographical references.

ISBN-10: 1-55002-622-4
ISBN-13: 978-1-55002-622-1

1. Freemasonry--History. I. Fanthorpe, Patricia II. Title.

HS403.F35 2006   366'.109   C2006-901336-5

1   2   3   4   5   10   09   08   07   06

  Canada

We acknowledge the support of the Canada Council for the Arts and the Ontario Arts Council for our publishing program. We also acknowledge the financial support of the Government of Canada through the Book Publishing Industry Development Program and The Association for the Export of Canadian Books, and the Government of Ontario through the Ontario Book Publishers Tax Credit program, and the Ontario Media Development Corporation's Ontario Book Initiative.

Care has been taken to trace the ownership of copyright material used in this book. The author and the publisher welcome any information enabling them to rectify any references or credits in subsequent editions.

J. Kirk Howard, President

Printed and bound in Canada.
Printed on recycled paper.

www.dundurn.com

Dundurn Press	Gazelle Book Services Limited	Dundurn Press
8 Market Street, Suite 200	White Cross Mills	2250 Military Road
Toronto, Ontario, Canada	High Town, Lancaster, England	Tonawanda NY
M5E 1M6	LA1 4XS	U.S.A. 14150

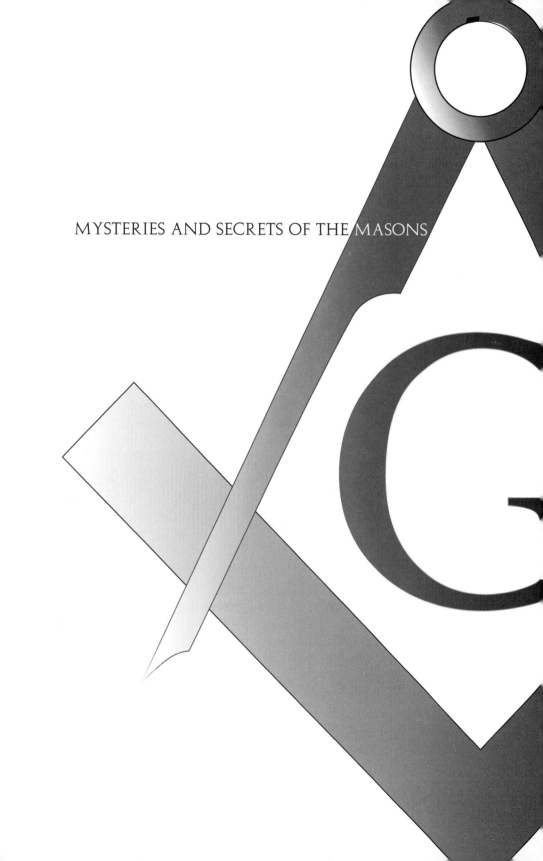

MYSTERIES AND SECRETS OF THE MASONS

This book is dedicated to all our Masonic friends worldwide — and especially to the Brethren of Bowers Lodge and the Wheatsheaf Lodge in Britain.

TABLE OF CONTENTS

FOREWORD

THE WRITER of this foreword is not a Freemason, never has been and, now at ninety-two, is never likely to be. However, he has had many friends over the years who are Masons and has come to understand something of what it means to them. Freemasonry has established itself as an impressive brotherhood of like-minded people, perhaps the oldest and largest in the world, numbering now, reportedly, some four million members. They join from all over the free world, from all occupations and professions, and to date, the movement shows no signs of diminishing in strength or influence.

Centuries old now, what gives it such appeal? Some of its qualities are obvious even to an outsider like me. First, there is its known strength in numbers. Success is always attractive as any good football team will prove. Crowds follow a winning side. The Masonic movement has never needed actively to recruit nor ever feared for its future. Where other organizations have come and gone, Masonry seems, over the years, as firmly rooted as ever.

Freemasonry has always had the attraction of high ideals and aspirations. The movement is not a religion competing with other religions, even if some of its meeting places seem to be called temples. However, all those who join the movement are religious people. All Masons are believers in God, and though, as in the finest of families and the strongest of churches, some few bring discredit on the faith they acknowledge, all Masons are people of principle and ideals and are believers in social justice and equality. Masons come from all walks of life and abilities but, as the movement demands, all are deemed equal one with the other.

Masons also have well-established and high humanitarian commitments. All Freemasons look after their own. The orphaned, the sick, and the elderly are never left friendless and uncomforted. In fact, Masons reach farther than their own to all others falling prey to the "slings and arrows of outrageous fortune."

Moreover, the movement has always had an aura of secrecy about it, which some will always find attractive. As far as this writer is aware, what secrets there are, be they matters of ritual or ceremonial or anything else, Masonic members are pledged to keep safe. However, where there are secrets the urge to expose them is ever-present. The great illusionists and escapologists have lived to face seeing some of their greatest exploits revealed to the outside world, and, sadly, often by members of their own craft. The Masonic movement has not been exempt from such disclosures, and books by the score, some written from inside the movement, are there on library shelves for all to read.

The writers of this book have been scrupulous in not following any such examples. Although I have known the Reverend Lionel Fanthorpe for more than twenty years, have read all of his recent books, and written the forewords to many of them, I believe, but am not certain, that he is or has been a Freemason. If so, knowing him as I do, he will have risen to be a grand master! Equally certain, from my knowledge of him, none of the secrets of the movement will be other than safe in his hands. He is not that kind of writer.

What the authors have done in this book is to delve deeply into the background, to the roots of the movement, and identify for us the people from whom worldwide Masonry took its inspiration. Those they highlight for us, they give the term *proto-Mason*. These will not have been Masons in our sense of the word, by name or profession, but as our writers see it, they represented in themselves and in their teaching and practices all the qualities and ideals accepted later as the foundation of the modern-day Masonic movement.

The Fanthorpes have probed deeply into diverse cultures, many civilizations, and through many centuries. The research work involved must have been immense, defeating most of us lesser mortals. Some of the proto-Masons they resurrect for us are of heroic stuff. One such is Cyrus, ruler of the once great Persian Empire, who set out the principles on which his vast conglomerate of peoples was to be ruled. They reveal a largeness of heart, deep humanitarian care, and benevolence to the downtrodden and displaced. Cyrus established a bill of rights even the most enlightened of modern-day nations would welcome. The Persian king has long gone to join the immortals. Even the name Persia is used no longer. His empire has long vanished. But our authors believe that he lives on in the work and fellowship of the Masonic movement of today.

Along with the obvious scholarship and research there are flights of imagination in this book and somewhat daring speculations. The Fanthorpes sometimes go in directions and make claims my more prosaic aged brain would never dare to go or make. Other readers may be more daring than I am. In any case, nothing diminishes my admiration for what they have achieved. This book follows almost immediately on their work on the Templars, equally well researched and now being widely read. *Mysteries and Secrets of the Masons* will prove to be a worthy successor to *Mysteries and Secrets of the Templars*. I wish it well. All Freemasons will be proud to read it. It brings nothing but credit to their movement. Hopefully, many who are not Masons will also read this book and accept the movement as a power for good and its ideals a worthy example for all.

Canon Stanley Mogford, MA
Cardiff, Wales, 2005

Chapter 1

WHAT IS FREEMASONRY AND WHAT ARE ITS OBJECTIVES?

THE GREATER a thing is, and the more important it is, the harder it is to describe, define, and analyze. To attempt to answer the basic questions about Freemasonry is almost as deep and wide an undertaking as asking what life itself is, what our universe is, and what our place within it is as members of the human race.

A march of 10,000 miles begins with the first step, and the first step in understanding the mysteries of Freemasonry is to consider it as a fraternal organization, a worldwide brotherhood, but a brotherhood that is not exclusively gender-oriented. The best Freemasonry includes a sisterhood, as well.

With the kinds of bonds between its members that exist in the best, the most loving, the most loyal, and the most mutually supportive extended families, Freemasonry, too, can be thought of as a family. Just as an ideal family is held together by certain shared ideas and ideals, so is Freemasonry. Freemasons from every walk of life, from every nation, and from every ethnic group share an extremely high moral code and excellent ethical principles. They also share profound metaphysical, theological, and philosophical beliefs. Freemasonry places great stress on the word *free*. There is immense tolerance and understanding within its codes of belief. Masons generally accept the existence of a Supreme Being and see the structural and practical aspects of architectural Masonry as reflecting the creative and sustaining work of that Supreme Being. Nevertheless, an honest, open, objective, unbiased, and inquiring mind is the surest mark of a real Freemason.

Freemasonry is also definable as an *esoteric* art. Just as every profession has its own special secrets, so there are aspects of Masonry that are carefully protected. Barristers, medical practitioners, and computer wizards all tend to have their own specific, internal, and professional knowledge that is usually kept within the group. Freemasonry, too, has its parallel secrets.

Part of this esoteric knowledge stems from the Masonic initiatory system. Understandably, there are various degrees within Masonry as more and more of the ethics and metaphysics of the Craft are revealed to the members one stage at a time. Those who understand the language of Masonry will readily describe these gradually unfolding mysteries as *a system of morality veiled in allegory and illustrated by symbols.*

All individuals and organizations — religious, social, or political — need to have aims and objectives, and Freemasonry is no exception to this general rule. Each Masonic lodge may vary slightly in the way that it phrases its aims and objectives, but every Mason and every lodge would agree about the following central aims and objectives:

- To practise, encourage, and advocate honesty, integrity, friendship, and charity as aspects of the individual's personal life and his or her social life.
- To serve and be loyal to one's own religious faith, but to acknowledge and respect different faiths and to accord them equal value. In the same way, where there are duties and responsibilities to a Mason's home community, he or she aims to comply with those communal duties and demands — insofar as they are in perfect harmony with the good of the wider community.
- Freemasons aim to do all in their power to show the world that in business and in private life, as well as in their personal relationships, they and the Masonic society they represent are upright, fair, and honest.
- Masons strive to be team players, to enjoy the company of other Masons, to participate in Masonic fellowship, and to work as members of the worldwide Masonic team.
- Freemasons attempt to do everything possible to make good people even better and more valuable to society. They believe in developing themselves as individuals and in trying to improve the outside world through education, social interaction, and discussion.

- Masons recognize the importance of time, our most precious commodity. They seek to balance leisure with work, religious thought with practical service to others.
- Freemasons regard human beings as having mental, spiritual, and physical gifts, and Freemasonry teaches its members how to make the best use of all of these gifts.
- Christ taught his disciples the Parable of the Talents. Masons follow the teachings of that parable. They seek to use whatever talents God has given them for the benefit of their families, friends, and neighbours. They aim to do this through their private life, as well as in their business and professional work.
- Freemasons endeavour to be totally honest and forthcoming about their membership in the organization, especially if there is any risk that a conflict of interest might arise.
- Despite what is often wrongly thought about the way that members of the Craft may seek to help one another, real Freemasons never use their membership to promote their own interests.

The above points are the laudable and unobjectionable surface definitions and the declared aims and objectives of Freemasonry. But there is much, much more, and although it is equally laudable and unobjectionable, it goes far deeper and raises enormous questions.

As a young newcomer to Freemasonry, co-author Lionel was talking confidentially to a far older and much more experienced, high-ranking Mason. They had recently been participating in a Masonic service in their temple, and referring back to the nature and purpose of that particular service, the wise old man said: "There has to be much more to it than this. It wouldn't have flourished, prospered, and survived as it has unless there were deeper secrets than these."

Co-author Lionel has pondered that wise man's words for more than thirty years. There are intriguing truths and mysteries behind them. The real secrets of Freemasonry are far older and more profound than anything that takes place at a lodge meeting in a Masonic temple.

There can be no full and proper understanding of the mysteries and secrets of Freemasonry without very deep and thorough research into its earliest history, and that enigmatic history goes back a great deal farther than is generally understood. The real beginnings of Masonry in its most archaic forms are lost in the mists of time. To understand its true nature and purpose, those mists have to be penetrated. But before we start to explore those unfathomable, secret depths we need to examine in finer detail exactly what it is that makes a man or a woman a Mason.

Chapter 2

WHAT MAKES A MAN OR A WOMAN A MASON?

IN CHAPTER 1 we looked at the basic nature and principles of Freemasonry, along with its aims and objectives. It is clear that all the good fellowship and charitable activities that take place in normal Masonic lodge meetings are totally unobjectionable, as are the broader Masonic aims and objectives in general.

But there are undeniably stranger, older secrets that lurk in the history, and ancient prehistory, of Masonry. Before we proceed to examine them, however, we need to look more closely and in finer detail at what constitutes a real Freemason. It is easier to examine the past once the present that grew from it has been thoroughly analyzed. It is easier to trace the causes once their effects are properly understood.

Although Masonry is ordered, arranged, structured, and organized, it is nevertheless *Free*masonry. It has its national and international hierarchies, its provinces, districts, and separate lodges, yet for all its administrative efficiency and the clearly designated and understood functions of its competent and experienced officers, there is a remarkable freedom about it. Masons are strong-minded and independent men and women, yet theirs is a strength and independence that comes from law, order, and regulation. There is an important paradox here, one that needs to be described and explained in depth. *The apparent freedom of so-called anarchy is not real freedom at all.* The anarchical society without any order or structure is amorphous — without shape and without form. Nothing is free to move in three-dimensional space unless that three-dimensional space has a definable structure. There has to be an *up*, a *down*, and a *sideways* before any choice of directed movement is possible. The random life is not a free life. It is merely submission to forces beyond the individual's control — a leaf floating over white water. Real decision-making freedom for any human being requires a social structure that offers choices.

Freemasonry by its very nature provides as wide a range of options as it is possible to find anywhere. Within its educational structure, for example, there is the opportunity to go on indefinitely acquiring the vast amounts of data, knowledge, wisdom, and skill that are available to members. Within Freemasonry's social structure a Mason can join fellowship group after fellowship group, making interesting new friends every time. Within the Craft's charitable structure, a Mason can give his or her talent, time, and money to making the world a better place for those who are less fortunate. Within the brotherhood's moral, ethical, philosophical, and metaphysical structures, a Mason can meditate on the real meaning of life — and how best to live it — in the company of kindred spirits who have embarked on the same vital quest.

There can be no genuine freedom of mental and spiritual movement — there can be no authentic autonomy — without structures like these within which the freedom-loving, independent mind can make its choices. A man or woman is truly a Mason when he or she recognizes that true freedom of choice is dependent upon an awareness of order and structure.

What else confers Masonhood on a person?

It is already clear that Freemasons enjoy learning and recognize that it is a never-ending process. Knowledge is power, and a Mason enjoys acquiring such power, not to control or restrict people, but to help others at an optimum level when Masonic aid is needed and requested. (Control freaks suffer from a particularly sad form of mental illness that is about as far removed from Freemasonry as ice is from fire.) The true knowledge that constitutes real power never interferes with other people's lives: it keeps its opinions to itself *unless and until help is requested.* Once invited to assist or advise, a Mason responds with alacrity and enthusiasm.

Freemasons are, above all, charitable. The man or woman who gives unstintingly of his or her time, money, wisdom, and experience — such a person is a genuine Mason.

A Freemason takes a great interest in every aspect of life, in society, in the people around him or her. It is all too easy to complain that life is boring and that there is nothing fulfilling or worthwhile to do. Freemasonry teaches that genuine interest in other people and society in general is the surest shield against boredom and lassitude. To a Mason no problem — social or personal — is insoluble. Freemasons have the attitude that it is infinitely better to light one small candle than to curse the darkness. Although modern, speculative Freemasonry is not *active* Masonry in the sense that our predecessors understood it when they hewed stone and built cathedrals, castles, and palaces, it is *attitudinally* active. A true Masonic response to a personal or social problem is to say: "I may not be able to do *much* about it, *but I can and I will do everything in my power.*" Masons are the men and women who answer life's questions with a fearless and resounding "*Yes!*"

When co-author Lionel studied psychology at college and later lectured on it for Cambridge University's E-MB, he was particularly interested in the theory that a great deal of human behaviour is governed by reference to the ideal images that people have of themselves. It seems that many of us carry a role model around inside our minds, often a composite of people we have known and admired over the years. Having created this idealized man or woman whom we aspire to be, we experience satisfaction when we can fit our real selves closely and accurately into that profile. Conversely, when we think a thought, speak a word, or perform an action that falls short of our ideals, we feel disappointment and frustration. Prolonged and repeated failure to reach our ideals can be one of the root causes of depression.

There are two remedies. First, we need to understand this whole psychological situation. Once we realize that we *have* an internalized role model, we have given ourselves the psychological sculptor's chisels and mallet with which to re-examine and recarve our mind-statue. Is it ridiculously too high? Is it too small and unambitious? Think carefully, then change it as necessary. The second remedy is to increase our determination to reach our goals and actually to become that ideal man or woman whom we rightly and realistically aspire to be. As Socrates said so profoundly, "The unexamined life is not worth living."

Freemasons are men and women who take Socrates's advice. They examine their ideals and they examine their progress towards them.

So far we have studied Freemasonry along with its aims and objectives, analyzing those factors that make a man or a woman into a genuine Mason. Having focused sharply first on Masonry as a whole and then on Masons as individuals, it is possible to proceed to study the earliest origins of Masonry.

Chapter 3

THE EARLIEST ORIGINS OF MASONRY

HISTORY IS not simple. As we delve farther and farther into the remote and shadowy depths of the past, we uncover small scraps of evidence that over time become increasingly rare. Yet when those scant scraps of evidence are carefully and open-mindedly examined and analyzed, and when their possible links with other discoveries are acknowledged, their implications can be awesome and portentous.

Leaving aside the Judeo-Christian fundamentalist simplicity of a six-day creation and Bishop Ussher's naive starting date of 4004 BC, we can explore a great many equally interesting attempts to explain how our astonishing universe — *and we ourselves* — came into existence. Once we get away from the unsophisticated cosmological literalism that overpowered Ussher's otherwise impressive mind, we seem to find early Masonic *symbolism* in the Judeo-Christian account of creation as recorded in Genesis. Were the learned authors and editors of those profound verses among the earliest Jewish Masons? Genesis 1:2 contains references to darkness, formlessness, and nothingness. In Masonic symbolism, darkness represents the state of the candidate prior to his or her initiation into the Craft before the light of Freemasonry dawns for him or her. Light appears in Genesis 1:3, and light is given symbolically to the newly initiated Mason.

Genesis 1:6 uses the symbolism of a dividing firmament, and there is a sense in which those initiated into the mysteries of Masonry are divided by their new knowledge from those who do not share it. Genesis 1:11 uses the symbolism of grass, herbs, and trees producing seeds and yielding a harvest. Does this represent the social and charitable "fruit" of an active, flourishing Masonic lodge, a caring fellowship providing food and shelter for the hungry, the homeless, and the destitute?

Close study of that first chapter of Genesis certainly suggests the *possibility* that it was the work of writers with Masonic knowledge and ideals who expressed their thoughts in characteristic Masonic allegories and symbols.

Other creation myths also seem to contain deep symbolism that has a distinctly Masonic flavour. Thousands of miles from the biblical Garden of Eden, Aztec mythology hints at *three* creations before ours, all of which ended in disasters of one sort or another. The first Aztec universe was the victim of a cosmic *tiger* (or any big, dangerous member of the South American cat family that would have been familiar to the myth-makers). Universe number two succumbed to a terrifying *hurricane*, the third was burnt in a vast cataclysmic *fire*, and we are currently living through what remains of the fourth.

In the profound moral and ethical symbolism of Masonry, which contains much philosophical, psychological, and sociological truth, there are clear warnings about what leads to destruction and what postpones it by preserving and protecting life. The tiger symbol stands for wild, dangerous, instinctive emotions and impetuous, uncontrolled behaviour — when calm, rational thought and action would avert suffering, disaster, and death.

Using deep Masonic symbolism again, we see that the hurricane can represent uncontrolled ambition and competitiveness. If every single molecule of air rushes destructively to outdo its rival molecules, then the air of human society as a whole will move like a hurricane, and in so doing will destroy everything in its path until finally it annihilates itself.

Wild, selfish, uncontrolled tiger *instincts* can destroy us, and so can the wild, selfish, uncontrolled hurricane of *ambition*. But what does their uncontrolled *fire* symbolize? In allegorical Masonic thought it can stand for any powerful, dynamic force that has not yet been properly harnessed, or which has been harnessed incorrectly. Such powers of themselves are neutral. Radiation can kill, or it can help to cure cancer. A pharmacist uses drugs to heal patients; a drug dealer uses them to destroy his victims while he grows rich on their suffering. A campfire provides warmth and protection, boils water, and cooks food. A fire that rages uncontrollably through a forest kills and obliterates everything in its path. Flames can protect and enrich life, but they can also wipe it out. Genetic engineering and cloning are like fire in this respect:

their potential for good is incalculable, yet so is their potential for evil. In the right hands they can open limitless new horizons for the future of medicine; in the wrong hands they can build monsters that would make Frankenstein's creature relatively about as dangerous as a zombified hamster.

Fire is the symbol of natural discoveries, or technical, scientific knowledge and skill. The element represents a power so awesome and challenging that the self-discipline of Masonic ethics and morality is needed to guide and control it.

Were the wise old creators of Aztec mythology influenced by symbolic Masonic thought? And if they were, where did they get it from? Did it reach them from the Middle East and Ur of the Chaldees, or did it *originate* among those ancient indigenous Americans and travel eastwards with their religious teachers and merchant adventurers?

An ancient Chinese creation myth relates how the giant Pangu was born from a cosmic egg. When the shell broke to release his vast body, the lighter elements floated upwards and formed the celestial regions. Heavier parts gravitated downwards and formed the Earth. Pangu exerted all his mighty strength and forced the Earth and Sky (Yin and Yang) farther apart. He held them like that for thousands of years until they became settled and stabilized, then, exhausted by the strain, even his colossal body could endure no more. He fell into a deep sleep and never woke again.

Although the heavier fragments of the egg had already given rise to the primeval semblance of the Earth, Pangu's body now devolved into various specific components. His breath became the winds and clouds. His mighty voice turned into thunder. His bright eyes formed the sun and moon, his vast body turned into the mountains, and his limbs became the four points of the compass: north, south, east, and west. His flesh became soil and his skin the plants growing in it. The rivers and oceans were made out of his blood. His veins and arteries became highways, roads, and tracks. Jewels and mineral deposits in the Earth came from his teeth and bones. The stars and planets were formed from his hair, what had once been parasites infesting his vast body turned into human beings, and various species of parasites became the different human ethnic groups.

Many other creation myths relate how the Earth and all its various components were formed from the body of some vast primal creature. These allegories and symbols of death followed by new creation are once again deeply Masonic in tone. At the heart of much Masonic teaching is the frank and fearless recognition that the longest human life is all too short and that death has to be faced.

In "Solomon's Mines and Temple," chapter 9 of this book, the teachings recorded in the *Book of the Wisdom of Solomon* are described and analyzed in detail. The core of these profoundly wholesome and erudite teachings is that the souls of the righteous are safely in the hands of God and that their future is full of immortality. Wisdom is partially personified, and the beauty and importance of Wisdom *as an entity* are expressed.

The first nine chapters of this book are very close indeed to allegorical, Masonic teaching about Wisdom, and the close relationship of Wisdom and Virtue. The following ten chapters move away from this *speculative* approach to personified Wisdom and look more directly at the way Wisdom is revealed in history.

The twin centres of the mystery here are the proximity of the highest and best Masonic teachings to the outstanding content of the *Book of the Wisdom of Solomon* and the riddle of its actual authorship. Most experienced biblical scholars tend to date the first known written copies of the *Book of the Wisdom of Solomon* to a period several centuries *after* the reign of King Solomon the Wise. However, there is another significant school of academic thought that argues that the principal body of theological and philosophical teachings enshrined within the book — its *metaphysics* in Masonic language — could well reflect the views of King Solomon himself.

If Plato passed on the teachings of Socrates, did the author of the *Book of the Wisdom of Solomon* perform a similar service for the great Hebrew king? If the best of the teachings the book contains really *are* the work of King Solomon, via a long line of intermediate disciples, then the many Masonic claims that Solomon was a most important and influential Freemason may well have solid foundations. Solomonic wisdom and Masonic wisdom are both crystal-clear in their respective teachings about human survival and a future comprising blissful immortality, reunion, and fellowship.

Returning to the detail of the creation myth centred on the dismembered parts of the body of the giant Pangu, we encounter another important area of Masonic allegory and symbolism. Masonic ethics and morality teach the importance of optimizing different human gifts, talents, and functions. Christ's parable of the talents enshrines this same deep allegorical truth.

The brilliantly perceptive C.S. Lewis once answered a question on the true nature and meaning of modesty and humility by saying in effect that true humility does not consist of an intelligent man trying to convince himself that he is a fool; neither does it consist of a strong man pretending to be weak. It does not consist of a beautiful woman trying to convince herself that she is plain and homely. True humility, according to Lewis, is the ability to design and build the best cathedral in the world, to know that it is the best, *but then to be neither more nor less pleased than if one of your friends had done it.*

Like human gifts and talents, the discrete parts of the giant's body each had their own distinct qualities: the ethereal nature of his breath; the fluidity of his blood; the hardness, brightness, and whiteness of his teeth; the flexibility and durability of his strong veins and arteries; and the variety of the tiny parasites on his great torso, which eventually became the different human ethnic groups.

One human being may have great strength of mind or body; another has remarkable courage and powers of endurance; a third is a brilliant mathematician; a fourth cooks delicious food; a fifth is a virtuoso musician; others are healers, poets, or teachers. Like the different parts of Pangu's vast body, every woman and man has some special gift or quality to offer to the community. That unique individuality is recognized in Masonic allegory. What is also clearly distinguished in Masonic ethics and morality is that every true Freemason is obligated to use his or her gifts *for the benefit of others.*

Just as St. Christopher used his strength to carry the child across the river, and Mother Teresa employed her gift of limitless love and compassion to help the sick and starving poor, so Masonry teaches its members to gaze inside themselves to find and identify their own special gifts and then to look outside themselves to see where their gifts can provide help and do good to those in most need in the community.

From these examples of allegorical Masonic teachings encapsulated in creation myths, we look at the myths and legends of *owls* — also potent Masonic symbols. The owl represents wisdom, just as surely as the *Book of the Wisdom of Solomon* extols it, and an owl also features in Apache creation myths.

Co-author Lionel with a wise and friendly owl from the Sanctuary.

In some cases, the best of ancient folklore, myth, and legend may have inspired Masonic teachings — or provided source materials and raw material for Masonic leaders and teachers to incorporate into their work — but it is never easy to determine the *direction* in which the ideas flowed. It may be more accurate to hypothesize that ancient Masonic allegories and symbols have inspired what is best and highest in folklore.

Owl folklore contains several references to human beings who were transformed into owls. In some instances, as with the baker's daughter, the transformation was a punishment for greed and selfishness, and this would certainly comply with Masonic ethical teaching about generosity and unselfishness. Other examples of transformation from human to owl form are voluntary. An old Amerindian story tells of a devoted young husband whose wife was turned into an owl by evil magic. She flew to him and explained that the magic was so strong she could never resume her human shape. Without a moment's hesitation her adoring husband transformed himself into an owl in order to be with her. Here, too, the Masonic ethic of unselfishness is clearly demonstrated, and the question of origins is raised again. Did Freemasonry spread from east to west or from west to east? Perhaps its high moral teachings came from *somewhere else*, reaching different parts of our Earth simultaneously a very long time ago?

The Amerindian owl folklore of the New World is balanced geo-graphically by the owl legend associated with Genghis Khan. Born Temüjin at Hentiy in Mongolia circa 1165, Genghis ruled the vast Mongol Empire from 1206 until his death on August 18, 1227. During the hazardous early stages of his rise to power, he and a small band of loyal followers were attacked by a far larger force and had to retreat. Genghis himself hid under a clump of bushes while the enemy looked everywhere for him. An owl sat unconcernedly a few feet above his head, and the bird's calm, unperturbed pose persuaded the searchers that no one could be hiding among the foliage below it. The owl sub-sequently became a protective symbol and is regarded as a bird of good fortune in Mongolia. This concept of protection and benign intention is, of course, Masonic: Freemasons will always endeavour to help and protect those in need whenever it is within their power to do so. The real historical episode of Genghis and the owl has become an allegory of the benign, protective, Masonic ethic. There is also the matter of the owl's calm dignity, which is also rightly and properly associated with Freemasonry.

Genghis Khan, the Mongol emperor.

If Bishop Ussher took us back as far as 4004 BC, the archaeologists working in the mysterious Chauvet Cave take us back six times farther. The cave itself is situated near Vallon-Pont-d'Arc in southeastern France. The entrance is at the foot of a cliff that forms part of the Ardèche Gorges. Fearless speleologists exploring there in 1994 discovered an Aladdin's cave of stalactites, stalagmites, glittering mineral curtains, very old animal bones, and a wealth of ancient cave paintings dating back more than 30,000 years!

Jean Clottes, an acknowledged expert in the highly specialized world of Palaeolithic art, vouched for the age and authenticity of the paintings that depicted many kinds of animals: horses, mammoths, lions, buffalos, rhinoceroses — *and the mysterious owl.* There is also a very curious representation of what *might* be a hybrid man-bull, reminiscent of the legend of the Cretan Minotaur.

Plan of a cave resembling a heraldic lion rampant.

These paintings were no mere primitive ochre daubs. They were the work of an artist, or artists, with the talent of Michelangelo or Leonardo da Vinci. The paintings have perspective, depth, poise, and composition. They could almost be the work of time travellers, or visitors from another world. If a Palaeolithic man or woman created them, then it will be necessary for historians to make radical reassessments of our remote ancestors' intelligence and abilities.

Masonic owl from the Chauvet Cave.

The owl symbol is undeniably Masonic, and the owl picture discovered in Chauvet Cave is clearly very ancient. The scientific name for one group of owls is *Athene*. The little owl is *Athene noctua*; the spotted owl is *Athene brama*; the forest owl is *Athene blewitti*; and the burrowing owl is *Athene cunicularia*. Athena was the Greek goddess of wisdom. Representations normally show her accompanied by an owl, and there were classical Greek coins (popularly known as *owls*) that featured a portrait of the goddess on one side and an owl on the other.

There are folklorists who identify the Greek Athena with the magnificent Queen Semiramis of Babylon. Her story, too, is full of Masonic allegory and symbolism. Some of the oldest and deepest of these secrets are concerned with ancient myths and legends involving strange *amphibian* beings credited with powers greatly in excess of those exercised by normal terrestrial human beings.

The story of Semiramis is inextricably bound up with the life of her husband, King Ninus, ruler of Nineveh. His name itself is intriguing as it seems to be derived from the Assyrian word *nunu*, meaning fish, a further link perhaps with the legends of strange, quasi-human, amphibian extraterrestrials.

According to the legend, an amphibian demigoddess named Derceto, also called Atargatis, made an enemy of Aphrodite (goddess of physical love), who cursed Atargatis by making her fall in love with a Syrian boy, by whom she had a daughter. Filled with shame and revulsion, Atargatis killed her lover and abandoned the baby girl to die on a lonely mountain. Hidden among acacia bushes, which protected her from the elements, she was miraculously rescued by doves.

Acacia is a very potent Masonic symbol indeed. It symbolizes resurrection and immortality, innocence and freedom from sin. Furthermore, it is regarded as the wood from which both the Ark of the Covenant and the tabernacle were constructed, and traditionally it is also associated with Moses's burning bush, the crown of thorns, and the wood of the cross. In other ancient traditions it was the tree of the knowledge of good and evil from the Garden of Eden. Apart from the myths, traditions, and legends associated with it, acacia was used by the ancient Egyptians as part of their funeral customs.

Acacia.

Later rescued and raised by local shepherds who gave her the name Semiramis (meaning, in Syrian, "the person who comes from the doves"), the little girl from the acacia bushes survived, grew up to be a beautiful woman, and married Onnes (also known as Menon). She was brilliantly intelligent and a great asset to him in battle. On one occasion she worked out a strategy that enabled an enemy citadel to be taken, and she herself led the troops up a steep cliff, reminiscent of the British General James Wolfe's assault on Quebec City.

It was Onnes's bad luck that King Ninus saw his beautiful young wife and wanted her for himself. Sadly, despite being offered Ninus's own daughter, Sosana, in exchange for the lovely Semiramis, Onnes refused and committed suicide. Semiramis was then compelled to marry Ninus, and they had a son called Ninyas.

After the death of Ninus, Semiramis became an exceptionally powerful and effective queen in her own right for many years. According to tradition, she led the army with great success and expanded her empire in the wake of her military conquests. Semiramis was also a great designer and builder in the best Masonic tradition. She is even credited by some authorities with being the creator of the Hanging Gardens of Babylon, one of the Seven Wonders of the Ancient World.

Most important, as far as Masonic history and its owl symbolism are concerned, is that Semiramis was identified in myth and legend with the goddess Athena and her mysterious owl. Traditional myths and legends also identify Athena with Ishtar and the Egyptian Isis, who was also revered for her wisdom. One of Isis's many titles was Tower Goddess, and she was credited with great skill as a builder — an early patroness of ancient Egyptian masons and craftspeople.

It is possible to trace ancient Hebrew Masonic influence in the editing of various Old Testament texts, where the owl symbolism is found frequently to occur. Superficial reading of the texts suggests that these references to owls are meant simply to imply the downfall of ancient empires, kingdoms, and city states — their former sites will be given over to wild birds and animals. It is *possible*, however, that there is a much deeper Masonic significance in these repetitive owl references. Examples include:

- Job 30:29: "a companion of owls."
- Psalm 102:6: "I am like an owl of the desert."
- Isaiah 13:22: "and owls shall dwell there, and satyrs dance there."
- Isaiah 14:23: "I will turn her into a place for owls."
- Isaiah 34:13: "and it shall be a habitation of dragons, and a court for owls."
- Jeremiah 50:39: "and the owls shall dwell therein."
- Micah 1:8: "a wailing like the dragons, and mourning as the owls."

Barn owl (*Strix flammea*).

Horned owl (*Strix otus*).

The editors and redactors of the Arthurian sagas often depict the wise and powerful magician Merlin with an owl on his shoulder, and a viable case can be argued for including the wizard among the prominent Masons of the past. But one of the most interesting and significant of all the potentially Masonic owl clues links the creatures to C.S. Lewis via *The Silver Chair* in his *Narnia* series. The fourth chapter is called "A Parliament of Owls," and it could easily be an allegory for a typical Masonic lodge meeting.

Lewis's owls are wise and helpful and make a major contribution to saving the lost prince in the author's story. Not surprisingly, there are researchers who believe that Lewis, J.R.R. Tolkien, and Charles Williams — the famous "Inklings" — were all Freemasons. Lewis had a pronounced sense of humour as well as an outstanding intellect, and it would have appealed to him immensely to allegorize his lodge brethren as a parliament of owls, knowing full well that all Freemasons who were aware of the owl symbolism would have seen the real meaning instantly.

Another aspect of the mysterious Masonic owl symbolism is the *secrecy* of the owl's nocturnal flight, and in looking at some of the stranger theories of the ancient roots of Masonry, the idea of *secret flights* from distant worlds leading to palaeocontact has to be invoked.

The term *palaeocontact* encapsulates the notion that extraterrestrial beings visited our Earth in very early times and that from those prehistoric visits a special group of Guardians was appointed. Some Guardians perhaps were the extraterrestrials themselves; others were a specially selected elite of trustworthy human beings — the very first prototype Freemasons. The concept of palaeocontact began to spread after the publication of Peter Kolosimo's pioneering work *Il pianeta sconosciuto* (*The Disowned Planet*) in 1957. Palaeocontact theory got another major boost when Erich von Däniken published *Chariots of the Gods* in 1968. This was followed by a number of sequels. Although von Däniken's work is undeniably controversial, the profound and radical ideas that form the basis of his palaeocontact hypotheses cannot lightly be discarded. In outline the theory postulates that humanity as we know it today has descended from prehistoric extraterrestrial visitors, or that those technically advanced visitors genetically engineered ancient pre-human species who then became our remote ancestors.

In 1958 the distinguished Russian mathematician Dr. Matest Agrest, who was also an expert ethnologist, put forward the theory that the ancient terrace at Baalbek in Lebanon was actually a launching and landing pad for spacecraft. There are stones at Baalbek that are estimated to weigh 1,000 tons each. The stones raise the profound question of how they could have been quarried and transported using the primitive equipment and slave labour that was supposed to have been all that was available thousands of years ago. Stonehenge and the pyramids of Egypt pose similar questions, as do the strange heads guarding Easter Island and the vast Olmec heads in Mexico and Central America. Many Mesoamerican and South American structures are not only built of massive stone blocks, but their *accuracy* creates as many questions as their vast size. Archaeologists confirm that many of the huge blocks there are fitted together so expertly that it is difficult, almost impossible, to insert a thin knife blade between them. Such accuracy points to the work of highly skilled masons.

Another of Dr. Agrest's theories was that the destruction of the cities of Sodom and Gomorrah on the plain of Jordan could have been brought about by nuclear explosions. If the palaeocontact theory is correct, then it may be also argued that some of the visitors seem to have possessed nuclear weaponry.

Further evidence suggests that if extraterrestrials really *were* here in ancient times they were more than ready to defend themselves with superior weaponry. A Neanderthal skull discovered in 1921 in what was then Rhodesia, now Zimbabwe, was found to have been pierced by a high-velocity projectile. Forensic experts who examined the skull felt certain that it was a fatal bullet wound. The skull was found more than twenty yards down, and experts agreed that the wound had ended the Neanderthal's life. It had not been inflicted posthumously. So who or *what* was firing high-velocity bullets in Africa thousands of years ago?

The evidence for the palaeocontact hypothesis and the associated secret of the *possible* extraterrestrial origin of Freemasonry comes in three main categories: anachronistic artifacts; primordial art like that in

Chauvet Cave; and ancient religious traditions referring to supernatural beings — "gods" and "demons" — that were able to fly.

Although the mysteries of ancient Egyptian Freemasonry will be examined in depth in chapter 5, the riddle of the so-called Abydos "helicopter" needs to be mentioned in this section. In the temple wall at Abydos is a hieroglyph that looks uncannily like a modern helicopter, and the same panel also carries other strange hieroglyphic shapes that *could* be representations of aircraft. Some small, ancient Egyptian artifacts, almost certainly originally intended as children's toys, are also shaped like model gliders, and when actually tested have been shown to be capable of short, gliding flights.

The most acceptable explanation among mainstream academic Egyptologists for the so-called "helicopter hieroglyph" at Abydos is that it has arisen more or less accidentally because temple and pyramid inscriptions were frequently altered, amended, and overlaid. When this happens to an old document on vellum or parchment, it is usually referred to as a palimpsest. An older, more historically interesting document was often washed and re-used in the days when vellum and parchment were relatively scarce and expensive. When the term *palimpsest* is applied to altered stonework inscriptions and engravings, it implies that older hieroglyphics have been cut away or plastered over to make way for a later inscription. In the course of such amending, curious hybrid shapes and forms may arise that are neither one character nor another, and which can look remarkably like some exciting anachronism such as a plane or a helicopter.

However, the traditional, academic explanation — logical and rational though it seems — is not *necessarily* the correct one in the case of the Abydos helicopter. Because the implications of what look like modern aircraft flying over ancient Egypt would radically alter the generally accepted view of history, evidence for such phenomena will tend to be resisted and excluded by every possible means rather than welcomed and accepted.

Ancient Masonic skills, such as those commended in the craftsmanship of Bezaleel, son of Uri, in Exodus 31:4, were by no means confined to later stone structures like Solomon's superb Jerusalem temple. Bezaleel was able "To devise cunning works, to work in gold, and in silver, and in brass ..." Where did he acquire those skills and were they from the same store of secret wisdom and knowledge that led to the astonishing 1901 discovery near the island of Antikythera off the Greek coast?

Divers working on a 2,000-year-old wreck there came up with a very advanced mechanism, rather like a contemporary clock or an astrolabe. This remarkable artifact is now safely in the Greek National Archaeological Museum in Athens. Its inexplicably complex mechanism provides grounds for speculating that its maker, or makers, had access to privileged knowledge far beyond that which was available to their contemporaries.

The mystery of the Antikythera device is reinforced by a curious discovery in the Coso Mountains of California. An unusual-looking stone found there in the early 1960s contained an odd piece of machinery. Witnesses maintained that there was a six-sided layer of *something* enclosing a cylindrical piece of porcelain, which in turn was bound with copper circles. Inside the porcelain cylinder was a shiny metallic rod about a quarter of an inch long fixed to a small spring. Those who examined it described it as reminding them more than anything else of a spark plug from a gasoline engine. The rock inside which it was discovered, however, was at least a half-million years old.

Whatever the true explanation of the Coso Mountains find, that mystery increases when it is considered alongside the enigma of the Salzburg steel cube. This item was found *inside* a block of coal in 1885, and when it was subjected to expert examination it was clearly seen to have been manufactured. The general theory at the time was that it had originally been part of a larger mechanism.

If these strange finds were parts of ancient machinery, was that machinery electrical? Curious evidence for the possible use of electricity in ancient times can be found among the ruins of what were once Persia and Babylonia. Some peculiar earthenware vessels excavated in Iraq were found to have been soldered with an alloy of tin and lead. They contained copper discs, just as the Coso Mountains object contained copper rings, and had been sealed with bitumen or pitch. When acetic acid (vinegar) and copper sulphate ($CuSO_4$) were added, a current of two or three volts was generated. Whoever designed and built these ancient electrical cells, also seems to have perfected a technique for electroplating jewellery thousands of years ago.

Is this further evidence of the palaeocontact hypothesis and the existence of secret knowledge in the hands of a select few? Were those wise men and women the earliest Freemasons?

In 1884 tough, practical, English quarrymen were blasting granite when they discovered a small golden object that had clearly been man-ufactured — totally inexplicable considering the age of the granite they were blasting out. A Mrs. Culp was shovelling coal in Morrisonville, Illinois, in 1891, when a piece broke open. It contained a gold chain of delicate and skilful workmanship, the kind of artifact that Bezaleel would have been proud of. Mrs. Culp's first thought, naturally, was that someone had dropped it accidentally among the coal before she began working on it. Closer examination, however, showed that both ends of the chain were firmly embedded *in* the coal, which had somehow formed around it. Who could possibly have lost an ornate gold chain millions of years ago? If palaeocontact theories are correct, did some of the wise alien visitors have time travel as well as space travel?

In 1938 it was reported that a team of Chinese archaeologists led by Professor Chi Pu Tei discovered a series of mysterious, labyrinthine tunnels in the Bayan Kara-Ula Mountains close to the Tibetan-Chinese border. Some aspects of their report were reminiscent of the Oak Island mystery in Nova Scotia, Canada, where an underwater camera lowered into the mysterious depths of Borehole 10X *seemed* to show that the maze of flooded tunnels below Oak Island was square in section as if the tunnels had been cut artificially. The walls of the tunnels that Professor Chi's team explored in 1938 were also said to have been rectangular and glazed, as though whoever, or whatever, had created them had used some sort of technically advanced thermal cutter.

Professor Chi's team reported that they had unearthed graves in neatly arranged rows containing small, crumbling, anthropoid skeletons. The bodies had apparently been relatively frail and feeble, and the heads were disproportionately large. The creatures were about the same height as Tolkien's Hobbits in *The Lord of the Rings*, but not nearly as sturdy as Bilbo, Frodo, and their friends. Furthermore, Hobbit heads are perfectly proportioned. An early theory put forward by some of the students in Professor Chi's group was that these odd little skeletons might belong to a hitherto unknown species of small mountain ape, but this contention was swiftly abandoned when it was pointed out that even the most advanced anthropoid apes do not bury their dead in neat rows.

The ape theory was discredited further when pictures and diagrams were reportedly found on the tunnel and cave walls. These images seemed to show stars and planetary systems connected by dotted lines, as though *indicating* the route by which extraterrestrial visitors had travelled to reach Earth.

Then came an even stranger discovery. One of Professor Chi's people found a most unusual stone disc partly buried in the floor of one of the caves. Perfectly circular, it was eight and a half inches across and almost three-quarters of an inch thick. It had a hole in the centre that was also approximately three-quarters of an inch in diameter. (If it had featured in a Fred Flintstone cartoon, it could well have been a Stone Age gramophone record!)

The circle, it must be remembered, is a very significant Masonic symbol. Just as *operative* stonemasons in olden times wore protective aprons when carving stone, so today's *speculative* Freemasons wear ceremonial aprons at their lodge meetings. The mystical, symbolic circle is represented by the strings of the apron that encircle the Mason's waist. Having no beginning and no end, the circle symbolizes the eternal nature of God, and the eternal nature of the life that God gives to human beings. The centre of the circle is invisible, and so represents the invisibility of God.

No single *straight* line can enclose anything. Using three straight lines, the triangle is the smallest figure that has the power to enclose an area. The circle, therefore, is the shortest *single* line, a uniformly and perfectly *curved* line that possesses this power to encompass or enclose. To Freemasons, therefore, the circle represents the all-encompassing power of God and the all-embracing unity and completeness of God. The circle reminds Masons of God's infinity, omnipresence, and eternity.

One mysterious stone disc would be strange enough, but there were reports that more than 700 of them were found in the Bayan Kara-Ula caves. Each disc had what seemed at first sight to be a groove running around it — again reminiscent of a gramophone record — spiralling from the centre to the rim. More careful and detailed inspection revealed that this was no mere groove; it was a line of extremely finely cut hieroglyphics.

For many years the Dropas stone discs, as they were known, lay carefully labelled and preserved in Beijing University until, in 1962, Professor Tsum Um Nui got to work on them. With infinite care and patience he examined disc after disc and symbol after symbol. He also minutely examined the actual material of which the stones were composed. Other scientists, including a Russian expert named Vyacheslav Zaitsev, came to the conclusion that the discs were made principally of some granite-like substance containing surprisingly high percentages of metals such as cobalt. It was also reported that under certain conditions, when subjected to oscillograph testing, the discs vibrated oddly, suggesting that at one time they had been powerfully electrically charged, or had perhaps been included as components in electrical circuits.

When the Dropas discs reportedly yielded their peculiar secrets, the story was an enigmatic one. Some investigators believe that an extraterrestrial race who referred to themselves as Dropas, or Dropa, had been visiting Earth with purely friendly and peaceful intentions some 12,000 years ago. Unfortunately, their ship had got into difficulties and crashed in the Bayan Kara-Ula Mountains. There, the survivors had used what remained of their technology to survive like troglodytes in the caves they had been able to adapt and improve with connecting tunnels. Their ship was damaged beyond repair, and there was no terrestrial technology available to assist them to repair it in that place at that time.

It must, in fairness, be acknowledged that the Dropa story *might* be nothing more than an elaborate creation myth manufactured by the small troglodyte race living in the Bayan Kara-Ula Mountains. If it is, then it leaves much to be explained, including the reports of 700-plus, extremely unusual Dropas discs and the messages they are alleged to carry.

What makes the Dropa episode stranger still is the existence of another enigmatic disc, the Phaistos Disc from ancient Crete. That, too, has a spiral message written around it in curious hieroglyphs that have not yet been deciphered.

The Phaistos Disc from Crete: is it connected with the weird Dropas discs and the *rongo-rongo* script of Easter Island? Was it an ancient Masonic code?

Easter Island's mysteries include the odd *rongo-rongo* script, also written on unusual discs and not yet deciphered. Is it possible that all three riddles have a common denominator? Are all those enigmatic disc artifacts carrying messages from a very long way away, and could those messages have something to do with our ancient extraterrestrial proto-Masonic guardians and guides?

Another intriguing discovery of what may be the remains of small extraterrestrial humanoids resembling Tolkien's Hobbits comes from the Indonesian island of Flores. During the early twenty-first century, researchers there found the remains of anthropoid skeletons barely half the size of normal *homo sapiens* and named these little people *homo floresiensis*. Older members of the island community have a legend that tells how their ancestors once shared the place with a race of very small humanoids whom the islanders referred to as *Ebu Gogo*, which translates as "the old ones who eat everything." Flores is heavily forested, and it is not impossible that a few of the ancient miniature race could still be living there in hiding. The most probable explanation is, of course, that they were simply the result of Darwinian evolution and a mutation that led to smaller size. It is not impossible that they are the remote descendants of small extraterrestrials. The Indonesian island mystery and the discoveries made in the Bayan Kara-Ula Mountains close to the Tibetan-Chinese border could be two sides of the same coin.

Midway between examples of inexplicable miniature people, ancient artifacts, and prehistoric art comes the mysterious *Venus of Willendorf*, which was found in Willendorf, Germany, during archaeological excavations in August 1907. The strange little female figurine, estimated to be 30,000 years old, is just over four inches high and carved from limestone. The most fascinating feature is the head. Some traditional archaeologists have described it as faceless and having an intricate hairstyle of tight, parallel plaits. Approaching it objectively, however, an open-minded investigator might think that it could equally well be an alien humanoid wearing a space helmet.

Prehistoric art is frequently puzzling and intriguing, and theories about its possible meanings abound. From a Masonic point of view, however, two of the very oddest examples yet discovered came from Blombos Cave about 198 miles from Cape Town, South Africa, near the southern Cape of Good Hope shore. The finds consisted of two ochre blocks carved with strange abstract symbols. The best scientific dating puts these carved blocks at 70,000 years old, more than *twice* the age of the amazing owl in Chauvet Cave in France.

Dr. Christopher Henshilwood from the State University of New York at Stony Brook is of the opinion that the mysterious geometrical markings on these primordial ochre blocks are symbols of some sort.

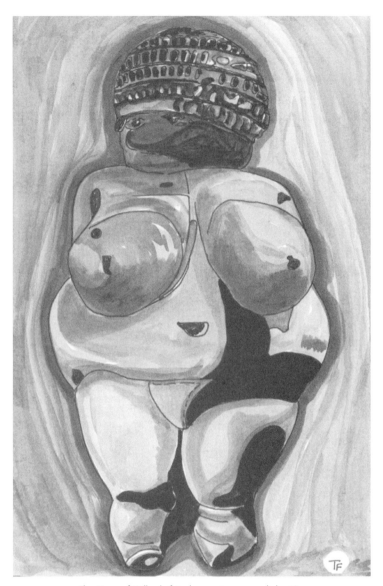

The *Venus of Willendorf*: is she wearing a space helmet?

What do those symbols mean? As the illustration on page 44 reveals, they are very close indeed to the modern Masonic square and compasses. Were the primeval artists and craftsmen working in Blombos Cave in Africa 70,000 years ago instructed by benign visitors from the stars — the ancient guides and guardians, the first Freemasons?

Do these strange ancient inscriptions in Blombos Cave include the Masonic square and compasses?

Based on samples of mitochondrial DNA through the female line, many palaeoanthropologists are of the opinion that what they term a "genetic Eve" may well have come from Africa. One widely discussed theory suggests that the earliest human ancestors were traceable to Africa some 300,000 years ago.

Dr. David Roberts, a South African geologist, discovered a set of small human footprints that were estimated to be almost 120,000 years old. The discovery was made in the Langebaan Lagoon about sixty miles north of Cape Town. So if there was a genetic Eve in Africa, these could even have been her footprints. The impressions show that the feet that made them were of the same type as twenty-first-century feet — about ten inches long, with a distinct big toe, arch, and heel.

After considering these very early African finds, the ancient civilization at Harappa in Pakistan seems relatively modern. Pottery fragments from there date back almost 6,000 years and contain what may well have been one of the world's earliest alphabets. As the illustration shows, the Harappan inscriptions contain a design that is *perhaps* similar to the Masonic square and compasses. Do these enigmatic pottery fragments suggest that the great Harappan civilization was nurtured and reinforced by Masonic guardians and guides?

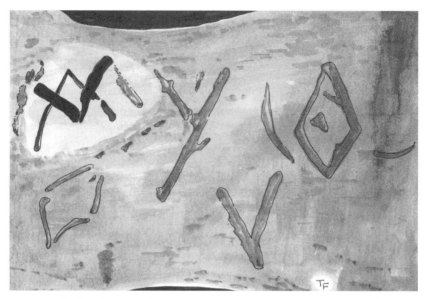

Do the Masonic square and compasses appear here, too, on this Harappan inscription?

Across the world from Pakistan, the ancient Taino cave art found in San Cristóbal in the Dominican Republic is just as mysterious. One drawing there looks for all the world like an enormous insect, yet also possesses strangely humanoid lines. Did the extinct Taino people encounter insectile extraterrestrials in the remote past? Despite its bizarre appearance, the entity's gestures need not necessarily be hostile or threatening. It could equally well be teaching or explaining something that will benefit the Taino people. Is it possible that this strange artwork is meant to demonstrate an early form of Masonic recognition gesture that will enable the elite, instructed Taino to know one another – and, perhaps, to identify themselves to future extraterrestrial visitors?

Another remarkable piece of ancient symbolic artwork is the vast Sun Stone or Calendar Stone, known to its Aztec creators as Cuauhxicalli. This is yet another major circle symbol, containing five concentric circles, plus squares and triangles, all of which are highly significant in Masonic symbolism.

There is an ancient Sumerian game, discovered by Sir Leonard Woolley when he was exploring the timeless city of Ur. The game is estimated to be around 5,000 years old and is also known as the Game of

Could this have been an intelligent extraterrestrial alien visiting San Cristóbal in the remote past?

Is it possible to discern Masonic symbols on this ancient Calendar Stone?

Twenty Squares. Like chess, the Royal Game of Ur has turned up during archaeological explorations in India, Egypt, and many parts of the ancient Middle East.

Board used for the Royal Game of Ur.

An excellent book entitled *Games* gives all the details and facilities for playing the Royal Game of Ur. The book is available from British Museum Press, and full details on how to obtain a copy are available from *www.britishmuseum.co.uk*. There are various forms of the game's rules, but the basic object is for a player to get all seven pieces off the board. Moves are controlled by dice throws, and the skill element is in deciding which piece to move, when to make a capture, when to double up pieces, and so on.

Pieces used for the Royal Game of Ur.

There seems to be a deep, religio-mystical, symbolic, and allegorical Masonic ideology underlying the Royal Game of Ur: the player's seven pieces probably represented the seven metaphysical stages of existence in ancient Sumerian thinking, and getting all seven off the board (escaping from the stresses, strains, and worries of the secular world into a wider, freer, happier sphere of spiritual existence) won the Game of Life.

A further fruitful historical area of exploration from the remote past, and one that is especially rich in what may well be ancient Masonic symbolism, is the game of chess and the riddle of its origins. Claims are made that the game originated in Uzbekistan, Ireland, Arabia, Persia, Assyria, Greece, Egypt, India, and China. The two last named probably have the strongest claims, and many an earnest quiz contestant has been cheated out of a well-deserved prize by saying one when the quizmaster, or mistress, had been given the other by the expert whom he or she trusted as the ultimate authority. Several experts assert that chess probably developed from a very old Indian game known as Chaturanga.

The Egyptian claim is based largely on an illustration in the tomb of Queen Nefertari (1295–1255 BC) in which she is shown poring over what looks like a chess-type game. If there was any contact between Egypt and China at this time, and there may well have been, the Egyptian version could have been based on an earlier Chinese variety known as Liubo. Rabbi Abraham ibn Ezra in the twelfth century voiced his opinion that Moses had invented chess. Another early, and rather romantic, historian, Zakariah Yahya, commented on the mythology of chess history in the tenth century. He reported that he had heard accounts of chess being played in Noah's Ark by Japheth and Shem, by Aristotle the Greek philosopher, and even by King Solomon the Wise. The reference to Solomon is particularly significant as far as the Masonic connection with chess is concerned. The allegories and symbolism of chess are especially pertinent to the high moral and ethical teachings of Freemasonry.

The ceiling of the Masonic temple symbolically represents the entire universe. The symbolism of the floor — black and white squares *like* a chessboard — represents the connection between the spiritual realm and the physical world. Black and white are also regarded as symbolic, allegorical representations of light and darkness, good and evil, life and death. They further signify such diametrically opposed concepts as heaven and earth, water and fire.

Ancient Egypt, where many early Masonic secrets were known and studied, will be examined in depth in chapter 5. But it can be noted here in connection with the Masonic association with chess that in ancient Egypt white was perceived as an expression of goodness, joy, and abundance. Black stood for death, the mysterious Underworld, and rebirth. It was also the colour associated with Osiris. Ancient Egyptian thinkers interspersed black and white to symbolize the reunion of spiritual and physical life. For them, as for Freemasonry, the chessboard is highly symbolic — and sacred.

A very learned and distinguished Masonic scholar writing in *Masonic Forum* says clearly: "The floor of the Masonic temple may be looked at as a chessboard."

Junior Warden	Steward	Junior Deacon	Tyler	Worshipful Master	Senior Deacon	Steward	Senior Warden
Master Mason	Master Mason	Master Mason	Master Mason	Master Mason	Master Mason	Master Mason	Master Mason

If a chess set was made with pieces showing the officers and members of a Masonic lodge, it could well be arranged as illustrated in the above table. The worshipful master would be the most important piece on the board and would occupy the square normally reserved for the king in ordinary chess. The king is not the most powerful piece in chess by any means, being able to move only one square at a time. His importance lies in the object of the game itself: once the king is checkmated, that is, forced into a position where he cannot avoid capture, then the game is lost. The tyler is the armed guard posted outside the Masonic lodge, but in the Masonic version of chess he would be placed next to the worshipful master to defend and protect him. The piece known as the queen in normal chess would be positioned next to the king, but calling that most powerful piece the queen, as though she were simply the king's consort and partner, is something of a misnomer. The queen moves any number of squares in any direction, laterally or diagonally, and this combination of range and mobility gives her more power than any other piece. When chess is regarded as a miniature war game, the queen is really the king's champion, his most powerful defender, a combination of his bodyguard and his army's commander-in-chief.

Chess pieces at the start of a game.

The chessboard bishops were probably meant to represent archers rather than senior clergy. However, it seemed appropriate to place the junior and senior Masonic deacons on the squares normally allocated to the bishops on an ordinary chessboard. This placing of Masonic deacons where chess bishops go is simply because of the religious links between deacons and bishops. Two Masonic stewards occupy the squares given to knights on the normal chess setup. The knights can either jump obstacles or move around them during play. Their range is short, but their manoeuvrability gives them a great deal of power and makes them dangerous opponents — pieces to be reckoned with. Masonic stewards need dexterity and flexibility to carry out their lodge duties satisfactorily, and these qualities correlate them with chess knights.

Second only to the queen, or commander-in-chief, in power are the two rooks, which occupy the end squares in the back row. The word *rook* is probably derived from the old Persian term *rukh*, meaning a chariot. Insofar as chess is a battle game, the lateral movement of the rooks — without any limit to the number of squares that they can move backward, forward, or horizontally — allows them to sweep down the board as a chariot would once have swept into battle. The senior warden and junior warden are the two most senior officers in the Masonic lodge after the worshipful master himself, so it is appropriate in Masonic chess to allocate them the roles of the powerful rooks, which are also referred to as castles.

A game in progress between master players Boris Spassky and Bobby Fischer.

In normal chess the front rank is occupied by eight pawns or foot soldiers — the infantry. In Masonic chess these are eight master masons. In the game a pawn that reaches the eighth rank — the enemy's back row — can become a major piece. Normally, the player whose pawn has made the hazardous journey successfully will opt to exchange it for an extra queen, but there are rare occasions on which a knight may be chosen for the conversion instead because of its ability to jump over or circumnavigate obstacles, the one power the queen lacks. In Masonic chess it can be seen that this conversion and promotion parallel is retained. A successful and faithful master mason can hope to be promoted up through the ranks as a reward for long service and merit.

But what other symbolic, Masonic, moral, and ethical teachings are to be found in chess? There are several very significant ones. The best and most skilful chess players think of their sixteen pieces as one whole gestalt, an organism, a totality, not as sixteen discrete units. Freemasons regard themselves in much the same manner. Each brother and sister is part of the Masonic community and family, and each does everything possible to help the others. During a chess game, a piece will frequently come under attack from the enemy and a defending piece will be moved up to protect it. In real life, just as in every other loyal, loving, and caring family, Freemasons guard and defend one another.

On the chessboard every piece has different powers and different ways of moving. In Masonry every member is different: we have different skills, different qualifications, different life experiences, and so on. Yet Masons work together harmoniously and successfully, just as a good chess player employs his pieces to create a closely integrated and unified team — a truly gestalt organism.

During a skilful chess game, there may be a need for *sacrifices*: one piece may be placed in danger and actually be captured by the enemy in order to improve the overall position of the remaining pieces, or to checkmate the enemy's king. Masonic ethics and morals also require sacrifices from time to time. For example, Freemasons respond generously when called upon to do without something they would have enjoyed, so that a brother or sister in greater need may have it. Ethics, morality, and integrity come first with every true Freemason, closely followed by the altruistic determination to help others, even when that entails sacrifices.

A case can be made, and an argument can be put forward, that the mysterious and controversial origins of chess are indicative of its very early Masonic connections. In terms of its deep symbolism and allegory, the game has great moral and ethical teaching value. Was it introduced in many ancient cultures *simultaneously* by the earliest Masonic guides and guardians?

In this chapter we have endeavoured to look at *some* of the possible origins of Freemasonry. In chapter 4 we shall explore the Masonic connections with the mysteries of Atlantis and Lemuria.

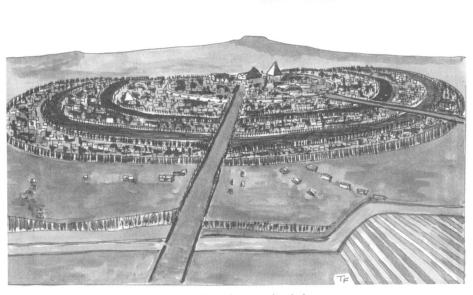

Atlantis as Plato and Socrates described it.

MASONIC IDEAS ABOUT ATLANTIS AND LEMURIA

ONE DARING, radical hypothesis of Masonic origins suggests that the roots of Freemasonry can be traced back to the dim dawn of prehistory, and that many of the wise, ethical, and moral teachings that lie at the heart of all true Masonry can be attributed to mysterious prehistoric guides and guardians. Where did those first extraordinary teachers come from? Were they in any way connected with the semi-legendary riddles of the lost continents of Atlantis and Lemuria?

Atlantean research begins with the brilliant Greek philosopher Plato. He said that Atlantis lay beyond the Pillars of Hercules, by which he meant present-day Gibraltar. Plato describes Atlantis in *Timaeus* and *Critias*, his accounts of two discussions that Socrates led.

To optimize the value of the material in those illuminating discussions, it is helpful to look at the characters who took part in them, or who are referred to in them. Except for Timaeus himself, for whose existence there is as yet no external evidence, all of the characters participating in the Socratic debates were real, historical people. But to what extent were they original, independent thinkers, and to what degree were they convenient puppets through whom Socrates and Plato spoke to posterity?

It is slightly confusing that there are *two* men named Critias. One is the debater, the other his grandfather. It was this older Critias who gave the account of Atlantis to his grandson who, in turn, relayed it to Socrates during the famous dialogues. Critias was also Plato's great-grandfather. Socrates, one of the finest thinkers of all time, was Plato's teacher. Both men were so typically Masonic in their wisdom that it is highly likely they were members of an early Greek lodge. Masonic involvement in classical Greek culture is examined in detail in chapter 6, "Masons in Classical Greece."

Socrates and Plato.

There is an element of irony in most tragedy and injustice. The ironically misnamed *Holy* Inquisition, for example, tortured and murdered good, honest, sincere men and women in the name of religion. Socrates, who lived from 469 to 399 BC, was the most ethical of men, but he was executed for "corrupting the morals of Athenian youth" when no one could have done more than he did to further the cause of truth and morality.

The Hemocrates who participated in the dialogues was a statesman and warrior from Syracuse. Solon (638–559 BC) was a poet, statesman, lawgiver, and traveller whose deep thought and high moral attitude qualified him as another distinguished Greek proto-Mason. It was the widely travelled, receptive, and perceptive Solon who learned about Atlantis from a wise old Egyptian priest, almost certainly another proto-Mason. Dropides, great-grandfather of Critias junior, heard the story of Atlantis from Solon, who was one of his distant relatives. Critias senior was the son of this Dropides and grandfather of the younger Critias, the one who participated in the vital dialogues.

This is how his account unfolded. Where the Nile River divided to form its delta there was a country called Sais, which was once ruled by King Amasis. The founder of that ancient kingdom was a goddess known to the Egyptians as Neith, who was regarded as identical to Athene. The people of Sais were great admirers of the Athenians and believed that they were related to them. Solon reached Sais in the course of his travels and was warmly welcomed there. During a discussion about ancient history and the origins of different peoples, Solon mentioned Phoroneus, often called the first man. Solon also talked about the flood and how Deucalion and Pyrrha had survived it. Then he tried to calculate how long ago these major events had taken place (an action strangely reminiscent of Bishop Ussher's attempts). At that point a very old Egyptian priest smiled and shook his head. "You Athenians are as young as children," said this venerable Egyptian, who then went on to say that many great civilizations and cultures had developed over the millennia, only to be destroyed, and he was certain that this cyclic pattern of growth, destruction, and reconstruction would happen again repeatedly in future ages.

The old Egyptian priest maintained that fire and water were responsible for many of these destructions. He then claimed that Egypt, and his district of Sais in particular, was usually protected from these cataclysms by the Nile. He also told Solon that carefully preserved in their ancient temples were the inscribed histories of great civilizations and major world events that had long since been lost and forgotten elsewhere. The old Egyptian priest informed Solon that there had been many deluges before the one that he had spoken of, and that the Athenians of Solon's time were descended from the remnants of a fair and noble race that had occupied their land millennia before.

These earlier Athenians, of whom the Egyptian priest spoke so admiringly, had not only been highly cultured and very well governed, but had also been the foremost warriors of their day, surpassing all other nations in military skill and courage. Fascinated by the priest's words, Solon begged him to go on with his account. The old Egyptian said that this earlier Athens had been founded by Neith-Athene 1,000 years before she had founded Sais. This fitted them into a time slot some 9,000 years before Solon's era.

To corroborate his argument that the same benign goddess had founded the two peoples, the Egyptian invited Solon to compare the laws of Sais with the laws of this earlier Athens. He spoke of the caste systems that he said were common to both Sais and proto-Athens:

priests were entirely separate from all other citizens, and each discrete group of craftsmen, or tradesmen, had its own caste, whose members did not mix with others. Shepherds, hunters, and husbandmen formed another social caste, while warriors, just like priests, were an elite group entirely separate from the main social body.

The wise old Egyptian then went on to describe how Neith-Athene had given the proto-Athenians such great knowledge of science, medicine, and law that they would be able to excel the rest of humanity. This account of the words of the wise old Egyptian priest to Solon seems to suggest that Neith-Athene was herself one of the early Masonic proto-guardians and guides who set up an elite group — the very early Freemasons — to help and protect humanity. The next section of the Egyptian's words to Solon shows how this protective, Masonic elite worked in practice.

A plan of Atlantis with its concentric circles as described by Solon.

According to the priest of Sais, a vast landmass bigger than Asia and Libya combined once occupied the Atlantic side of the Straits of Gibraltar, known in Solon's time as the Pillars of Hercules. Forces from this great kingdom of Atlantis already controlled many countries adjoining the Mediterranean, including Libya and Tyrrhenia, but they now sought to extend their empire yet farther. Only the warriors of Athens made a successful stand against them, and after a long and bitter struggle, the valiant proto-Athenians were finally triumphant. They drove out the invading Atlanteans and liberated their former Mediterranean subject territories. After this great victory, there was a cataclysmic tragedy that engulfed not only Atlantis but the gallant proto-Athenians, as well.

The second of the Atlantean dialogues is called *Critias*, and in it the vast island of Atlantis is described in detail. The gods allocated different areas of the Earth to one another, and Poseidon was given Atlantis. He took a beautiful human girl named Cleito as his partner, and they produced a large family — five sets of male twins. Their sons duly became kings and princes of Atlantis, and for many years all was happiness, peace, and prosperity on their vast island continent.

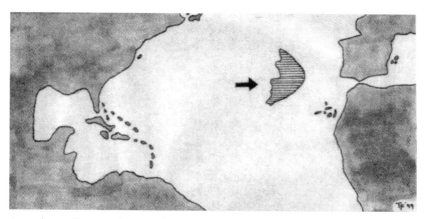

A map showing the projected position of Atlantis according to the Egyptian priest who told Solon about it.

In the centre of Atlantis was a beautiful, fertile plain that surrounded a small hill, and Poseidon built concentric circles of land and sea around it. Because of their divine parentage, and their genetically acquired strength and skill, the Atlanteans ruled an empire that extended well into the Mediterranean. The Egyptian priest described the Atlantean kingdom to Solon as being exceptionally wealthy and that it imported every kind of luxury from overseas. Part of the Atlanteans' great wealth was founded upon a mysterious precious metal known as *orichalcum.*

There are numerous theories about what *orichalcum* really was, or what it might have been. The old but reliable *Dictionary of Greek and Roman Antiquities* edited by Dr. William Smith and published by Murray in London in 1885 carries an article on *orichalcum.* According to Smith, it was a metallic compound, or alloy, probably made by fusing copper and an *ore* of zinc, rather than using properly extracted *pure* zinc. There is Masonic allegory and symbolism to be found in the parallel of the rough *ashlar,* the large square-cut stone employed in building. *Orichalcum* teaches that even rough-hewn stone (ore) can be transformed into precious metal by Masonic wisdom and teaching. Some ancient metallurgists believed that the word should be written *aurichalcum,* since they thought gold was incorporated into the alloy.

The Masonic allegory and symbolism of gold within *aurichalcum* is an important one. It teaches the same spiritual, personal, and social truths as Christ's parables of leaven and salt. Ordinary society and the monotonous routines of everyday life can be metamorphosed by the addition of some special, inspiring, dynamic, transforming ingredient: salt, leaven, or gold in the case of *aurichalcum.* The ethical and moral impact of Freemasonry can perform this function for the community that local Masons help and serve.

Jim Allen, who has made a profound study of Atlantis, cites Karen Olsen Bruhns, author of *Ancient South America.* Olsen Bruhns is of the opinion that *orichalcum* is a mixture of gold and copper, known to the ancient South American craftsmen as *tumbaga. Orichalcum* is much harder than copper but keeps its malleability and is, therefore, conveniently flexible when hammered. The substance melts at a lower temperature than copper and is an excellent metal for casting. Here, too, the allegory and symbolism of Masonic moral teachings are very clear. Skilled stonemasons working with *orichalcum* in ancient times would have demonstrated its social implications. By uniting the gold of Masonic wisdom with the utilitarian copper of everyday life, great gains could be achieved: improved flexibility, greater strength to withstand the hammer blows of life, a lower melting point signifying greater adaptability and readiness to flow in ways that aid society. Diligent Masonic accuracy and close attention to fine detail are represented by the excellent casting quality of *aurichalcum*.

In this sense, Masonic morality and ethics teach a Mason to pay close attention to what other people really need and want. The metal that casts well, as *tumbaga* does, is like the caring Masonic judge or lawyer who goes into every paragraph and every clause of a complicated legal document in order to achieve justice. The allegory also applies to a compassionate Masonic doctor who studies all of the patient's symptoms with great care and then takes equal care with the surgery and medicine necessary for healing.

In *Critias* there is considerable detail about the many other major advantages Atlantis offered its prosperous people. Carpenters had no shortage of wood on which to use their strength and skills, and there was ample vegetation and pasturage for both wild and domesticated Atlantean animals. There were all kinds of creatures from the largest to the smallest; even elephants were plentiful. From mountain peaks to marshes and verdant valleys, the whole of the vast island was inhabited. In *Critias* the flora of Atlantis is described in depth and detail. Every good thing the Earth could produce grew there — above and below ground. Every benign essence that could be extracted or distilled from herbs, fruits, roots, bark, and florets was in Atlantis. Everything that provided wholesome nourishment and delicious flavours could be found in abundance.

Here again Atlantis is rich in Masonic allegory and symbolism. This part of the Atlantean description is so close to the heart of Masonic ethics, morals, and philosophical ideals that it is impossible to separate them. The more deeply the student of mythology, folklore, and prehistory studies the riddles posed by Atlantis, the closer that student comes to understanding the origins of Freemasonry.

The Atlantis documents tell of a world of almost idyllic plenty — the country itself was one huge cornucopia. Every prospect pleased, and yet somewhere, somehow, the seeds of discontent germinated. The Masonic moral and ethical symbolism was also clear and vivid here. Atlantis was described as an ideal state, but the first faint shadows of its approaching disaster were also visible.

That sombre juxtaposition teaches deep Masonic wisdom. Masonry says: "Give profound thanks for all that is good, enjoy and share your prosperity, be happy, be content with your life. Explore all the bounty that the Creator and Sustainer of the Universe has provided for your pleasure and satisfaction — and help others to find it. Overcome selfishness, avoid greed, shun discontentment, resist the temptation to try to control others, live and let live, be free, and revel in your freedom, but always allow others to be free alongside you. Remember that your freedom to seek happiness ends at the line where your search interferes with theirs."

What are these threatened changes in Atlantis, these divergences from its idyllic origin and blissful past? What more does *Critias* have to say about it?

The old city had been surrounded by water, but now people were building bridges. A new road ran from what was once the old, well-protected royal palace of Cleito and her ten sons down to the great harbour. The later Atlantean kings did not strive to build better and greater structures out of love or respect for their fair city and their fruitful, fertile lands. They built bigger and more ornate edifices competitively, simply to declare in stone: "I am greater than you are."

And then they constructed a canal 300 feet wide, 100 feet deep, and fifty stadia long. (A stadium in the Greek measurement system was just over 600 feet. Fifty stadia would be about five and a half miles.) This canal was excavated from the citadel of Atlantis all the way through to the ocean itself, thus providing access for the biggest ships. Access was a positive factor commercially, but a negative factor defensively. Further inadvisable changes were made at the bridges: the zones of land were divided in such a way that a trireme could pass from one zone to another. Once again accessibility took precedence over defence. Channels, according to *Critias*, were covered over to leave a way below them for the ships to pass. Three kinds of stone were quarried from beneath the central part of Atlantis: red, white, and black.

The Masonic symbolism is again clear: Freemasonry caters to all human needs and conditions. The red, white, and black stones of Atlantis represented mind, body, and spirit — *physical* power to carry out practical craftwork and build castles, temples, and palaces; *mental* power to design, plan, and make the necessary structural calculations for such physical craftwork; *spiritual*, moral, and ethical power to work and plan with honesty, integrity, and the highest possible purpose — in other words, to build, as devout Masons have always built, for the greater glory of God, the supreme Architect and Geometrician of the Masonic universe.

The three great concentric walls that encircled the citadel of Atlantis were coated with three different metals: the outer wall was covered with brass, the one inside that was covered in tin, and the innermost wall was covered with *orichalcum*. What were the secret Masonic meanings of these three metals that protected the concentric walls of Atlantis? Gold and *orichalcum* were both used to represent the sun. Gold was often referred to in ancient symbols and allegories as "the tears of the sun." The tin wall represented "the tears of the moon" in much the same way; silver had exactly the same meaning, but tin could be substituted. The wall of brass represented defensive social strength — protection of the community as a whole. The Masonic allegory of the three Atlantean walls was also intended to teach the need for human strength in a difficult and dangerous world — strength of mind, spirit, and body.

The tin or silver "tears of the moon" can also represent the need for perceptive compassion towards others. The golden *aurichalcum* "tears of the sun" symbolize the need for compassion towards ourselves. Figuratively, the bright, penetrating light of the sun reveals weaknesses that we have to overcome if the citadel of our personality is to be defended from within as well as from without. When there is too wide a gap between the ideal man or woman we strive to be and the actual man or woman we are, then we need this metaphorical sunlight of self-examination to reveal the gap so that we can make the necessary decisions and take the necessary actions to close it. In Freemasonry, therefore, the allegory of the three Atlantean walls represents the need to defend society as a whole, the need to guard and protect other people, and the need to nurture and develop our own personalities and individual identities to their full potential.

Did Atlantis really enjoy a geographical and historical existence, or was it an ingenious Masonic teaching allegory? Was Atlantis an ancient proto-Masonic kingdom, or an intricate and elaborate Masonic moral fable? If the account of Solon's meeting with the ancient Egyptian priest of Sais is not historically accurate, what other possible theories of Atlantis need to be scrutinized?

What is sometimes referred to by Atlantean researchers as the Andes theory, or the Bolivian hypothesis, concerns the possibility that although *Timaeus* and *Critias* are broadly accurate and correct, they refer only to the sinking of the citadel, not the whole continent. Modern geology and geography, and contemporary tectonic plate theory, find it difficult to accept the sinking of a whole continent in a single day. But what if, as described in Plato's two dialogues, it was only the *city* that sank, and that it sank into a very large lake or inland sea, not into the depths of the vast Atlantic Ocean itself? Satellite pictures of Lake Poopó, close to the Bolivian Altiplano, or Pampas Aullagas, indicate that it would have been the right size and shape to accommodate the citadel of Atlantis and its immediate environs, and it would certainly have been geologically possible for that to have gone down in a very short time if subjected to earthquakes or volcanic disturbances. This Bolivian hypothesis argues that the whole of present-day South America was once called Atlantis. In chapter 22, "Canadian and American Masonry," the link between ancient Mesoamerican and South American peoples and the origins of Masonry will be examined in detail.

The Bolivian hypothesis is strengthened by the presence of the mountains surrounding the Altiplano and the occurrence in those mountains of copper, silver, tin, gold and, most significantly, *orichalcum*. Red, white, and black stones are also found there. There is also an interesting linguistic clue to the mystery — in South America *atl* meant water and *antis* meant copper.

Another factor that favours the Bolivian hypothesis is the mysterious Legend of Desaguadero, an account of an ancient South American city built near a lake. The city and its people were punished by the gods for some real or imaginary offence. Just as Plato's version involving the Egyptian priest of Sais and Solon spoke of a submerged Atlantis, so this South American variation is about the sinking of Desaguadero. Did the Desaguadero legend cross the Atlantic millennia ago and become the inspiration for Plato's *Critias* and *Timaeus*? Once again a Masonic allegory is built into the story, just as it is in the account of Noah and the biblical flood. In essence the story teaches that sin is punished and righteousness is rewarded.

Yet another interesting parallel is found in the rings — Masonic circle symbolism again — surrounding Desaguadero, just as they surrounded Atlantis in Plato's dialogues. Furthermore, Poseidon, the water god, was credited with creating Atlantis, whereas Tunapa, a South American water god, is recognized as the founder of Desaguadero.

Other fascinating theories regarding Atlantis are dealt with in depth in Herbie Brennan's outstanding definitive 1999 study *The Atlantis Enigma*. These theories include Viatcheslav Koudriavtsev's proposition that Atlantis vanished off the coast of Cornwall, as supposedly happened to the lost land of Lyonesse, which was believed to have disappeared off Land's End during a terrible medieval storm. The Aran Islands off the Irish west coast are also said by some Atlantean researchers to be the mountaintops of the lost continent.

Dr. John Dee, an exceptionally strong candidate for being an early Elizabethan Mason, was of the opinion that the newly discovered North American continent was Atlantis. He believed that Christopher Columbus and his successors were re-establishing a trade route over 10,000 years old. Another hypothesis regards Minoan Crete as the historical Atlantis and suggests that when volcanic activity destroyed the island of Thera, the ensuing tidal waves and other major disturbances annihilated the ancient Cretan Empire, as well. Albert Hermann, a German geographer, put forward the idea that Atlantis had been in what is now Tunisia. His attention was focused on a large dried-up marsh there. Another German adventurer, Jurgen Spanuth, discovered ancient, submerged walls off the coast of Heligoland and suggested they might have been part of ancient Atlantis. Leo Frobenius put Atlantis in Nigeria after comparing the characteristics of the Yoruban sea god, Olokun, with those of Poseidon. In the Bahamas, Dr. Manson Valentine discovered a very large and impressive submerged wall to the west of Bimini that could well have been part of Atlantis or part of an Atlantean colony.

Pioneering researchers Rand and Rose Flem-Ath came up with the exciting, original, and thoroughly argued suggestion that Atlantis had not so much sunk as *slipped*. They concluded that what is now Antarctica was once Atlantis, and they have put a great deal of painstaking thought into their theory. As a solution, it is among the best worked out so far.

Atlantis may well be much more than a myth or fable. The daring, radical, Masonic hypothesis cannot be lightly discarded. Atlantis may well have existed, and in ancient times an idyllic, utopian society could have flourished there for long centuries. If proto-Masonic, extraterrestrial guides and guardians did help, protect, and advise our earliest ancestors, they might well have established the kingdom of Atlantis and spread their wisdom from it all around the world. Atlantis presents the historian with a puzzling riddle, one in which Masonry may well hold the essential keys. But Atlantis is not the only conundrum: the strange history contained in the *Oera Linda Book* makes equally curious reading. That book refers frequently to a large landmass called either Atland or Aldland that vanished under the North Sea between Britain and the Netherlands. Trubners of London published the *Oera Linda Book* in 1876, which purported to be an English translation of a thirteenth-century Frisian manuscript. The volume contained an account of how Inka, a Frisian king, had sailed towards the setting sun and founded a great empire in a vast new country many miles west of Europe. Was *Inka*, the Frisian adventurer, the founder of Atlantis, of the *Inca* Empire, or *both*?

Yet another submerged land mystery centres on Lemuria. Those researchers who believe they have found evidence that Lemuria once existed place it deep below the present Pacific Ocean. Far less technical than the Atlanteans, but much more spiritual, philosophical, and meditative, the Lemurians spent much of their time in prayer and in sending out positive mental energy for the benefit of all life in the terrestrial biosphere. Here, yet again, sound and benign Masonic principles can be detected. The concepts of meditation and prayer, and of intercessionary prayer in particular, are found among the most important Masonic teachings. The joint existence of both Lemuria in the Pacific and Atlantis on the other side of the world carries a strong Masonic message, a symbolic and allegorical ethical concept. The surging technical energy and inventiveness and the material ambition of Atlantis are balanced and harmonized by the calm reflection and spirituality of all that is associated with Lemuria.

The search for Atlantis still goes on, attracting a significant number of serious-minded, reputable academics. As recently as August 2005, for example, researchers working on the Atlantis mystery discovered evidence for a severe earthquake and tsunami in the vicinity of Spartel Island west of the Straits of Gibralter, just as Plato described it. This 2005 evidence lying under nearly 200 feet of water indicates a probable disaster date of around 12,000 years ago, and that fits well with Plato's *Timaeus* and *Critias*. Another fascinating piece of contemporary Atlantean research is in the capable and enthusiastic hands of Robert Sarmast. He maintains that he has found impressive evidence of Atlantis 3,282 feet down and a little more than four miles off Cyprus. That doesn't fit Plato's location, but Sarmast is immensely confident about what he has seen down there.

The two great continents of Atlantis and Lemuria, now both lost beneath the waves, if they ever *had* any real, concrete, historical existence, provide Masonic lessons for all who are willing to learn from them. *Life must have balance.* Materialism without deep spirituality and genuine moral purpose is futile and tawdry. Withdrawal from the hectic struggle, cut, and thrust of the world into hermit-like spirituality is equally useless and totally unproductive. The great Masonic lesson is that human beings need to balance both sides of their lives — the dynamic activity of secular, material life and the deep tranquillity of meditative spirituality.

The Great Pyramid and the Great Sphinx in Egypt.

Chapter 5

ANCIENT EGYPTIAN MASONRY

TO PURSUE the basic hypothesis that a very high level of culture, ethics, morality, and technology reached our earliest ancestors from somewhere else, we now need to examine ancient Egypt. We ask where the *first* Egyptians came from, and we study the significant links between ancient Egypt and Freemasonry.

Early Dynastic Period	Old Kingdom	Middle Kingdom	New Kingdom	Late Dynastic Period	Greco-Roman Period
3000 BC	2500 BC	2000 BC	1500 BC	1000 BC	500 BC

As the table shows, Egyptian history may be broadly divided into six major categories. How did the Early Dynastic Period begin and where did the first Egyptians come from? The pioneer researcher in this area was Emile-Clément Amélineau. In 1895 he began work at Abydos, where the strange, controversial "helicopter" hieroglyphic was later observed. Working his way steadily and systematically towards the west, Amélineau reached Umm el-Ka'ab, which can be translated as Mother of the Pots. Its name is derived from the vast number of pottery fragments strewn all over the sand there. A mile farther west than the last cultivated area, Amélineau discovered a group of very early brick pit tombs dating from the Early Dynastic Period. His scholarly Coptic background made him totally familiar with the Coptic language and alphabet, and that was a great advantage for an Egyptologist.

The most important clue to this Early Dynastic Period and the mysterious pre-dynastic times that preceded it is that it was the time of Horus, the strange falcon-headed god. The earliest pre-Egyptians in the

Nile Valley seem to have worshipped the falcon as the symbol of cosmic power. These first proto-Egyptians appear to have had an inexplicable amount of wisdom and knowledge. Where did they get it from? Were they taught by extraterrestrials, by Atlanteans, or by an early Masonic elite who had themselves learned it from mysterious super-beings who had travelled to Earth from elsewhere?

The Mysterious Coptic Alphabet

Ⲁ ⲁ	Alpha (a)	Ⲥ ⲥ	Seema (s)
Ⲃ ⲃ	Beta or Veta (b or v)	Ⲧ ⲧ	Tav (t or d)
Ⲅ ⲅ	Gamma (g)		
Ⲇ ⲇ	Delta (d)	Ⲩ ⲩ	Epsilon (v, u or y)
Ⲉ ⲉ	Ei (e)	Ⲫ ⲫ	Fel (f)
Ⲋ	Soo (s)	Ⲭ ⲭ	Kai (k, sh or kh)
Ⲍ ⲍ	Zeta (z)	Ⲯ ⲯ	Epsee (ps)
Ⲏ ⲏ	Eeta (long, heavy e)	Ⲱ ⲱ	Omega (long o)
Ⲑ ⲑ	Theta (t or th)	Ϣ ϣ	Shai (sh)
Ⲓ ⲓ	Iota (i)	Ϥ ϥ	Fai (f)
Ⲕ ⲕ	Kappa (k)	Ϧ ϧ	Khai (kh)
Ⲗ ⲗ	Lambda (l)	Ϩ ϩ	Horee (h)
Ⲙ ⲙ	Mei (m)	Ϫ ϫ	Cheema (ch)
Ⲛ ⲛ	Nei (n)	Ϯ ϯ	Tee (t)
Ⲝ ⲝ	Exsee (x)	Ⳉ ⳉ	Janja (g or j)
Ⲟ ⲟ	Omicron (Short o)	ˋ	Jinkim (Splits words.)
Ⲡ ⲡ	Pi (p)		
Ⲣ ⲣ	Ro (r)		

These intricate old Coptic letter forms could easily have concealed secret Masonic codes.

Very curious mysteries germane to the Masonic history of Egypt are associated with the all-seeing eye of Horus, the falcon god. The eyes of Horus are complementary, balanced, and harmonized like the Ying and Yang of Taoist mythology. His right eye symbolizes the sun, which represents so-called *masculine* energy, logic, reasoning power, and mathematical ability. His left eye is the moon, which symbolizes flexibility and liquid power such as the movement of flowing waters, so-called *feminine* energy, intuition, and magic.

Horus is also associated with the extremely powerful and knowledgeable Thoth, scribe of the Egyptian gods and keeper of all their secrets. These secrets are interpreted as magical spells and incantations by some researchers but as ancient scientific and technological data by other investigators. Some Masonic historians suggest that Thoth, alias Hermes Trismegistus, creator and keeper of the Emerald Tablets on which his vast knowledge is reputedly inscribed, was actually a high-ranking Freemason in that ancient world.

According to some of the oldest Egyptian myths and legends, when the evil god Set gouged out the left eye of Horus, it was recovered for him by the benign power of Thoth. Some folklorists would regard this particular Egyptian incident simply as an aetiological myth indicating that when the moon wanes it is because Set has stolen the eye of Horus, and when it waxes again, the eye has been restored by the power of Thoth. There may, however, be much more to it than that. In its earliest days ancient Egypt was a hotbed of political competition, military conquest, and dangerous intrigue. The work of the proto-Masons there was part of the battle between freedom and oppression, between tyranny and justice, between — in its simplest and most basic terms — good and evil.

Horus can be seen as a benign, humane, and kindly ruler. The cruel and evil Set planned to usurp his throne. Thoth, alias Hermes Trismegistus, was a powerful proto-Masonic source of goodness. He and his followers worked with Horus against the evil Set, and some of that work had to be accomplished in secret. In the sense that there were Masonic conspiracies from these earliest times, and right through history, they were conspiracies against evil — secret alliances to preserve and protect society, never to harm it.

Sadly, the opponents and detractors of Freemasonry are swift to embrace the negative side of conspiracy theory and to attribute all manner of evil schemes to members of the Craft. These accusations range from grandiose Masonic attempts at world domination via political dynasties to international financial corruption and Masonic control of organized vice and crime. Freemasons are also accused of favouring one another unfairly in matters of appointments, promotions, and business contracts. Sadly, some fundamentalists, evangelicals, and cautiously traditional Christians even suspect that Freemasons are secret Satanists or undercover worshippers of Lucifer. *Nothing could be farther from the truth.* Such sensational accusations are as wide of the mark and unfounded as those levelled against the noble and honourable Order of Knights Templar in 1307 by the unprincipled and unscrupulous king Philip le Bel of France and his feebly vacillating accomplice, Pope Clement V, a man who should certainly have known better.

There have been a great many historical events, however, in which Freemasons both individually and as a group have worked together, sometimes in secret, for the good of all. During the horrors of Nazism in occupied Europe during World War II, for example, generous-hearted and courageous Freemasons would always have lived up to their high moral and ethical code and done everything in their power to conceal Jewish friends from Adolf Hitler's psychopathic exterminators. That kind of work in those hazardous circumstances had to be done in the greatest possible secrecy.

Hitler's deplorable *Mein Kampf* condemned Jews and Freemasons alike, and both groups were victims of the brutal and mindless Nazi persecutions. As a small but significant personal case study from those days, co-author Lionel's father, Robert, was a high-ranking Freemason in Sondes Lodge, Dereham, Norfolk, England, in the 1930s and 1940s. He helped and befriended a family of Jewish refugees who had reached England just in time. Robert's warmly welcoming attitude towards them was typically Masonic.

Following on from Amélineau's important pioneering work, an English Egyptologist, J.E. Quibell, was working in Hierakonpolis in 1897 and 1898. He discovered the interesting Narmer Palette and fragments of a ceremonial mace that had once been used by King Narmer himself. Other fragments discovered there well over a century ago included references to the Horus Scorpion King, a pre-dynastic ruler from times even earlier than Narmer's. On the Narmer Palette the king's name appears sandwiched between two bulls with human faces.

Carved from slate, the mysterious Narmer Palette contains what looks like ancient proto-Masonic symbolism.

These mysterious humanoid-bull carvings link immediately with the Minotaur, the man-bull in the Cretan labyrinth; the golden calf the Israelites worshipped; and the cult of Mithras. There is also an interesting connection between bull symbolism and the important Masonic emblem of the Seven Stars, the Pleiades, in Taurus the Bull. The Roman author Virgil, Publius Vergilius Maro (October 15, 70 BC–19 BC), is the author of the *Georgics* and the *Aeneid* and is arguably the greatest Latin poet. There are strange, hidden messages concealed in his work, and we examine these in detail in chapter 11, "Roman Masonry and the Secrets of Como." In book 1 of the *Georgics*, Virgil refers to the stellar bull symbol: "*Candidus auratis aperit cum/Cornibus annum taurus* — the shining bull with horns of gold opens the year." There are several other important symbolic implications here, and this early Masonic metaphor of the Seven Stars in the Taurus constellation refers to Masonic teachings concerning immortality among "the starry hosts of heaven."

Close-up view of the mystical bulls' heads from the Narmer Palette.

Over and above the intriguing bull symbolism on the palette, there is what *could* be a reference to the central Masonic theme of the history of Hiram Abiff. (The *Abiff* part of his name may well have come from the Middle Eastern term of respect *abi*, "father," which also implied "master" or "teacher.") To Masonic historians the three small human figures *might* symbolize the murderous fellow craft workers who killed Hiram Abiff; the large central figure delivering the death blow could be an enlargement of the fellow craft mason who actually committed the crime; the kneeling victim is Hiram Abiff himself. Horus, the falcon god, is looking on appalled by the crime.

This interpretation, however, raises vast problems of dating. The Narmer Palette is 5,000 years old, possibly older. It was carved at least two millennia *before* the reign of Solomon the Wise in Jerusalem. In the Hiram Abiff story (parts of which are corroborated in II Chronicles 2, and in I Kings 7) there are three prime figures involved in the building of King Solomon's great temple in Jerusalem: Solomon himself, King Hiram of Tyre, and Hiram Abiff, who was their chief architect and master craftsman. He was the son of an Israelite widow and a Tyrian father, who had been yet another master craftsman.

Does the Narmer Palette show the murder of brave, idealistic Hiram Abiff? If it does, then the
Masonic allegory of his murder may be much older than the reign of King Solomon.

It is possible, however, that the deep Masonic symbolism in the
account of the murder of brave and faithful Hiram Abiff during the
reign of Solomon of Jerusalem *may* be much older than the reign of
Solomon. Some of the greatest and most significant pieces of moral
folklore and ethical legend tend to recur age after age. The setting
changes and the characters are different, but the central narrative and its
deep symbolic meaning remain the same. In the Hiram episode a good,
wise, skilful, and honourable man possesses vitally important secret
knowledge. His courage and integrity are such that not even the threat
of death will force him to reveal those precious secrets. Avaricious enemies with no morals strike the good man down. But as the *Book of the
Wisdom of Solomon* teaches, "the souls of the righteous are in the hands
of God." In an infinitely better, eternal world, brave and faithful men
and women of integrity are richly rewarded — and this again links with
Taurus, the Heavenly Bull symbolism of the spring equinox, and the
Seven Stars of the Pleiades. Could an earlier version of the Hiram Abiff
story have been known during the life of Narmer?

Narmer was also referred to rather strangely as the Catfish King —
is this a pointer to the widely discussed theory that the hypothetical

extraterrestrials who brought technology and culture to Earth millennia ago were amphibians?

There were several major building programs during Narmer's reign, and they would have provided opportunities — just as there were opportunities during Solomon's reign — for jealous and unscrupulous rival building workers to threaten a true master mason in order to try to steal his precious secrets to further their own ambitions. Men like Hiram Abiff, with the strength of character and high moral principles that true master masons have, will *never* capitulate. So the *essence* of the moral teachings behind the tragic death of Solomon's Hiram Abiff, the Jewish widow's talented son, could have been in place as an ethical allegory long *before* the historical Hiram ever assisted Solomon.

Another archetypal proto-Masonic figure is the mysterious and shadowy Nimrod. In the traditional genealogies following the deluge, Noah's son, Ham, fathered a boy named Cush, who in turn became Nimrod's father. Nimrod is described as a man of abnormal strength and physical prowess — a mighty hunter, warrior, and conqueror. He built city after city and is traditionally regarded as one of the founders of the Assyrian and Babylonian empires, which will be studied in depth for their Masonic connections in chapter 8. Nimrod's era was often a violent and dangerous one, although expert Masonic historians tend to regard him favourably. It may be suggested that in such times and places a strong leader like Nimrod feels the need to command respect and obedience before he can begin to civilize and teach his people better ways, higher morals, and more positive ethical standards.

In a growing and developing empire like Nimrod's, with new cities being established everywhere, there would be an ever-increasing need for skilled architects, designer, planners, and stonemasons. Just as in the Hiram allegory from Solomon's much later era, there could well have been an envious attack on a skilled master mason who courageously refused to betray the Craft's secrets. This also raises the vexed question of what those secrets were that the murderers wanted so desperately. If the prototype Hiram from the very earliest times had *technological* secrets that conferred great power on their holder, it goes some way to explaining why his jealous rivals set such store by them. The allegorical truth behind the courageous death of Hiram Abiff is independent of time and place. It teaches that loyalty, honour, and integrity are more important than life itself, because without them, life degenerates into mere meaningless existence. If the great secrets the good man guarded in pre-Egyptian days concerned the powers of Horus, and if Horus was an extraterrestrial, these early proto-Masonic mysteries deepen.

Horus with the symbolic hawk on his shoulder.

Horus, the falcon god, is a very diverse and complex deity. In his original form he appears to have been a god of the skies. Does that imply that he and his people came *from* the sky? His name seems to have developed from an old Egyptian word that can be rendered as *her, hor,* or *har,* which means "the being on high" or "the distant being." This might refer to the sun itself, which is seen in folklore and mythology as the right eye of Horus. The falcon's speckled feathers represented the stars, and the moon was his left eye. The winds that swept across the Arabian and African deserts were caused by his gigantic wings, and it was in the form of an enormous birdlike sky god that Horus was worshipped by the earliest proto-Egyptians at Nekhen, which the Greeks called Hierakonpolis, meaning "the city of the falcon" or "the city of the hawk." Horus became the patron of the Nekhen rulers, and when they in turn grew into the later national state, ruled by the pharaohs, Horus achieved the status of a national deity.

Other symbolic aspects of Horus that must have been well-known to ancient Egyptian proto-Masonry included the image of the great hawk god with its wings outspread as it crossed the sky, like the sun, in a celestial boat. When this image is studied alongside the controversial helicopter hieroglyph from Abydos, it seems to be a tantalizing hint that those who came to teach the proto-Egyptians in the pre-dynastic ages came from beyond the skies.

Could these mysterious hieroglyphics be meant to represent planes and helicopters?

Also known as Horakhty, or Horus of the Two Horizons, this mysterious sky god travelled, like the sun, from east to west. Masonic historians and folklorists who understand the allegories and symbolism behind this path-of-the-sun interpretation will suggest that it may indicate an elite group of teachers and leaders — the ancient Egyptian proto-Masons — whose advanced technology included the power of flight. It also suggests the deep Masonic teachings about immortality: the reborn are symbolically resurrected in the east, just like the reborn sun. Horus was also known as the god of the east.

Another piece of early Masonic symbolism is the lion — and Horus was depicted as a lion as well as a falcon. Among the Hebrews, the lion was the symbol of the tribe of Judah, the messianic tribe. In the Bible's Revelation 5:5, Christ is referred to as the Lion of the Tribe of Judah. The lion as a Masonic symbol appears again and again in the medieval cathedrals where active Masons revealed their Craft identity to one another in their beautiful and meaningful carvings. Whether as Horus, the ancient Egyptian sky god, or as Jesus, the Jewish Messiah and Son of Yahweh, the lion was a uniquely potent and significant symbol. It has already been suggested that C.S. Lewis, J.R.R. Tolkien, and the other Inklings were Freemasons, so it is no surprise to find that Aslan, the Hero-God of Lewis's *Narnia* series, was a lion.

Just as Jesus, the pre-existent Logos, or Word of God, was incarnated as a tiny human baby at Bethlehem, so Horus, the mighty and powerful sun god and cosmic falcon, was born as a tiny, helpless child, son of Isis and Osiris. In this form he was called Harparkered, meaning Horus-the-Child, and his name in this context became Harpokrates in Greek. In ancient Egyptian art he is depicted sitting on the knee of his mother, Isis, and being fed. What becomes extremely interesting for Masonic historians is that Isis was already widowed when Harpokrates was born. So, like Hiram, Horus is the son of a widow.

Here, too, in connection with the infant Horus, Masonic theologians, folklorists, and historians understand the deep underlying symbolism: Masonic ethical and moral teachings reveal that vast power and childlike helplessness are at the opposite ends of the spectrum, yet the spectrum curves like the rainbow so that, paradoxically, strength can be expressed through weakness and weakness can express itself through an appearance of strength. The paradox can be resolved by considering the tenderness that a powerful father expresses when he takes his infant son into gorilla-like arms that could uproot a tree and cradles the boy as gently as his mother would. Conversely, the feeble, uncertain, weak, and insecure mind of a cruel and vicious tyrant reveals its weakness by ostentatious acts of cruel and ruthless brutality: pathetic weakness masquerades as strength.

In his Greek guise as Harpokrates, Horus-the-Child wards off danger from snakes, crocodiles, and scorpions. He is also seen as uniting two divine parents with different attributes. This miraculous birth took place in Khemmis, in the Nile delta, after his wicked brother, Seth, uncle to Horus, had treacherously murdered his father, the good and great Osiris.

What followed was an eighty-four-year battle between Horus and Seth. In Masonic numerological symbolism 8+4=12 and subsequently 1+2=3. *Three* is a highly significant Masonic number. It represents the three sides of the Pythagorean triangle; the three Divine Persons of the Christian Trinity; the Bethlehem birth trinity of Mary, Joseph, and Jesus; and the three sacred symbols of Masonic geometry — the square, the circle, and the triangle. *Three* also signifies Solomon of Jerusalem, Hiram of Tyre, and Hiram Abiff. The symbolic Masonic *three* further stands for body, mind, and spirit — the complete human being.

Some of the oldest Egyptian legends describe the way in which Horus's mother protected him by hiding with him among the papyrus reeds. Here again is deep Masonic symbolism. Truth and goodness, morality and ethics, have to be protected by being hidden in allegory and symbolism — the metaphorical papyrus reeds. The falcon in these ancient depictions is shown on top of a pillar of papyrus reeds, which also symbolizes written records and important archives. The benign Horus, therefore, achieves his power through the data inscribed on the papyrus: power is the child of knowledge, just as Horus-the-Child is the son of Isis and Osiris.

There is a very strange Masonic allegory in the legend of Haroeris, the adult Horus grown from Harpokrates, the infant. In this powerful adult form, Haroeris performs the all-important ceremony of the opening of the mouth for his dead father before wreaking his vengeance on Seth, his wicked uncle, and winning back his father's throne. The moral, ethical teaching here shows a vital order of priorities: the giving of life is infinitely more important than mere revenge.

Horus is also represented as a serpent, and that image is important in certain Masonic rites. The twenty-eighth degree of the Scottish Rite Southern Jurisdiction incorporates the Serpent Ouroboros, and its twenty-fifth degree is that of the Knight of the Brazen Serpent.

Another question that intrigues Masonic historians is the connection between the Egyptian legend of Hathor, goddess of love, music, dancing, and art, and the destruction of the evil Seth. In one version of Seth's overthrow the otherwise beautiful, gentle, and benign Hathor turns into a deadly serpent and kills him. The deep, symbolic, allegorical teaching here is that human nature can contain both qualities: the gentle, loving, artistic, and beautiful woman can turn into a terrifying destroyer when evil threatens her husband or children. The gentle, peaceful, protective, and benign Mason can become a fierce and formidable warrior in defence of those in his or her care.

Tem, also called Atum, was yet another serpent god. He was originally the local god for Heliopolis and was said to be one of the forms assumed by Ra — Tem was the setting sun. His identification as both a serpent god and a sun god came about because the tail-in-mouth serpent could be understood as the solar disc as well as the Ouroboros type of serpent that encircled the Earth. The proto-Masonic symbolism here is that the day is divided into three parts: the morning belongs to Ra as Khepera, he is simply Ra at noon, and he becomes Tem in the evening. Once again the highly significant *three* is represented in the proto-Masonic allegory of the tripartite sun god.

In Greek mythology, dealt with in chapter 6, Zeus's two eagles meet at the centre of the Earth, where they encounter the gigantic snake, Pytho. *Serpens Candivorens* (also called Ouroboros) is the ancient Greek symbol of the snake with its tail in its mouth. To Masonic historians it is the allegory of the endless cycle of nature: death, new life, growth, and maturity. Chinese mythology has a pair of entwined snakes encircling the world; they symbolize a combination of power and wisdom and so represent the Creator, an idea that is very close to the Masonic teaching about God as the Supreme Architect and Geometrician of the Universe.

In an important segment of Buddhist teaching, a huge snake wound its coils seven times around Buddha's waist in an attempt to kill him. So great was Buddha's goodness and inner strength, however, that the serpent could not harm him and became one of his disciples instead. This story is clearly in accord with the highest principles of worldwide proto-Masonic teaching: goodness and inner strength are impervious to evil. The true Freemason is proof against all that is negative and harmful. His or her inner strength and goodness also protect those whom the Mason guards.

Eric Rucker Eddison was a British civil servant and author who lived from November 24, 1882, until August 18, 1945. His best-known work, *The Worm Ouroboros*, was published in 1922. It is interesting to note that both J.R.R. Tolkien and C.S. Lewis went out of their way to praise Eddison's writings. If, as is widely believed, Lewis, Tolkien, and their close friends, who were known as the Inklings, were Freemasons, they would have understood and enjoyed the Masonic allegory and symbolism in Eddison's *The Worm Ouroboros*. It is a fast-moving, heroic narrative in which, after a great struggle, good defeats evil — the fundamental truth at the core of all true Masonic teaching.

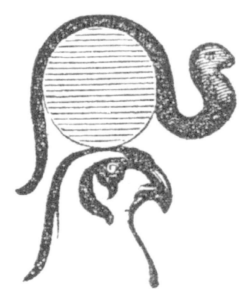

Strange ancient Egyptian, proto-Masonic symbolism shows the serpent around the solar disc, or the Earth, with Horus, the falcon god, above.

Masonic students of the history of astronomy and its predecessor, astrology, will be aware that there was once a thirteenth sign of the zodiac called Ophiuchus Serpentarius, meaning "the holder of the snake." In more recent times the thirteenth sign has also been referred to as Alpheichius. It lies between Sagittarius and Libra, close to Scorpio. Zeus transformed Asclepius, the healer god of the Greek pantheon, into the constellation Ophiuchus. Asclepius's famous caduceus — the physician's healing staff — has a serpent wrapped around it, and this characteristic ties in very closely with the strange biblical references to Moses and the brazen serpent.

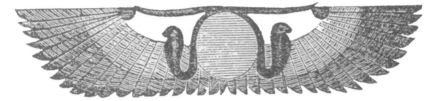

Ancient Egyptian, proto-Masonic symbolism that depicts serpents around the Earth, or the solar disc, with the wings of Horus, the falcon god.

The Bible's Numbers 21: 4–9 tells how "fiery serpents" attacked the Israelites, and many of those who were bitten by them died. Moses then made a serpent of brass and set it up on a pole, similar in some ways to a caduceus. And any Israelites who were bitten after that had only to look at the brazen serpent on the pole in order to be healed.

This curious tale is rich in Masonic symbolism. To begin with, the account in Numbers says that the Israelites had been complaining bitterly about their general conditions and the difficulty of the route they were following *before* the fiery serpents attacked them. To a Masonic historian the first part of this allegorical narrative is a clear warning against negative criticism and bitter complaints. Moses, their leader, was doing his best for them. Unnecessary, unhelpful comments were not going to help him, nor would they improve morale during the arduous journey, a situation in which high morale was essential to success. The second part of the allegory — the attack by the fiery serpents — clearly indicates just how groundless the Israelites' earlier complaints were. There is another interesting

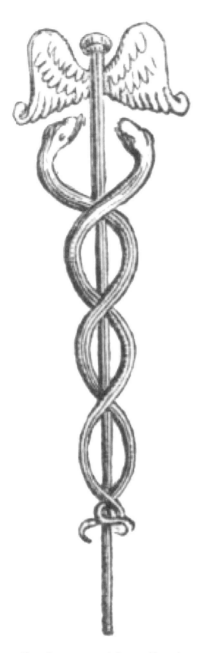

The caduceus: some scholars would say that the wings represent the Greek god Hermes, but they could equally well be the wings of Horus, the Egyptian falcon god.

reference to "flying fiery serpents" in Isaiah 30:6. Some scholars have seen a connection between the Hebrew word *saraph* (meaning "fire," "burning heat," or "brilliancy") and the *seraphim* (bright angels with powers of flight).

There are parallels here perhaps with Aesop's fable of the foolish shepherd boy who cried wolf when no wolf was threatening the flock. Those who grumble unnecessarily about trivia change their priorities when serious trouble arrives. A monotonous diet and steep, rough terrain were not *real* problems: fiery serpents with potentially fatal bites *were*. Another aspect of the rich Masonic symbolism here is the curative power of the brazen serpent that Moses made. Masonry teaches the basic truths of death and resurrection to a happier, fuller, richer life. Those who had been bitten *before* Moses made the life-giving brazen serpent had frequently succumbed to the bite. Now, once the curative serpent was there, looking at it healed those who had been bitten. Some scholars have suggested that, like the caduceus, the brazen serpent's main purpose was to indicate where the camp's medical centre was so that bite victims could go there quickly for treatment.

Formerly, a snakebite had been a death sentence; now it was curable. The brazen serpent remedy for what had formerly been a terminal condition was close to the idea of resurrection from the dead. To a Masonic historian the allegory of seeing the brazen serpent and being healed was equivalent to seeing a Masonic symbol such as the square and compasses. Led by that benign symbol, the inquirer could find Masonic brethren, apply to join a lodge, and so come to understand the new and better way of life that Masonic truth made available.

It is a pity that some anti-Masonic religious fundamentalists and overly simplistic religious traditionalists have totally misunderstood the Masonic symbolism of the snake and mixed it up with the tale of the evil serpent in Eden. For knowledgeable Freemasons, the serpent symbolizes healing and wisdom — excellent Masonic hospitals and schools put that healing and wisdom into practice.

The pyramids and the Great Sphinx are well-known aspects of ancient Egyptian culture, and they also have strong links with proto-Masonic allegory and symbolism. Immortality and lives that continue after death are indispensable parts of the core of Masonic wisdom. It was an essential aspect of ancient Egyptian belief in eternal life that the dead person's *material* body should be preserved as long as possible on Earth to assist his or her immortal essence, the soul, or true and eternal personality, to make swift and certain progress through the different spheres of the afterlife. Understandably, using their logic and reasoning powers, the ancient Egyptians thought of the afterlife as an amplified and vastly improved version of the life they had enjoyed on Earth. They also wanted to live in close proximity to the families and friends they had loved on Earth. Here, too, their ideas were similar to proto-Masonic ethical and moral teaching: loving fellowship and blissful community life were recognized as the most important ingredients of true happiness.

The king or pharaoh, however, had rather different expectations. He was regarded as already semi-divine while still on Earth. At death he took up his full divinity in the celestial court of Ra. Whether king or commoner, the dead still had to be nourished, and some, at least, of the different parts of the new-world body (the *ba*, the *ka*, the *akh*, and the *shadow*) required food. Here, too, the Egyptian ideas about the care of their dead can be tied to proto-Masonic teachings. After the spiritual work performed in a Masonic temple, the brothers or sisters enjoy a shared meal. Here Masonry teaches the practicalities and realities of life: spiritual worship and fellowship are followed by the equally important shared meal at what Masons call the festive board. Masonic harmony and balance between spiritual and physical life are essential. When Christ himself had taught his disciples and prayed with them, they all ate together.

What is thought to be the oldest pyramid, the Step Pyramid of Saqqara, is associated with King Zoser, and estimates of its age vary around the 3000 BC mark. Mainstream Egyptologists have dated the Medum Pyramid as belonging roughly to the same period as the Saqqara Pyramid. It was created originally as another step pyramid, but a few years later Pharaoh Snefru filled in the ninety-degree angles separating the steps and added a limestone casing. This, unfortunately, collapsed so that what is visible now in the twenty-first century is a wide, squat tower-like structure.

Another early pyramid is the one situated at Dahshur. Known as the Bent Pyramid, it dates from around 2600 BC. When this pyramid was partially constructed, the builders realized that its slope was too steep and that it could not be completed at that precipitous angle. Accordingly, the gradient was reduced, producing an effect similar to the refraction of light.

There is a great deal of important proto-Masonic symbolism and allegory here. This curious structure is associated with Snefru, first king of the fourth dynasty, who reigned for a quarter-century. If, as some Masonic historians have conjectured, Snefru was a high-ranking proto-Mason, then the Bent Pyramid may be regarded as a moral and ethical allegory. The life teaching it contains within its massive stones is the determination to circumvent all obstacles and *never* be defeated by them. The best and highest Masonic aims and objectives, in accordance with the best and highest Masonic ethics and morals, must always be achieved as long as there is blood in a Freemason's veins. Snefru's goal was to complete his Dahshur pyramid and, despite the gradient problem, he finished it.

The Red Pyramid, also known as the Lower Pyramid, was built at this lower gradient. This pyramid provides a further proto-Masonic allegory and life-teaching principle. We must learn by our mistakes. It is a Masonic principle that experience is a great teacher. A fool constantly repeats his or her mistakes; a sensible man or woman never makes the same mistake twice; a wise master mason observes the world of cause and effect very carefully and is able to learn from the mistakes of others. He or she is ready and willing to pass on that vital wisdom to those who ask for help and advice.

Snefru's wife was Hetepheres, and their son was the famous Khufu, *allegedly* the builder of the Great Pyramid. However, there are substantial reasons for believing that the Great Pyramid was already built long before Khufu saw fit to claim it as his own.

In chapter 22 we deal in depth with Canadian and American Freemasonry, including the amazing old pyramids of Mesoamerica and South America. Their style of structure argues strongly for the existence of a global, technologically developed, pre-Egyptian culture, possibly centred on Atlantis or Lemuria. It is, nevertheless, relevant to make brief mention of them here in connection with the pyramids of ancient Egypt that they closely resemble.

The Mayans, Toltecs, Aztecs, and their ancestors seem to have built pyramids in the New World that bear an uncanny similarity to those in Egypt. The Mesoamerican pyramids can be seen in El Salvador, Honduras, Guatemala, and Mexico. The New World pyramids look as though they were intended to serve as vast plinths for temples. As such they follow the stepped pattern of the Zoser pyramid in Egypt rather than the smooth "proper" pyramid.

Again the gradient problem is evident. The smaller Mesoamerican pyramids have slopes that are occasionally steeper than the incline of Egyptian pyramids; the larger Mesoamerican pyramids have gentler slopes than their Egyptian counterparts. The terraced pyramid of El Tajin in Veracruz, Mexico, shows clear signs of proto-Masonic influence. It has seven levels corresponding to the seven ranks of Freemasonry: steward, tyler, junior deacon, senior deacon, junior warden, senior warden, and worshipful master. On each of the terraces of the El Tajin pyramid there are recessed storage spaces where the secret wisdom leading up to the next level of Masonic knowledge could have been stored, ready for the candidate to study before proceeding to more advanced duties.

No reference to Mesoamerican pyramids would be complete without including the Pyramid of the Sun in Teotihuacán. At close to 230 feet high, it is one of the largest pyramids in Central America. Another imposing New World structure, the Castillo Pyramid, can be seen at Chichén Itzá on the Yucatán Peninsula.

The Castillo Pyramid at Chichén Itzá on the Yucatán Peninsula may have strange Masonic connections.

The unanswered questions remain. Did an alien culture from the stars pass its secrets to east and west, to Egypt in one direction and to Canada and the Americas in the other? Did the Atlanteans transmit pyramid knowledge in both directions? Did eastern wisdom travel west, or was it western wisdom that journeyed east? It is a high principle of Freemasonry that knowledge paradoxically needs to be both guarded *and* disseminated, sent to those who need it and will benefit from it, guarded from any who would misuse it to bring harm to others.

If ancient proto-Masons knew the secrets of the pyramids, were their secrets preserved over millennia and passed to the builders of the Louvre Pyramid in Paris? Ieoh Ming Pei, the brilliant Sino-American architect who won the prestigious Pritzker Prize in 1983, designed the Parisian pyramid. The amazing glass structure was completed in 1989. Masonic numerologists would comment on the year as being a significant one — 1+9+8+9=27, the cube of three, one of the most significant symbolic numbers. There are *three* fundamental Masonic symbols: the square, the circle, and the triangle. There are *three* fundamental Masonic ranks: entered apprentice, fellow craft, and master mason. There are *three* leaders of a Masonic lodge: the junior warden, the senior warden, and the worshipful master. So the cube of three is an important Masonic number. Very few Freemasons would think that opening the Louvre Pyramid in 1989 was a simple coincidence. The genius of Ieoh Ming Pei would have worked out the ideal opening year for his masterpiece, and it must always be remembered that architecture and Masonry are very close companions.

If the ancient Egyptian pyramids contain proto-Masonic symbolism and allegory, what about their companion, the Great Sphinx? Its age-old riddle is filled with proto-Masonic symbolism: what walks on four legs, then two legs, then three legs? The answer is a human being. A baby crawls on all fours, an adult walks on two legs, an elderly person with mobility problems walks with a stick, hence three legs. Once again the vital, proto-Masonic *three* features in the answer.

Carved from the surrounding limestone, the Sphinx is about 240 feet long and around twenty-three feet wide. Approximately sixty-six feet high, it stands on the Giza Plain on the west bank of the Nile. It faces east, and there is a temple between its huge front paws. Its Arabic name is Abu al-Hôl, which translates literally as Father of Terror. Sphinx is its Greek name, and refers to a legendary creature with the body of a lion and the head of a beautiful woman. The Sphinx at Giza, as it can be seen today, has the body of a lion and the head of a man, *which seems too small for the gigantic lion's body*. Did the Sphinx originally have the head of a lion to match its huge body? If so, and that seems likely, *why* was it changed and *when* was it changed? In Masonic allegory, the lion is the symbol for strength and courage: the strength to live with high moral and ethical principles in a world that is all too often immoral and unethical; and the courage to challenge things that are wrong, and to fight against them. The lion is also a messianic champion — like the Lion of Judah, a deliverer of the oppressed.

If a human face was carved on the Sphinx to replace the ancient lion's head, then whose face is it? One idea is that it is intended as a portrait of Pharaoh Khafre, who was also known to the Greeks as Chephren or Khephren. His period was between 2723 BC and 2563 BC during the fourth dynasty. His father was Khufu, but Khafre's half-brother, Redjedef, ruled before Khafre acquired the throne. Although some Egyptologists credit Khafre with constructing the Sphinx, the arguments against him seem stronger than those that favour his workmanship.

A substantial number of Egyptologists regard the face on the Sphinx as that of Harmachis, the sun god. He was one of the many forms of Horus, and his title Harmachis means Horus on the Horizon. As the Sphinx faces east, it may be said to carry the face of Horus look-ing towards the eastern horizon in the form of Harmachis.

Yet again there is proto-Masonic symbolism and allegory behind the supposed change of head and face from the lion to the man. Masonry teaches that by acquiring Masonic ideals, a man can change for the better and acquire the characteristics of the great and noble lion, the universal symbol of strength and courage.

If the face on the Sphinx is intended to be that of Khafre, then the symbolism demonstrates that this relatively undistinguished pharaoh acquired leonine characteristics by learning from the elite Egyptian proto-Masons of his day. Masonic teaching symbolically turned a man into a lion. If, however, the face on the Sphinx is that of Harmachis, the sun god, an aspect of the mighty Horus, then the Sphinx reveals that the courage and strength of the lion are synonymous with the power of the divine Horus. The Masonic teaching is again clear: good-ness creates further, higher goodness; leonine strength and courage are rewarded by divine approval and identification with the divine. The identification problem is exacerbated by the Sphinx's having been almost completely buried under the sand for a very long time.

One account of the Sphinx having been cleared of the sand that almost enveloped it dates back to around 1400 BC when the future Tutmosis IV, then a very young man, dreamt that if he cleared the Sphinx he would become pharaoh. His excavators struggled hard to uncover the front paws, and Tutmosis duly became the ruler of Egypt. The proto-Masonic allegory is clear: nothing is achieved without hard work, and it is the mark of a wise and honourable man to keep his word. The granite dream stela was placed between the Sphinx's paws to commemorate Tutmosis's work.

In 1817 Captain Caviglia carried on with the work that Tutmosis had started more than 3,000 years earlier. Caviglia uncovered most of the Sphinx's chest. Well over a century later, the whole of the gigantic statue was freed from the entombing sand. Stones from the bedrock out of which the Sphinx was carved were used to construct the nearby temple; some of those stones weighed in the region of 200 tons. How was it done without the cutting, lifting, and moving machinery available to construction workers in the twenty-first century? Who brought such knowledge to the ancient Egyptians? Was it the elite corps of proto-Masons? If so, who were they and where did they come from?

Mainstream Egyptologists estimate the Sphinx's age at a little less than 5,000 years, but there is compelling evidence suggesting that it is actually far older. Much controversy has raged over the nature of the erosion on its huge body: was it done by airborne sand, or by water? If the arid desert around Egypt today was once a fertile and well-watered plain, the Sphinx might well have been subjected to water erosion. No great civilization could rise and flourish for millennia unless it had ample food supplies. Was today's barren desert once the granary of the ancient world?

Of all the great civilizations that have risen to their zenith, then slowly declined to their nadir as millennia passed, the glories of ancient Egypt are in a class of their own. They have achieved a level of durability that ensures that their proto-Masonic symbolism and allegory will be passed on to succeeding generations — a rich Masonic heritage of ethics, morality, and wisdom set in stone.

Mount Olympus, traditional home of the Greek gods.

Chapter 6

MASONS IN CLASSICAL GREECE

THE GREEK pantheon of gods and goddesses provides the first fascinating clues to the existence of a proto-Masonic elite in ancient Greece that helped to spread culture, philosophy, and science. The divine family tree began with Chaos, from whom were descended Gaea, Tartarus, Eros, and Erebus. The next generation of Greek gods included Cronus, Coeus, and Oceanus, and the generation after that gave rise to the mighty Zeus, Poseidon, Hades, Hestia, and Demeter. The following generation saw the appearance of Athena, Ares, Hebe, Hephaestus, Hermes, and Aphrodite. The myths show conflict and rivalry among these ancient gods, and the interface of widely different aims and objectives. Some were keen to help human development; others sought to rule, exploit, and dominate our earliest ancestors.

If we look deeper than the romantic, mythological, and magical elements of the Greek myths, we find what sound suspiciously like accounts of advanced, cultured, and technological extraterrestrials with formidable weaponry and powers of flight. From the legends it would seem that Zeus in particular frequently blended his genes with those of attractive human females, not only because he seemed to find the experience pleasant, but because he was endeavouring to father an improved race of stronger, more intelligent terrestrial humanoids — either to *be* the proto-Masonic elite or to *serve* the proto-Masonic elite, and in so doing advance human welfare. The Greek gods' escapades parallel the Old Testament account of mysterious super-beings referred to as the Sons of God who interbred with attractive human females and produced offspring with additional powers (Genesis 6:1–4).

There are students of folklore and mythopoeia who argue that the Greek gods behaved as they did in the stories simply because the creators of those stories had anthropomorphized their deities. This school of folklorists contends that the writers of the mythology created fabulous gods in their own human image and gave them imaginary powers that their creators longed to have for themselves. Modern "gods" like Superman and Batman, they argue, also fit this wish-fulfilment pattern.

But other experts present an entirely different case. They consider the strong possibility that the influential ideas flowed in the opposite direction. For these investigators it was not terrestrial humanoids who created imaginary gods that behaved as they would have liked to behave themselves, if only they had had the power; rather, it was the highly advanced extraterrestrial humanoids with *genuinely* amazing powers who seemed godlike to early human beings. This second argument suggests that it was those astounding visitors whose immense powers provided the fertile fields from which the ancient Greek myths and legends grew.

If this contention is true, those extraterrestrials were, therefore, either early proto-Masons themselves, or they were the creators and teachers of the early *human* proto-Masons. Stories of hybrids (like Herakles) who finally achieved full godhead, thus acquiring the power and longevity of their extraterrestrial mentors, are remarkably similar to the ancient Egyptian ideas of semi-divine pharaohs doing much the same thing.

Herakles was the son of Zeus by Alkmene, a human girl. After many adventures, and much earthly grief, Herakles became a complete god and joined the other immortals on Mount Olympus, where he married his half-sister, Hebe, the daughter of Zeus and Hera. Here, too, there is a remarkable parallel with the Egyptian custom of semi-divine pharaohs marrying their sisters. If extraterrestrial super-beings were involved in genetic engineering and a program of in-breeding aimed at improving human stock, such brother-sister marriages could well have formed part of their long-term plan. In this context it is interesting to re-examine the relationship between Abraham and Sarah and his otherwise puzzling half-truth to the pharaoh about Sarah being his *sister* rather than his *wife* when she was, in fact, *both*. If, as seems possible, the pharaoh was also connected with the extraterrestrial elite and knew many proto-Masonic secrets, his understanding of the relationship problem — and his prompt return of Sarah — becomes easier to explain.

Abraham's goodness, expressed in his high ethical and moral standards, his unselfishness, courage, and military and pastoral successes, makes him a clear candidate for high rank in the proto-Masonic elite. There is also his strong sense of mission, of being called from Ur of the Chaldees to accomplish a task of vast, global importance.

The positive encounter of Abraham with the mysterious Melchizedek, the priest-king of Salem, is also germane to this argument. Melchizedek was said to have no human genealogy and "neither beginning of days nor end of life," which would seem to make him a prime candidate for senior rank in the ancient, proto-Masonic hierarchy. Some researchers have also identified him with Thoth, powerful scribe of the Egyptian gods, and with Hermes Trismegistus, who may well have been one and the same entity as Melchizedek.

There is also the question of the Emerald Tablets on which it is alleged that Thoth, or Hermes Trismegistus, had inscribed vitally important secrets. It also needs to be recalled that in at least one ancient legend Sarah found Hermes Trismegistus asleep, or in suspended animation, in a cave. She fled when he began to stir. Did she take at least one of the Emerald Tablets with her? And were the secrets engraved on it *Masonic* secrets? Did the stones that she took become the strange *urim* and *thummim* used by early Hebrew priests to ascertain the will of Yahweh? These questions will be examined in more depth in chapter 8, entitled "Ancient Chaldean and Hebrew Masonry."

The Greek gods were believed to have their headquarters on Mount Olympus, the highest mountain peak in Greece with a summit reaching nearly 10,000 feet. Olympus is close to the Gulf of Thérmai of the Aegean Sea. Bordering both Macedonia and Thessaly, it connects northern and southern Greece. Mount Olympus is also known as Óros Ólimbos, and its map reference is 40°5′ North, 22°21′ East.

Olympus's plant life is among the most varied in the whole of Europe, which raises further questions about genetic engineering, plant breeding, and botanical culture. Were the hypothetical extraterrestrial proto-Masons interested in developing medicinal plants for the human beings they were teaching and helping?

As for the actual dwelling places of the Greek gods, many of the old myths and legends housed them in crystal palaces on Olympus. Was there a reason for that? Had an adventurous early goatherd tending his flock high on the slopes of Olympus actually glimpsed sunlight flashing on what was unmistakably a crystal mansion?

According to myth, the Greek gods of Olympus lived in crystal palaces like this one.

Masonic historians, especially those who are academically oriented towards psychology — and towards the study of early, pre-scientific attempts to understand and explain the mysteries of human nature and behaviour — are interested in the theory that each of the Greek gods and goddesses on Olympus represented a facet of the incredibly complex human psyche. This hypothesis is parallel in many important ways to Carl Jung's theory of archetypes and would tie in with the idea that extraterrestrial mentors were keen to study our ancestors' thought processes, to monitor the ways in which human personalities were growing and developing.

The inhabitants of the crystal mansions on Mount Olympus were: Zeus, king of the gods, and his wife, Hera; Poseidon and Hades, Zeus's brothers; Demeter and Hestia, his sisters; and his children, Aphrodite, Apollo, Ares, Artemis, Athena, Hephaestus, and Hermes.

There was a sense in which these ancients Olympian gods were regarded as personifications of abstract human attributes and human goals, aims, and objectives. These were very close indeed to the high ethical principles characteristic of proto-Masonry. Zeus represented the mind at its best, the pursuit of philosophy and intellectual ability, all of which are reflected in Freemasonry. It was thought by some historians and theologians that worshippers of the Olympian gods used them as personifications to increase the relevant desirable qualities within themselves. In other words, according to this theory, people believed that worshipping Zeus, for example, helped them to develop their minds. Zeus also represented the highest Masonic ethics of protecting those in need, especially sojourners in a strange land. Zeus stood, additionally, for integrity and the vital importance of keeping an oath or promise, a particularly Masonic virtue.

Hera was the representation of femininity, fertility, and marriage. Apollo was another recognizably Masonic Greek god. He stood for self-discipline, law, and order, but he also signified the wisdom of tolerance, inclusiveness, and moderation in both social and intellectual life. Apollo would have been appalled by the death of Socrates. Aphrodite symbolized wild, uncontrolled passion, irrational behaviour, and the high risk of consequent tragedy that can spring from it when control is lost. She also stood for the indescribable delight that passion can bring to lovers when it is not corrupted or warped by selfishness, treachery, betrayal, or disloyalty. She personified the need for self-control, which is a vital part of Masonic morality and ethics. Hermes protected travellers and represented the human desire to travel and in so doing to experience new and different things. Just as dreams were regarded, in a sense, as a form of mental or spiritual travel, so Hermes was concerned with travelling to the dream world as well as actual movement through space.

Athena was the personification of wisdom, an essential ingredient of Masonry. Hephaestus, sometimes called the blacksmith of the gods, was the embodiment of science, art, and technology. He stood for that drive towards practical knowledge and discovery that was to lead from walking to charioteering, and from charioteering to supersonic aircraft and space travel.

According to this theory of the gods of Olympus, acting as sounding boards and personifications of human nature in all its complexities, the dark side of being human was also represented. Ares, the god of war, stood for the savage, aggressive, ruthless, and merciless aspect of the human mind. He was not so much a representation of evil as a warning of where human viciousness could lead if it was not kept under the tightest control. He was, in that sense, the equivalent of the admonition against uncontrolled sexual passion that Aphrodite typified. There are acceptable and legitimate occasions for violence — in defence of the weak, for example, in order to save them from an evil and predatory enemy — just as there are acceptable and legitimate occasions for explosive sexual passion. Because both are so strong, the warnings personified in Aphrodite and Ares are vitally important and must be heeded. Here yet again Masonry teaches the vital moral and ethical self-control that prevents misery and tragedy.

Yet another theory, which appeals to reflective and meditative Masonic historians and philosophers, is the hypothesis that the wise ancient Greeks did not actually believe that their gods were sentient entities who dwelt in crystal mansions on the mountain. According to this speculation, it was the peace and tranquillity of the mountain that made it possible for deep thinkers to encounter their personified gods within themselves. A mystic alone on the beautiful, wooded slopes of Olympus could reach his or her own deepest mind levels in a way that was not possible when distracted by the bustle of a city marketplace. Such a thinker, alone among the trees, could find within himself or herself the intellectual power of Zeus, the sensitive femininity of Hera, the orderliness of Apollo, the passion of Aphrodite, the wanderlust of Hermes, the wisdom of Athena, and the scientific and technological drive of Hephaestus. Counterpoised against these virtues and abilities would be an awareness of the danger that the instinctive violence of Ares could invoke unless strict self-control was maintained against it.

In classic Greek, Mount Olympus means "the shining mountain" or "the luminous place," and whichever theory of the gods of Olympus is considered, it is undeniable that a great many sensitive and perceptive thinkers have found enlightenment on the mountain's awe-inspiring slopes. Such men and women would say, in a symbolic and allegorical way, that they have experienced an awareness that the Greek gods still linger there. Masonic historians would know exactly what such mystics were talking about.

Another fascinating field of study for Masonic historians is Homer's account of the adventures of Odysseus, the siege of Troy, and Odysseus's troubled journey back to Ithaca. Every encounter that Odysseus has can be understood in terms of Masonic allegory, and that raises the question of whether Homer was one of the ancient proto-Masons who used his narrative powers to spread Masonic wisdom, ethics, and morality.

The simple outline of Homer's basic narrative is too well-known to need anything but the briefest reminder. Odysseus, king of the peaceful island of Ithaca, is the husband of the beautiful Penelope and father of their infant son, Telemachus. Odysseus, also known as Ulysses, is deservedly liked and respected by his subjects. He is a fair, just, and honest ruler, a man who represents exactly that type of good citizen to whom Freemasonry opens with alacrity the welcoming doors of the lodge. At this stage of the narrative, however, Odysseus signifies what is very much an *ordinary* world. There is peace and prosperity in Ithaca, but adventure and character development are yet to come. Odysseus is a *good* person, but an *incomplete* and *unfulfilled* man.

Challenge and adventure come to Odysseus because of the wild love affair between the exquisitely beautiful Helen, wife of King Menelaus, and her impetuous lover, Paris, prince of Troy, with whom she elopes in one version but is abducted in another. Agamemnon, brother of Menelaus, rouses the Greek army to attack Troy and bring Helen home again. Odysseus is one of the Greek kings invited to join the Trojan expedition. He refuses at first, much preferring peace and Penelope. Masonic historians would understand this mental conflict very clearly as the incompatible demands of duty on the one hand and domesticity on the other. *The Cloister and the Hearth* by Charles Reade, a seriously underrated Victorian novelist with great literary talent, reflects this same mental conflict. The religious life (symbolically the *cloister*) and patriotic duty pull people in different directions, as do home and family life (symbolically the *hearth*).

Born in Oxford in 1814 and educated at Magdalen College, Reade's best-known work, *The Cloister and the Hearth*, was published in 1861 and is as informative about the medieval European world as Homer is about the ancient Greek world. Reade was almost certainly a Freemason, and it is ironic that his last work, *A Perilous Secret*, was finished only a few months before his death in 1884.

Masonry, as an excellent life system, lays considerable emphasis on receiving and acting upon good advice. The idea of having a wise and reliable mentor is very much a Masonic idea. The worshipful master of any good Masonic lodge relies upon the help and advice of the immediate past master. The importance of mentoring in this Masonic sense is clearly illustrated in Homer's work where Pallas Athena, the wise daughter of Zeus, assists Odysseus time after time. He, in return, is devoted to her. This quality, too, is a well-known Masonic ideal: good advice and sincere gratitude for it are the complementary sides of the same ethical coin.

Freemasonry also understands the clearly defined stages of life, and what might be termed its *thresholds* that have to be crossed as human beings grow and develop. For Odysseus the first great threshold is the Trojan War. During this conflict, he is distinguished by his mental and physical abilities, his high intelligence, and the way that he applies it to overcoming the Trojans. Odysseus has courage as well as intelligence, and that combination takes him safely over this first great threshold. The ranks in Freemasonry plainly reflect these stages and thresholds. Odysseus may be seen to rise from the role of entered apprentice, to fellow craft, and finally to master mason.

Masonic historians would agree that the moral and ethical lifemanship lessons that all human beings have to learn are clearly set out in Masonic allegory, and in its ethical and moral teachings. Odysseus has to pass many tests and overcome numerous difficulties and temptations before he is finally reunited with his beloved Penelope and re-established with her as the benign ruler of Ithaca.

Homer has carefully introduced the idea of *secrecy* into the story of Odysseus, and this, of course, is clearly understood by Masonic historians. When Odysseus finally returns, he keeps his identity secret. The suitors who seek to replace him are persecuting Penelope. His son,

Telemachus, is in deadly peril from these avaricious would-be usurpers of his father's kingdom. Secrecy at this point is as important a weapon as the great bow with which Odysseus finally dispatches his enemies.

After this vitally important secrecy, there is the equally crucial Masonic allegory of *resurrection*. Odysseus has not won some vast new kingdom; he has been restored (resurrected) to his former kingdom. This resurrection ingredient in the Masonic allegory that Homer created is something that brings great happiness — to Odysseus's sick and aged father, to his brave and faithful bride, to his fearless son, and to the whole kingdom of Ithaca. Here yet again is clear Masonic allegory: goodness and courage not only bring happiness to the hero, but to all who are associated with him. Resurrection, in this Masonic sense, sets in motion a widely shared joy.

Another significant factor in connection with Homer's writings is the historical dispute over whether he ever existed at all as an individual poet, or whether he was a collective noun for the *group* of Greek poets and storytellers who immortalized the Trojan war and the journeys of Odysseus of Ithaca.

A reputable case has been made that Homer was a woman, and the issue of his or her blindness has been the central theme of several learned academic papers. Masonic historians would argue that Homer was probably a real, historical character and that he or she was a proto-Mason who transmitted ethical Masonic allegories in his or her poems.

However, it must also be noted that during medieval times in Europe there were fraternal bands of minstrels and troubadours who were evidently Masonic in their attitudes to one another and in the moral and ethical contents of their songs. It has been suggested that several of their songs were actually codes and ciphers. More is said of these Masonic minstrels and their secret messages in chapter 14, "Medieval Masonry and the Cathedral Builders." In Homer's time there were similar bands of poets and storytellers. Were they the forerunners of the mysterious, medieval minstrel groups? Did they share the same great secrets?

Another mysterious proto-Masonic feature in the old Greek myths and legends is the strange account of the Minotaur in the labyrinth at Knossos. Bull worship and rituals were ubiquitous in the ancient world. Mithraism provided only one widespread example. In India there was a sacred white bull belonging to Siva; Persians, Assyrians, Phoenicians, and Chaldeans revered the bull; a golden calf was worshipped by the Jews when Moses was a long time returning from the mountain; Jupiter turned himself into a white bull in order to abduct Europa; excavations in the Serapeum in Memphis in Egypt have uncovered more than fifty mummified bulls, interred as though they were Egyptian nobles, or even Egyptian gods.

The work of Daedalus: part of the Cretan architecture at Knossos shows the sacred bull motif.

Several proto-Masonic strands in the story of the Minotaur intrigue Masonic historians. As has already been noted, if the hypothetical extra-terrestrial visitors were involved with genetic engineering, then a hybrid man-bull such as the Cretan Minotaur is not entirely beyond the bounds of possibility. In the legend it is Daedalus whose technical ingenuity makes it possible for Queen Pasiphae to satisfy her zoophilia. He builds a hollow wooden cow for her. She climbs inside and conceives the Minotaur. Daedalus is then called upon again to design and build the Cretan labyrinth in which to house the creature. Bypassing the colourful legendary and mythological aspects of the story, what remains is an ingenious technologist, a master craftsman far ahead of his contemporaries, and a strong suspicion of genetic engineering.

Daedalus has another strange quasi-Masonic link with the mystery of Roslyn Chapel near Edinburgh, which is crammed with Masonic symbolism and imagery. The chapel is examined in depth in chapter 18, "Masonic Symbols in Roslyn Chapel." In particular Roslyn contains a beautiful and elaborate pillar, known as the Apprentice Pillar. In essence, the story behind this pillar is that a master craftsman was so furious that his gifted apprentice had produced better work than his that he killed the boy with a savage blow from a mallet. Daedalus was said to have committed an almost identical crime when he murdered his talented young apprentice. Neither event may have had any historical basis, but the moral, ethical, and allegorical purpose of both stories is clear. They are timely warnings against envy and jealousy, especially the kind of jealousy that can beset a great craftsman who is in danger of becoming too proud of his own work. C.S. Lewis teaches this same Masonic moral truth when he says that true humility consists of the ability to create something superb — to *know* that it is the best, but then to be neither more nor less pleased than if one of your friends had created it.

Masonic historians are also interested in Daedalus because of his genealogy. He was reportedly a descendant of Erichthonius, who in mythology was the son of Athena, the wisest goddess, and Hephaestus, the blacksmith and craftsman god. This genealogical symbolism suggests that Daedalus had a genetic combination of a brain that could cope with abstract wisdom as well as practical science and technology. Whatever crimes he may or may not have committed, Daedalus came to Crete, and thus into the service of King Minos, as an exile. Here again is the rich Masonic symbolism of a traveller or sojourner.

Perhaps Daedalus can be understood as repenting of his supposed crime against the murdered apprentice by doing everything he is asked in Crete. When Ariadne seeks help for Theseus, who has to enter the bewildering labyrinth to find and kill the carnivorous Minotaur, it is Daedalus, in some versions of the legend, who tells her to use the ball of twine. He is also credited in some accounts with providing the "magic" sword that Ariadne passes to Theseus to dispatch the fearsome man-bull.

Strange numerological symbolism also filters down into the story of the Minotaur. Seven and nine are significant numbers in Masonry. The mystical *seven* governs the number of youths and maidens who are sent from Athens as tribute to be eaten by the monster — and they are sent every *nine* years. Ancient Greek illustrations of bull-jumping, as a religious practice, as a sport, or as pure entertainment, also make an important contribution to an understanding of what really lay behind the Minotaur stories.

Another significant moral teaching in the Daedalus narrative is the airborne escape from Crete that ends in the death of his son, Icarus. Masonic ethics, as taught by allegory and symbolism, are characterized by *warnings*, as has already been noted. The ideal Masonic individual is someone who never shirks from danger or holds back from risk-taking in a worthy cause, such as liberty from captivity on Crete. But Masonry also stresses the importance of safety and the necessity of taking sensible precautions. Masonic lifemanship is encapsulated allegorically in the account of the flight from Crete. Icarus is told to fly neither too high nor too low. Too high means that the excessive heat will melt the wax that holds his wings together. Too low means that the water splashing up from the waves will destroy his wings and bring him down. In the legend Daedalus's flight technology is effective, but it is limited, frail, and vulnerable.

Metaphorically, the danger of flying too high in life, being too ambitious, and attempting to go beyond our powers is one of the characteristic Masonic warnings. A wise master mason is taught by Masonic allegory to take strength and talents to their utmost limits, but he or she also realizes that there *are* limits. Conversely, Masonic allegory teaches that there are equally grave dangers inherent in flying too low — in failing to make optimal use of the gifts and talents we have and setting our sights below our real potential.

In this chapter we have considered proto-Masonry in conjunction with some aspects of ancient and classical Greece: its gods, legends, allegories, and achievements. One of the greatest Greek thinkers, Pythagoras of Samos, was a combination of mystic and mathematician. He founded, at Crotona in southern Italy, what was almost certainly an early Masonic society that made vast contributions to science and mathematics. Pythagoras and his mathematical, Masonic mysteries form the subject of the next chapter.

Chapter 7

MATHEMATICAL MASONIC MYSTERIES AND THE PYTHAGOREANS

MASONIC HISTORIANS have the greatest respect and admiration for Thales of Miletos; his student, Anaximander, the astronomer; and for the outstanding mystic and mathematician, Pythagoras. Thales is usually included in the roll of honour of the Seven Sages of Greece, although the list varies occasionally. His parents were Examyes and Cleobuline, who may have been Phoenicians rather than Greeks.

Thales of Miletos, one of the Seven Sages of Greece.

Irrespective of whether Thales's parents were Greek or Phoenician, he was highly revered by Mestrius Plutarchus — generally referred to as Plutarch — who lived in the town of Chaeronea from around 45 AD to 125 AD. Plutarch was one of the two priests of Apollo at Delphi, the site of the famous Delphic Oracle and only eighteen miles from Plutarch's home.

Over and above his fulsome praise for his wise proto-Masonic hero, Thales, and the other six Greek sages, Plutarch was himself an exceptionally able and astute man, and well qualified for a senior role in Greek Freemasonry during the first and second centuries AD. His brilliant writings are collected in *Moralia*, where his belief in life after death is revealed as especially Masonic. When Plutarch and his wife lost their beloved two-year-old daughter, he did his best to console his wife with these words: "The soul is immortal, and flies like a caged bird that has just been released when death changes our lives…. The soul that stays within the body only for a short time quickly recovers its immortal fire and speeds on to higher things."

The Seven Greek Sages whom Plutarch admired so much were distinguished philosophers, statesmen, and lawgivers and included, besides Thales, Solon of Athens, Chilon of Sparta, Bias of Priene, Cleobulus of Lindos, Pittacus of Mitylene, and Periander of Corinth. Some Masonic historians believe that these seven famous sages were also outstanding leaders of early Greek Freemasonry.

Bias of Priene is among Masonry's favourite candidates for the title "wisest of the wise." By Masonic standards of ethics and morality, he was a man whose kindness and generosity matched his great wisdom. One of his typical acts was to pay the ransom for some women prisoners, and then, after caring for them and educating them as if they were his own daughters, he sent them safely home to their families in Messina in Sicily.

Another proto-Masonic allegory concerning Bias is the legend of the brazen tripod. Some fishermen discovered it and read its inscription: For the Wisest of the Wise. The fathers of the girls whom Bias had saved wanted to award it to him, but he modestly declined saying: "Apollo is the wisest."

Another essential characteristic of these proto-Masonic sages such as Bias was their collections of proverbs and wise sayings; King Solomon and Confucius had that same attribute. Two pieces of typically Masonic wisdom attributed to Bias were: "Do not speak rapidly for it is a sign of foolishness" and "Choose your path wisely and carefully, then adhere to it faithfully." Perhaps his most profound Masonic saying was: "Value wisdom as the ship on which you may sail safely from youth to old age — that ship is your most precious possession." These sayings of Bias's may be described as "gems for keen ears" which, rather curiously, is a perfect anagram for "Greek Freemasons"!

Bias's noble and dignified death also had singularly Masonic characteristics. He was a brilliant advocate and in great demand but would never take on a case unless he believed firmly in the justice of the cause he was asked to defend. At last, when Bias was a very old man, despite his frailty, he took on one more case because he believed fervently in the rightness of the cause. His grandson loved and admired Bias greatly and accompanied him to the court.

The great old sage presented his case magnificently, but it exhausted him and he lay back to rest with his head on his grandson's shoulder. The opposing advocate presented his case, and after some deliberation the court decided in favour of Bias. When the officials came to tell the grand old man of his victory, they found him dead, still resting gently on his grandson's shoulder as though he were merely asleep.

Any close and detailed study of Pythagoras and his outstanding mathematical and scientific work needs to include the life of Thales and his major contributions to geometry. Like Solon, Thales travelled extensively in Egypt and acquired much deep Egyptian knowledge, including the advanced geometry that he brought home to Miletos.

Anaximander, widely regarded as another Greek proto-Mason, was interested in astronomy and cosmology and was the inventor of the gnomon, a perpendicular sundial. His treatise *On Nature* was venerated by classical scholars and widely read. There seems to have been copies in the great library of Alexandria, which tragically destroyed, but no copies of Anaximander's great book are thought to have survived the fire.

Chilon of Sparta lived during the sixth century BC and was another worthy member of the Seven Sages of Greece. He believed in hard, disciplined training of the kind that made the Spartans such formidable warriors, and under his direction their training became even more rigorous. His work as an *ephor* also had a distinctly Masonic flavour. The role of an *ephor* in the ancient world gave him responsibilities similar to those of an ombudsman combined with being chair of a Senate committee in the United States. In Sparta the five *ephors* exercised judicial, legislative, and executive authority in the land. Their powers varied over the centuries, but under Chilon's leadership the *ephors* had more power over the two Spartan kings than *ephors* were normally able to exercise at other times. When the two kings disagreed, the *ephors* had the deciding vote. They were the power of the Spartan citizenry balanced against the power of the two kings.

Cleobulus of Lindus was the son of Evagoras, and like Solon and Thales, Cleobulus learned many strange mysteries in Egypt. Like all the other thoughtful proto-Masons of antiquity, Cleobulus left numerous wise sayings, many of which clearly encapsulate Masonic ethical and moral teachings. Among his proverbs and maxims were: "Seek wisdom and shun vice; never be ungrateful; be of steadfast purpose; the foolish man speaks, the wise man listens; be swift to make peace after a quarrel; moderation is best; fight against injustice." Cleobulus's hatred of injustice brought his thinking very close to that of Bias, who gave the last of his strength to protecting an innocent man in court.

Periander was prominent in Corinth during the fifth and sixth centuries BC. His most famous aphorism is: "Act moderately during times of prosperity and show great care and wisdom during times of adversity." He was also credited with originating "Practice makes perfect," but what he actually said was: "Practice is everything."

The seventh sage was Pittacus of Mytilene, a general in charge of the Mytilenaean army that defeated the Athenians, led by Phrynon. He became ruler of Mytilene for some ten years and then handed constitutional power back to the citizens whom he had served so well in both peace and war. He provides a great example of Greek proto-Masons, and his high ethical and moral standards are also encapsulated in his sayings, proverbs, maxims, and aphorisms: "Pardon is better than punishment; it is extremely hard to be a good person; never disclose what you are intending to do in advance because if you fail you will be ridiculed; never speak ill of either friends or enemies; cultivate hard work, friendliness and openness, rich experiences, wisdom, and truth." It would be hard to find proto-Masonic moral and ethical truth expressed more succinctly or more profoundly. Pittacus knew a great deal about the art of living.

To a perceptive Masonic historian the Seven Sages represent a complete proto-Masonic lodge in ancient Greece. Thales stands as worshipful master with Solon of Athens as senior warden. The junior warden is Chilon of Sparta, the senior and junior deacons are Bias and Cleobulus respectively, while Pittacus and Periander are stewards. The tyler, not one of the seven in most accounts, is Anaximander, or perhaps even Pythagoras himself.

In this ancient Greek lodge Socrates and Plato are distinguished past masters, and their Allegory of the Cave is clearly proto-Masonic teaching of the deepest and wisest sort. Plato's Academy on the outskirts of Athens was an extremely noble and worthwhile institution that was run on Masonic lines and made a vast contribution to human wisdom and culture from 387 BC to 529 AD. Sadly, it was closed in 529 on the orders of the Byzantine emperor Justinian I (born in 483 at Tauresium; emperor from 527 until his death in 565).

Plato's allegorical use of the cave is a proto-Masonic masterpiece of moral and ethical teaching encapsulating the problems that beset humanity and offering a solution to them. Plato believed that the universe that we experience through our senses is not *real* in the philosophical sense of *reality*. Sight, sound, and touch convey only very poor, inaccurate copies of the true universe. In Plato's view the real world can only be understood by using the mind. His fundamental educational approach was not to teach his students by *telling* them, but to create for them an intellectual environment in which they would be stimulated to ask questions and carry out research. Plato believed that such research would direct their minds to the good, the important, and the eternal things that made up the real universe. The philosopher also believed that this real universe was benign and positive and that it was the solemn duty of the wise and enlightened to inspire and stimulate others so they would be able to find it for themselves.

In the mysterious cave allegory, prisoners have been confined since birth and secured in such a way that they can see only the wall in front of them. Behind them a fire is burning brightly so that when a procession of people between the fire and the prisoners carry objects of metal, wood, or stone above their heads the chained prisoners see only the flickering distorted shadows of the carried objects that are themselves only copies. The impression that the prisoners have of the universe in which they are so strangely confined is, therefore, one that is based on distorted two-dimensional shadows of objects that are themselves only *copies* of what is truly *real*. If a prisoner escaped and saw the true state of affairs and then later returned to explain it to the others, his life might well be in danger.

The Platonic allegory of the prisoners in the cave.

Plato and Socrates believed in the vital importance of truth, and both recognized the significance of free and independent thought as a *pathway to truth*. This is what made both of them distinguished Greek proto-Masons. The observer who has escaped from the cave of deceptive shadows and discovered reality is someone who has learned Masonic truth.

Pythagoras, like Socrates and Plato, saw clearly what was wrong with his contemporary world and did everything in his power to reform and improve it. Born in Samos, Pythagoras met Thales, took that wise man's excellent advice, and went to Egypt to study its ancient mysteries. After many years of study and travel, which probably took him to Assyria, as well, Pythagoras returned to his native Samos. Not liking the society he found there under the dictatorship of Polycrates, who reigned from 540 until 522 BC, Pythagoras went to the flourishing Greek city of Crotona, situated on the south Italian coast.

In Crotona, Pythagoras established an academic brotherhood along moral and ethical lines that were very close indeed to the highest Masonic principles. Members were very carefully chosen: they had to be intellectually able and have unblemished characters. In the mission statement of Pythagoras's Crotona Brotherhood, the members vowed to do all in their power to make public and private life better — to create happy, healthy citizens in a happy, healthy society. Crotona, famous for its advanced gymnastic exercises and its high standards of hygiene, was an ideal base for Pythagoras's proto-Masonic brotherhood.

Both men and women were eligible for membership, and there was a lengthy period of preparation and training. There were also three levels of membership, corresponding to modern Freemasonry's entered apprentice, fellow craft, and master mason.

Pythagoras left many wise sayings behind him as well as his significant mathematical discoveries. His proverbs rank alongside the highest moral and ethical Masonic wisdom:

> The oath you make is sacred and binding. Cultivate friendship with the best people. Overcome greed, sloth, lust, and anger. Learn to save money carefully and to spend it wisely. Take care of your physical health. Never fall asleep until you have thought carefully through all that you have done during the day. If you have done well, rejoice. If you have made mistakes, determine how to avoid them in future. Honour and respect your parents, your family, and worthy heroes.

The life and aims of Pythagoras can be summed up under three main headings: work to improve society and those who live in it with you; be morally pure; study and carry out research to improve your mind — this will help you to achieve your objectives. Pythagoras was also a distinguished proto-Mason by virtue of his understanding of science and his belief that scientific study of the universe and everything in it was an essential way for human beings to make real progress. He saw clearly that shape, space, and number were essential instruments for scientific investigation of the natural world.

The theorem by which Pythagoras is best remembered is $a^2+b^2=c^2$. It can be expressed in words as: in any right-angled triangle, the square on the hypotenuse is equal to the sum of the squares on the other two sides.

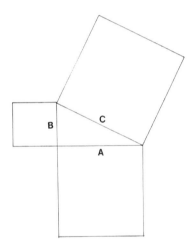

Pythagoras's great discovery: $a^2+b^2=c^2$.

Although the theorem bears his name, Pythagoras, with his strict regard for truth and morality, would have been the first to accept that the earliest known statement of this right-angled triangle theory as such was said to have been discovered on an ancient Babylonian tablet dating back to perhaps 2000 BC. What is particularly interesting is that the theory is *reversible*: if a triangle has sides of lengths that fit the $a^2+b^2=c^2$ formula, then it must be a right-angled triangle.

What Pythagoras and his proto-Masonic Crotona Brotherhood did such excellent innovative work on was the *proof* of the ancient $a^2+b^2=c^2$ formula dating back more than a millennium before them. Was it ancient Babylonian proto-Masons who carved that tablet? The Pythagorean triangle diagram is not so very different from the square and compasses, especially when the Euclidean construction lines are added for the proof. Euclid of Alexandria, another very able early mathematician, may well have been yet another Greek proto-Mason. He lived from 325 BC until 265 BC.

The first part of the proof is to prove that triangle ABF equals triangle AEC. One way to prove that triangles are equal is to demonstrate that both of them have two sides and an included angle that are the *same* in each triangle. Side AE must equal side AB as each is a side of the square ABDE. Side AF must equal side AC as each of them is a side of the square ACFG. Now we need to find an equal angle in each of our triangles ABF and AEC. We do this by looking carefully at angle BAF and angle BAE. The first clue is that the acute angle CAB is an integral part of *both* the obtuse angles BAF *and* CAE. To make angle BAF we simply add the right-angle CAF at the corner of

Euclid, the great proto-Masonic mathematician.

the square ACGF. Now we have an angle of CAB plus ninety degrees making up angle BAF. Angle CAE is exactly the same: it comprises the shared acute angle CAB and the ninety-degree corner of the square ABDE. We have now proved that angle BAF equals angle CAE. As we have now got two equal sides and an included equal angle, triangle BAF equals triangle CAE.

The area of a triangle is half of its base multiplied by its vertical height. Take AF as the base of triangle ABF. Its vertical height is AC because any point along the line GCB will be the vertical height of triangle ABF when we take AF as its base. Triangle FAC, therefore, has exactly the same area as triangle FAC, and triangle FAC is exactly half of the square ACGF.

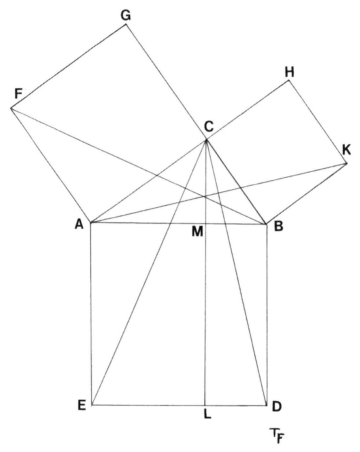

The proof of Pythagoras's Theorem that the square on the hypotenuse
is equal to the sum of the squares on the other two sides.

Construct the vertical line from point C through the top of the square ABDE at M and continue down as far as point L at the base of the square ABDE. Look carefully at the rectangle AMLE. Take any point on the line CML as the height of triangle CAE when we use AE as its base. Triangle AME must therefore have the same area as triangle CAE, and this new triangle AME is half the area of rectangle AMLE because EM is a diagonal of that rectangle.

We now take two new triangles ABK and CBD and prove that they, too, are equal. The next step is to show that because BM is the vertical height of triangle CBD with BD as the base, triangle BMD is equal in area to triangle CBD. Because MD is a diagonal of rectangle BMLD, triangle BMD has half the area of rectangle BMLD.

This proof makes it clear that the two small squares together are equal in area to the large square on the hypotenuse. The truth of Pythagoras's Theorem's $a^2+b^2=c^2$ is *proved*.

It is in that indomitable search for *proof* that we see Pythagoras at his most truly Masonic. To conjure up a hypothesis is one thing; to be able to *prove* it is vastly more important. Proof, logic, reason, and truth are the guardian angels of intellectual progress. Mindless, fanatical adherence to unproven dogma has been the cause of untold misery, suffering, and death throughout human history. One of the great Masonic principles is independent thought and a demand for proof. The more closely that principle is followed, the safer and better the world will become.

From this pioneering work of the great Greek proto-Masons, Pythagoras and Euclid — and their determination to *prove* what they knew — have come some of the most important and advanced mathematical developments that are still of vital importance in our technological and scientific twenty-first century. Science relies on mathematics. Without the proto-Masonic wisdom of Pythagoras and Euclid, today's technology would not have developed as well as it has.

CHAPTER 8

ANCIENT CHALDEAN AND HEBREW MASONRY

ANAGRAMS INTRIGUE Masonic researchers and historians, and the words "Chaldean Masonry" are a particularly interesting example. They can be turned into "Land so many reach" and "monarchy and seal." Both of these strange, anagrammatic, proto-Masonic phrases are potentially significant and meaningful, and they are just two of many odd and intriguing mysteries that can be traced back to the oldest stages of Chaldean, Sumerian, and Hebrew history.

In chapter 5, which dealt with the Masonic mysteries of ancient Egypt, a passing reference was made to Nimrod, biblical grandson of Ham and great-grandson of Noah. In chapter 3, mention was made of the legends associated with the beautiful and talented Queen Semiramis, who is usually regarded as the wife of Ninus, ruler of Nineveh. One set of theories involving Ninus's name is that it came from the Assyrian word *nunu*, meaning a fish, and that he was in some strange way a "fish king" associated with legends of quasi-human, amphibian extraterrestrials. There are other quasi-historical myths and legends associated with Semiramis that suggest she was the wife of Nimrod. Does that mean that Ninus and Nimrod were one and the same ancient emperor?

Nimrod is regarded by some researchers as *more* than a normal human descendant of Noah: it is conjectured that he *might* have been one of the superhuman offspring of the mysterious Sons of God referred to in Genesis 6:1–4, super-beings who interbred with attractive human females. Semiramis herself was thought to have been more than mortal. Her mother was alleged to have been an amphibian demigoddess known as Derceto or Atargatis, who abandoned the infant Semiramis on a lonely mountain. Miraculously rescued first by doves and then later by shepherds, Semiramis grew up with superhuman powers and achieved greatness.

Yet another set of curiously confusing myths and legends associates Nimrod with the ancient Mesopotamian god Marduk. He in turn is linked with the Sumerian Enki, the god of wisdom, and Mars, the Roman god of war. His beautiful consort, Queen Semiramis, is then translated into the goddess Astarte. Enki was also known as Apsu, and some experts believe that this name gave rise to the name Poseidon (Neptune to the Romans), the Greek god of the seas. To the Canaanites, Phoenicians, Syrians, and to some Egyptians, Marduk was also known as Baal, whose name simply meant lord or master. An ancient Babylonian cylinder seal shows him riding over the waves accompanied by his symbolic dragon, a depiction that strengthens his connection with Poseidon.

Biblical references to owls and dragons, and the potent symbolism of both, are noted in chapter 3. The prophets Isaiah, Jeremiah, and Micah all make use of the images.

What is the proto-Masonic significance of these obscure and convoluted linkages between the so-called ancient Mesopotamian gods? When all the fanciful religious myths and legends are removed, a process not unlike unwrapping an Egyptian mummy, what emerges is another persuasive argument for the mysterious origins of proto-Masonry. Nimrod, alias Marduk, is an outstandingly powerful individual, mentally and physically. He is closely associated with the equally formidable Semiramis. Both had abilities that made their subject peoples regard them as more than mortal. Were they themselves extraterrestrials? Or were they the genetically engineered, quasi-human offspring of extraterrestrials? And were they two of the proto-Masons responsible for the great social and technical advances of the early Mesopotamian peoples? Was it proto-Masonic teaching that led to the architecture, the canals, and the hanging gardens for which the Mesopotamians were rightly renowned?

In the Babylonian creation myth known as the Enûma Elish, there is a terrible internecine war between the gods, and Marduk is chosen to lead the forces of good against the legions of chaos and evil. After he triumphs, he becomes leader of the gods and recovers the *Tablets of Destiny* from their enemies. There is a significant parallel here with Hermes Trismegistus, alias Thoth, scribe of the Egyptian gods, and his famous Emerald Tablets, which contained the knowledge on which the gods' power depended. Could these mysterious Babylonian *Tablets of Destiny* be the same as Hermes's Emerald Tablets? Are the two accounts simply variants of the same story, an epic cosmic narrative in which one group of extraterrestrials (who have benign plans for the human race) are at war with another extraterrestrial faction whose members are malign exploiters of Earth and its peoples?

The ancient Hebrew texts contain a number of intriguing accounts of apparently unnatural births that *could* be regarded as clues to genetic engineering of the kind alluded to earlier and *possibly* connected with extraterrestrial proto-Masons. Strange circumstances surround the birth of Abraham's son, Isaac, when Sarah is by all accounts past childbearing age. It is also important to remember the curious legend to the effect that Sarah entered a mysterious cave where Thoth, alias Hermes Trismegistus, lay in suspended animation with the Emerald Tablets beside him. Attracted by their beauty and brilliance, Sarah picked up two of them. As she did so, Hermes began to stir, and Sarah fled from the cave. Did she take those two tablets with her, and did they ultimately become the famous *urim* and *thummim* stones by means of which Jewish high priests were thought to be able to foretell the future?

The birth of the super-strong Hebrew judge Samson is, if anything, even more mysterious than the nativity of Isaac. According to the account in Judges 13, Samson's father was a Danite named Manoah whose wife had apparently been unable to have children. Circumstances change after she is visited by a being whom the story in Judges describes as "an angel of the Lord." He tells her that although she has been barren, she will shortly conceive and bear a son. The angel then instructs her to be particularly careful about her diet during pregnancy — to avoid alcohol and any foods that are defined as "unclean" under Hebrew law. Furthermore, the child is to be a Nazarite.

Occasionally, there seems to be a slight, derivational, linguistic problem concerning *nazir* with its plural *nazirim* that appears to have troubled some earlier translators. In this form it is thought to refer to leaders of the people, or princes, as it does when rendered *nezerim*.

The *religious* Nazarites, however, were regarded as being totally different from rulers, prominent men, or leaders of the people. These Nazarites were seen as being set aside to serve God in a particular way. They were dedicated and committed to such service. It was generally assumed that they never cut their hair and that they abstained from alcohol. In addition to lifelong, *perpetual* Nazarites, there were devout Hebrews who took Nazarite vows for a period of time in fulfilment of a sacred, religious vow.

By whatever means, Samson is duly born to Manoah's wife and grows up to be abnormally strong. His adventures in battle against the Philistines, his ability to kill a lion with his bare hands, and his final *coup de grâce* when he pulls down the Philistine temple are all very well-known episodes in a dynamic but tragic life. There are remarkable parallels between the biblical stories of Samson and the legends of Heracles, Herakles, or Hercules in Greek mythology. Both, for example, kill a lion. Despite their prodigious strength, each enjoys only limited success and each suffers profoundly. Both serve as tragic examples that physical strength and power are never enough to overcome the evils and problems of the world.

Here, too, the possibility may be considered that both great physically powerful heroes are part of a deep proto-Masonic ethical and moral allegory. The lives of Samson and Hercules both say clearly that physical strength alone is not enough: the successful hero needs intelligence and, more important, Masonic moral and ethical principles with which to guide that intelligence.

The miraculous birth of Samuel creates the possibility of another proto-Masonic, genetic-engineering mystery. The details appear in 1 Samuel 1. Elkanah the Ephraimite has two wives: Peninnah, who has several children, and Hannah, who has none, just like Sarah and Manoah's wife. Hannah visits the Holy Place at Shiloh where Eli is high priest. Hannah prays fervently for a child, and Eli prays that her prayers will be answered. Shortly afterwards she gives birth to the future prophet Samuel. He is taken to live in the Holy Place at Shiloh as soon as he is old enough.

Just as Samson is abnormally strong, Samuel is abnormally perceptive. According to the biblical account in 1 Samuel 3, he hears a voice calling him in the night when old Eli the high priest at Shiloh is asleep. Obediently and helpfully, young Samuel reports to Eli to see what the priest needs. Eli denies calling the boy, whose sleeping quarters are next to the Ark of the Covenant. The inexplicable call is repeated three times, and the biblical account explains it as a message from God.

If genetic engineering gave Samson supernormal physical strength, did it give Hannah's talented son mental powers that most people lacked? Had it made him what might be described as *psychic* with unusual gifts of clairvoyance and clairaudience? If proto-Masonic genetic engineers were striving to produce a superior, more moral, more ethical human being to help and guide others, was it logical for them to aim at heightened perception after enhanced physical strength had not produced particularly successful results? But what if those proto-Masons who were engaged in the quest for improved human beings had considered improving their *environment* as well as their DNA?

The argument between nature and nurture is one that greatly interests psychologists and sociologists as well as geneticists. To what extent are we the product of our biological inheritance? To what extent are we the result of our environmental experiences? Studies of identical twins who were separated at very early stages of their lives have proved largely inconclusive: the relative significance of both genetic and environmental input is still unresolved.

Moses, born with all the benefits of Hebrew genes and then nurtured in the richest possible Egyptian cultural environment, presents yet another proto-Masonic riddle from the ancient world. Were the very odd circumstances of Moses's birth, adoption, and upbringing *deliberately controlled* in order to study the effects of combining excellent genes with an excellent environment? It must be remembered that Moses, like Samuel centuries later, was highly perceptive. His experiences with the burning bush and on Mount Sinai could perhaps be translated as abnormally perceptive contact with something, or *someone*, of immense power: Moses, it may be argued, was genetically able to make a type of contact that appears to be beyond the normal human range of psychic perception.

Brought up as he was by an Egyptian princess and her family amid the luxuries and high culture of the Egyptian court, Moses had golden opportunities to acquire the ancient proto-Masonic wisdom of the Egyptian priests and scholars. He also had the massive advantage of acquiring Hebrew wisdom from his mother, who was employed as his nurse and carer during his impressionable formative years.

A closely detailed study of Moses reveals another fascinating aspect of this truly remarkable man: he was immensely strong physically, as well as being highly intelligent and perceptive. As evidence of this, consider first the episode with the Egyptian taskmaster in Exodus 2:12 where Moses kills and buries him in the sand. It takes a powerful fighting man to do that. Was Moses's abnormal physical strength also the product of genetic engineering, as Samson's may well have been?

There are further clues concerning Moses's abilities in the episode of Jethro's daughters and the belligerent, bullying shepherds who jump the queue ahead of the girls when they are watering their father's flock. Moses, who has left Egypt in a hurry after killing the taskmaster, tells the shepherds to stand back and give the girls their proper turn at the watering place, where he helps them with the work (Exodus 2:17). Would one man alone dare to take on a dozen or so burly shepherds unless he was totally confident that he was more than a match for all of them put together? What confronts the shepherds is a tall, powerful, assertive Hebrew fighting man, in the prime of life, rippling with muscle, brimming with confidence, and carrying a ruthlessly effective Egyptian sword that he clearly knows how to use. Very prudently, the shepherds back off.

Even more important than his courage and physical prowess is Moses's hatred of injustice. This is what makes him so clearly Masonic. The ethics of Freemasonry deplore unfairness. Honesty and integrity are the foundations of Masonic morality — the deepest meaning of being *on the square*. He kills the Egyptian taskmaster because the man is striking a defenceless Hebrew slave, for whom Moses feels great fraternal sympathy. He confronts and subdues the shepherds of Midian because of the unfair way in which they are treating Jethro's daughters.

Another clearly Masonic aspect of Moses's life and character was his generous appreciation of the craftsmanship of his friend Bezaleel. In Exodus 35:30 and onwards, Moses declares that such brilliant, skilful workmanship is a gift from God. Appreciation of craftsmanship is another indication of Masonic ethics and morality. To admire without envy is the nature of a true Mason. It is thought by some researchers that part of the mystical teachings found in the Kabbalah, or Cabala, refers to the Sefirot — in their theology, the powers that emanate from God. In Cabalistic thought these Sefirot powers created and now maintain the universe. Proto-Masonic beliefs run parallel to Cabalistic thinking at this point as far as skill and craftsmanship are concerned; God makes part of the Sefirot accessible to craftsmen to help in the work of sustaining the universe.

It is significant to Masonic historians that traditionally the secret wisdom of the Cabala was handed on by Abraham himself. The earliest written versions can be traced to eleventh-century France, and then spread into Spain. There are strong possibilities that medieval European Freemasonry owed much to these mystical Cabalistic secrets. Scholars can also establish a link between the medieval Cabala of France and Spain and the much older Merkava teachings. One of the most significant aspects of the Cabala was that members of Cabalistic groups believed that every word, letter, and number in a sacred text had a secret meaning of its own, and that it was necessary for an initiate to understand these in order to fathom the deepest Cabalistic secrets.

Secret Cabalistic texts were made into so-called "magical" amulets, which were believed to protect the wearer. Over and above any superficial, superstitious concepts concerning these amulets were the deeply serious proto-Masonic moral and ethical allegories. The profounder meaning was that the amulet enshrined and encapsulated vital principles by which the wearer should aim to live. It was not merely sacred truth expressed in the form of numbers, letters, and words that was being carried; it was that abstract truth itself that gave life its true and worthwhile meaning. The eternal verities were not just there in the form of verbal and numerical signs and symbols, nor were they merely reminders. Actually, they were really present. At this point the deep, mystical, Merkavan teaching approached the theological doctrine of consubstantiation. The amulets were not simply *reminders* of power; they were iconic *vehicles* of power.

The heart of these Merkava teachings (which were known in the first century AD and probably long before then) was concerned with the strange visions of the aerial chariot-throne experienced by the prophet Ezekiel. Merkava can also be spelled Merkabah, which is the Hebrew term for a chariot, and the followers of its mystic teachings spread from Palestine to Babylonia. To the Merkavan initiates, who were referred to as the Tzenuim, there were Seven Heavenly Spheres through which the soul seeking perfection slowly ascended. There is evidence of proto-Masonic thought here. The allegory of the Seven Spheres can be paralleled by the arrangements of ranks in Freemasonry, and up through the various Masonic degrees and side degrees. It can also be compared with the statuses of entered apprentice, fellow craft, master mason, tyler, steward, deacon, and warden.

These proto-Masonic, Merkavan, Tzenuimistic teachings are centred on Ezekiel's vision of the extremely mysterious aerial vehicle and its awesomely powerful controller. Numerous serious researchers, including reputable and experienced flight engineers, have read the Book of Ezekiel closely and critically and have concluded that a man from Ezekiel's background, with its limited awareness of science and technology, would have described a spacecraft in much the same way as the prophet did. Authorities in this area such as Zecharia Sitchin and Josef F. Blumrich have also argued that what Ezekiel witnessed was an advanced spacecraft visiting Earth from some distant part of the universe. The evidence is undeniably compelling, but not yet conclusive. Whoever, or whatever, visited Ezekiel created a dramatic enough impression to have triggered the Merkavan teachings and the mystical Tzenuim brotherhood. The similarities between Freemasonry and these moral, mystical groups are more than coincidental. It must also be remembered that the biblical account of the Prophet Elijah tells how he left the Earth in a whirlwind accompanied by *horses of fire and chariot of fire*. Was that also a spacecraft of the type that Ezekiel saw (2 Kings 2:11–12)?

One of the most significant followers of the early proto-Masonic, Merkavan doctrines was the saintly Akiba ben Joseph (50–132 AD). Deservedly holding high academic rank, he was to his Jewish disciples what Socrates and Plato were to the Greeks.

Akiba ben Joseph, a proto-Mason who was filled with wisdom and goodness.

Akiba was also known and revered as a *tanna*, a Hebrew word lit-erally meaning one who repeats or recites holy texts and ancient wis-dom. Akiba, however, was a great independent thinker and religious philosopher in his own right, as well as a reservoir of priceless ancient wisdom that he recited to his numerous disciples and followers. Much of Freemasonry and good Masonic teaching depend upon skills of memorizing and reciting ancient Masonic texts, and the effective Masonic teacher in the twenty-first century is very like the ancient Hebrew *tanna*. Akiba's full and worthwhile life ended tragically in martyrdom, but not before his kindness, generosity, unselfishness, and all-round moral and ethical goodness had made him a living legend. Of all the men of his time, Akiba ben Joseph has the strongest claim to be an outstanding, high-ranking, Hebrew proto-Mason.

Artist's impression of Solomon's Temple.

Chapter 9

SOLOMON'S MINES AND TEMPLE

THERE ARE expert Jewish historians, like the scholarly Rabbi Ken Spiro, with access to impressive old scriptural archives, who have suggested that the great and wise King Solomon, reputedly "the wisest human being who ever lived," was only twelve years old when his father, King David, died. If he was, this information appears to create yet another mystery.

The proto-Masonic ethical and moral codes of fairness and honesty, however, are vehemently opposed to the offensive fallacy of ageism — in either direction. Masonic wisdom can accept that a young man of twelve who is wise and mature beyond his years can rule a kingdom as well as a thirty-year-old. The fearless military commander and brilliant tactician, Field Marshal Joseph Radetzky (1766–1858), was the best leader the Austrian army had when he was over ninety.

Field Marshal Joseph Radetzky, military hero at ninety years of age.

So it is certainly *possible* that Solomon the Wise was twelve years old when he succeeded his father, David. A man or woman with the right moral attitude and ethical spirit can be a valuable and active supporter of the Craft at *any* age.

If the proto-Masonic riddle of Solomon's youthful accession encapsulates one mystery, the background history of his mother, the exquisitely beautiful Bathsheba (Bathshua in some accounts), presents another, greater one. Some versions of her genealogy regard her as the daughter of Eliam (2 Samuel 11:3), or of Ammiel (1 Chronicles 3:5). A number of academic, Masonic, biblical scholars believe her father could have been the same Eliam who was the son of Ahitophel. If this is correct, it might explain some of her tortuous relationship problems involving the rivalry for her affection between King David and Bathsheba's husband, Uriah the Hittite.

King Suppiluliuma II, the last ruler of the Hittite Empire.

This Hittite connection with the David and Bathsheba mystery opens new dimensions of their contribution to the proto-Masonic enigma. The Hittite Empire was a significant one in its day. The Hittites were a very ancient people who spoke an Indo-European language and may well have come originally from India. At its height the Hittite Empire included Anatolia, the northwestern parts of Syria as far as Mugarit, and Mesopotamia all the way down to Babylon. The unified empire lasted 500 years, from roughly 1700 BC until 1200 BC, but fragments of it lingered on for a few centuries more. Hittites were skilful builders and chariot makers and were among the earliest workers in iron. Some archaeologists regard them as pioneers of the Iron Age. Proto-Masonic historians have great respect for their craftwork.

Remains of their achievements can still be unearthed in Boğazköy, where archaeologist William Wright made important discoveries as far back as 1884. Links were later established between the Hittite Empire and ancient Egypt. Correspondence between Pharaoh Akhenaton and his father, Amenhotep III, provides evidence of this. Proto-Masonry in Egypt was apparently in contact with proto-Masonry in the Hittite Empire. The mysterious Uriah, therefore, came from a highly cultured and technically competent civilization, renowned for its iron weaponry and military charioteering skills. It is probable, therefore, that Uriah was one of a much sought after group of itinerant Hittite mercenaries working alongside David's men under Joab's command.

If that was the case, Uriah, as a mercenary soldier of fortune, might well have been responsive to a cash offer from Eliam to marry the beautiful Bathsheba and take her back to Boğazköy well out of David's reach. The immediate war situation, however, postponed the planned move to Boğazköy and gave the cruelly opportunistic Eliam other ideas.

The background to the theory is complex. Ahitophel, Eliam's father, sided with David's rebellious son, Absalom, in the internecine war that threatened the stability and integrity of David's kingdom. That war ended in victory for David and the death of Absalom and the defeat of his supporters. Ahitophel committed suicide by hanging himself. Clearly, his son, Eliam, would have harboured thoughts of revenge. The plot is given a dangerous twist if it is then surmised that Eliam, alias

Ammiel, forced his lovely daughter into a marriage with the itinerant mercenary soldier, Uriah the Hittite, when he *suspected* that David might have been interested in her.

Is it possible that Uriah was instructed to get Bathsheba back to Boğazköy as soon as possible, and to keep their temporary Jerusalem location as private as he could so that David could not find out where Bathsheba had gone? The king would hardly have been likely to ask Eliam about her after the death of Ahitophel, for which Eliam would have held David responsible and accordingly harboured a long and bitter grudge against him.

The famous, controversial episode in which David sees a delectable girl bathing (and promptly sends for her) is now much easier to explain. Can it be assumed that this is the same beautiful woman he originally hoped to add to his own royal harem long before Uriah the Hittite came on the scene as part of Eliam's plot?

Seen in this light, Bathsheba is far from being an amoral adulteress, and David is not indulging in casual and superficial lust. Once Bathsheba has been brought to the palace, David tells her of his true and deep feelings for her. The closeness of their long-lasting, loving relationship, one that endures right through their lives until David's death, is indicative of something far more durable and permanent than sexual chemistry alone. Bathsheba, reunited however temporarily with the man she knows she *should* have married, gives herself joyfully to David regardless of the consequences.

If Uriah, the Hittite mercenary, *is* part of Eliam's bitter, vengeful conspiracy to bring down David where Ahitophel failed, he now determinedly and deliberately refuses to sleep with Bathsheba so that her adultery with the king can be proved by her subsequent pregnancy. Eliam calculates that David's reputation will be ruined, and his hapless pawn of a daughter can swiftly be stoned to death for adultery before she can reveal any mitigating facts about her forced marriage to Uriah.

The conspirators, however, fatally underestimate the king in two respects: his capacity for love and his facility for decisive action. David, the man who took on Goliath of Gath, never lacks courage, nor is he the man to hesitate when his hand is forced and ruthless action is essential.

His immediate concern is for Bathsheba, the woman he truly and deeply loves, rather than for his life, crown, or kingdom. Uriah's death is not to save David's reputation or his throne. No, Uriah, assuming for the sake of this scenario that he *is* one of Eliam's co-conspirators, has to die to rescue the innocent Bathsheba from the venomous, self-righteous hypocrites who will otherwise stone her.

David has an entirely loyal, discreet, and trustworthy ally in the ruthless Joab, the pragmatic warrior who combines the roles of military commander-in-chief and hit man. The magnanimous David has done his best to preserve the Hittite mercenary's life, but when all else has failed Joab eliminates Uriah.

Another intriguing theory concerning the proto-Masonic mystery of Bathsheba's name and possible ancestry takes her a long way from the hypothesis of cruel victimization at the hands of her father, Eliam, and her enforced husband, Uriah. *Bath*, or *Beth*, can signify "daughter of," just as *bar* means "son of." When this is considered in connection with Solomon's later acquaintance with the Queen of Sheba, it may be asked whether his mother, Bathsheba, came from the land of Sheba and that her name simply meant Daughter of Sheba or Woman of Sheba. To have been known simply as "daughter of" or "woman of," with the place of her origin, could imply that she had been brought to Israel as a slave girl and was subsequently bought by Uriah.

This hypothesis would replace the Eliam conspiracy theory. When Bathsheba's great and famous son, Solomon, eventually became king of Israel, it was more than probable that she told him all she could recall of her old homeland. Her love for her son was warmly reciprocated, and Solomon might well have invited the Queen of Sheba for a state visit at Bathsheba's request.

The whole question of proto-Masonic genetic engineering and the vital preservation of the right kind of DNA is dramatically reopened. It now seems possible that Bathsheba and David were *deliberately* brought together for a specific genetic purpose, and that Solomon and the Queen of Sheba were later paired to serve that same genetic purpose.

If Sheba and Ethiopia are one and the same kingdom, then the accounts of the queen bearing Solomon's son, Menelik, whose name means "the son of the wise man," may well be true and could link the Ethiopian dynasty to Solomon and the Sheban queen who visited him. According to venerable Ethiopian traditions, the Ark of the Covenant was taken from Jerusalem to Axum in Ethiopia after Menelik, as a young adult, had gone to visit his royal father in the city where he was conceived.

Guardian Obelisk at Axum: does it protect a unique sacred relic?

Some Masonic historians and researchers would consider the intriguing possibility that benign proto-Masonic planning could well have been going on here. Solomon the Wise was all too aware of the potential political unrest surrounding the closing years of his reign. He was realistic about the limited abilities of his son, Rehoboam, who was to succeed him, and about the threat from the popular rebel leader, Jeroboam, son of Nebat, who hid out in Egypt, biding his time until a coup was likely to succeed.

To Solomon the wealthy and powerful kingdom of Sheba, with his son, Menelik, securely on the throne, now seemed a much safer place for the Ark of the Covenant than the Temple of Jerusalem. The removal of the ark to Axum can be no more than a theory, but it is a supposition that is strongly supported by Ethiopian history and tradition.

The ark itself, an object of great reverence to the Hebrews, neverthe-less presents an array of very puzzling proto-Masonic questions. Careful consideration needs to be given to the very strong possibility that Moses brought it with him from Egypt. Raised as an Egyptian prince, he would have known all the Egyptian proto-Masonic secrets connected with the sacred Egyptian arks. He would also have been aware of their strange and secret powers.

The pharaoh's suicidal launching of his charioteers across the tem-porarily dry Red Sea bed might have been motivated by his discovery that Moses and the Israelites had taken the most prized of all the Egyptian arks with them. The later Hebrew accounts of the making of the Ark of the Covenant could have been records not of its original construction but of additions and modifications to this same mysterious, ancient, awesomely powerful ark, which Moses had brought out of Egypt. The great, proto-Masonic craftsman Bezaleel, son of Uri, of the tribe of Judah, a very skilful artisan whom Moses particularly praised and admired, was one of those involved in the work. Bezaleel was almost certainly a very high-ranking proto-Mason.

The Ark of the Covenant was described as being made of acacia wood which, as mentioned earlier in chapter 3, has special Masonic significance. The ark was one and a half cubits wide and the same meas-urement high. Its length was two cubits. In modern measurements it was approximately four feet long with a width and height of about two and a half feet. The ark was covered in gold, a very effective shield against nuclear radiation. What was referred to as the mercy seat, which was the lid of the ark, was embellished with a gold rim. Other very significant features of its curious design were the wooden poles that went through golden carrying rings. Were these arrangements more than decorative? Were the nonconductive wooden poles intended to insulate the bearers from whatever power was contained in the gold-shielded box? Might the contents of the ark have included some type of high-voltage electrical battery or a capacitor?

And what about the two enigmatic golden cherubim adorning the top of the ark and facing each other? Could they have been the terminals or contacts linked to the power source inside? Another interesting detail is that the carrying poles actually touched the veil inside the tabernacle when the ark was stored in there. Did that arrangement joining the veil to the poles also indicate some magnetic or electrical power circuitry?

Aron habrit, the Hebrew name for the Ark of the Covenant.

The traditional Hebrew history of their adventures during the Exodus recounts how the ark had the power to burn away thorny undergrowth that blocked their way, and mysterious sparks flying between the golden cherubim killed scorpions and serpents. On one occasion after the Philistines had captured the ark, they placed it in the Temple of Dagon. The next morning the statue of Dagon was found prostrate before the ark. Subsequently, it was discovered not only prostrate but in pieces. When the ark was located in the Philistine cities of Ashdod, Gath, and Ekron, the inhabitants suffered skin problems that were described in the biblical account as boils. Those researchers who hypothesize about the possibility of some dangerous technological contents in the ark, perhaps a hazardous atomic radiation source, would speculate about the Philistines' skin problems being due to exposure to nuclear energy.

On another occasion Uzzah, a well-meaning cart driver, put out his hand to steady the ark, which seemed to him to be in danger of falling. He died after touching it. Some early authors mistakenly assumed that Uzzah had been struck dead as a punishment for his presumption in daring to touch the ark, but the Judeo-Christian-Islamic God of love, mercy, and justice would never have punished a well-meaning carter who sought only to protect and preserve something precious and holy. Proto-Masonic understanding of morality and ethics could never ascribe Uzzah's death to a deliberate act of God. Realistically, there are two possible causes of Uzzah's sudden death: the psychological shock of realizing that he had inadvertently touched the sacred ark while instinctively seeking only to safeguard it, or some mysterious power within it, possibly electrical, that had given him a fatal blast when he touched it.

A huge question mark hangs over what happened to the Ark of the Covenant after the Babylonians plundered Jerusalem and Solomon's Temple. One theory says that it was hidden under Temple Mount in Jerusalem, which adds credence to the idea that the Templars found it there during their twelfth-century excavations and took it somewhere safe.

After Philip le Bel (Philip IV of France) treacherously attacked the noble order of the Templars in 1307, knowledge of the ark's hiding place may have been lost except perhaps to an elite group of high-ranking Freemasons who had access to the vital medieval secrets of the order. Another hypothesis places the ark in Axum in Ethiopia. According to this theory, it was brought there during Solomon's own lifetime, and with his full knowledge and consent, by Menelik, the son he gave to Sheba. A third theory suggests that Jewish priests removed the ark and hid it safely during the evil reign of Manasseh.

Other theories as to the ark's concealment are referred to in the Mishnayot. The Mishnayot is comprised of ancient sacred texts that are missing from the Mishna, the opening section of the Talmud. The Talmud itself is best described as a written record of the scholarly legal and theological discussions of the leading learned rabbis on matters of Jewish law, customs, morals, and ethics. It also covers certain relevant stories and germane case histories.

There has been great speculation over the centuries as to what the ark really was, what its powers were, and how they could be directed and employed. Historians of proto-Masonry believe there is a strong nexus between the secrets of the ark and the secrets of early Egyptian and Hebrew Freemasonry.

Was it perhaps some immense power within the ark that enabled the Israelites to cross the Red Sea in safety, while those same powers unleashed the returning water on the hapless Egyptian charioteers? The ark's reported power over water is described in Joshua 3:15–17, where

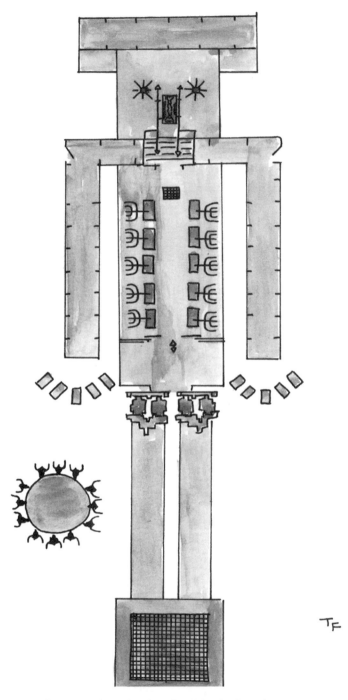

Solomon's Temple may have been designed in the shape of a man.

the priests carrying the ark stood still in the middle of the Jordan River while the host made its way across the dry bed. In Joshua 4:18 there is a record of the way in which the Jordan returned to its original course as soon as the priests carrying the ark stepped out of its path.

A great deal of Masonic teaching is centred on Solomon's Temple. In fact, the design and structure of that unique building are a significant part of Masonic history. Although Solomon's ancestry has posed a number of interesting questions, especially on his mother's side, Masonic historians are more concerned with the mystery of his temple than with the mystery of his antecedents. According to the history of Freemasonry, the temple was the work of three very great and talented men. The first was King Solomon the Wise; the Second was Hiram, the sensible and statesmanlike king of Tyre; and the third was Hiram Abiff, an artisan with the same level of skill as the great Bezaleel, the craftsman whom Moses praised so fulsomely. This third member of the triumvirate was the son of a widow, something of great importance in Masonic tradition. Hiram Abiff was brutally murdered when he courageously refused to reveal the secrets of the Craft.

Among the many fascinating riddles of Solomon's Temple is the mysterious human shape of its floor plan. Some specialist historians and expert archaeologists even suggest that the temple was deliberately laid out to represent not one but *three* human figures. The floor plan has to be read in conjunction with the temple furnishings in order to reveal these secret proto-Masonic designs.

One school of thought proposes that the three humanoid outlines are meant to represent Jacob, father of the twelve sons who became leaders of the Israelite tribes; the current high priest; and, thirdly, *something* very strange and esoteric, *something* that ties in with the myths and legends of the terrifying golem, *something* that at least one daringly unconventional historian has referred to as a *metal messiah*.

This metal messiah theory suggests we envisage that the figure consists of a golden head and thorax, arms of silver terminating in brazen fingers, and a pelvis and legs made of bronze. The Holy of Holies is the golden head, the priests' cells along each side are silver arms, and the ten brazen lavers (the vessels in which the officiating priests washed) form the fingers, five at the end of each arm. In 2 Chronicles 4:6, the precise details of these finger-like lavers are provided, while in 3:17 of the same book there are detailed descriptions of the two pillars known as Jachin and Boaz. These are fitted into the metal messiah theory as comprising the legs of the huge human figure.

But what did Solomon the Wise *intend* this metallic figure to represent? Was he passing on some strange, ancient, proto-Masonic wisdom about the mysterious appearance of the original guides and guardians?

There is a possibility that the metal messiah temple design theory may be associated with the old Hebrew golem traditions. Numerous myths and legends are linked to the animated clay monster known as the golem, but one that is of particular significance to Masonic historians concerns Rabbi Bezalel, or Bezaleel. His name is significant because of his famous forerunner, the great craftsman who worked with Moses during the Exodus. This original Mosaic Bezaleel was a strong candidate for high proto-Masonic rank, and it seems reasonable to assume that Rabbi Bezalel, who lived in Europe during the sixteenth century, had been so named because of his important Masonic connections.

Rabbi Bezalel's wife gave birth to their son, Judah Arya, during Passover in 1579 (Jewish year 5273), and his father prophesied that he would be a potent force for good and would be instrumental in bringing an end to the mindless anti-Semitic persecutions of the time. The talented boy grew up benefiting from his father's proto-Masonic wisdom and depth of secret, ancient knowledge and became a rabbi himself, first in Posen in Poland and later in Prague. When the persecution of the Jews in Prague reached an intolerable level, it was said that Bezalel's wise and skilful son used his mystical powers to create a golem that defended them from their enemies.

Is it possible that the story of the golem of Prague is *more* than myth and legend? Is there a mysterious connection between that golem legend and the metal messiah theory of the Jerusalem temple? There is a persistent historical seventeenth-century tradition that when things were particularly bad for the Jewish community in Prague, someone or *something* mysterious and powerful delivered them. If the tale of a golem of clay animated by Jewish mysticism is set aside as myth and legend, *who* or *what* intervened on behalf of the persecuted Jews of Prague?

If the oldest proto-Masonic thinking contains vestigial truth about the extraterrestrial origin of the first proto-Masonic guides and guardians of humanity, then a being of paranormal power operating benignly in seventeenth-century Prague is not impossible. What if the learned son of Rabbi Bezalel did not *create* something abnormally powerful to defend his people, but rather *summoned* it?

A detailed description of the temple layout and its building processes can be consulted in 1 Kings 6. Those ancient records show that in modern measurement terms the interior was eighty-eight and a half feet long by twenty-nine and a half feet wide and about 44 feet high. These details provide interesting corroboration for the theory that the temple actually *was* built according to an enigmatic triple-anthropoid design. The Old Testament, or Hebrew Tanach, account goes on to say that the entrance room was twenty-nine and a half feet wide and almost fifteen feet deep, which made it as wide as the sanctuary itself. Most significant of all, as far as the humanoid shape theory is concerned, is the detailed description of the three-storied annexes that were constructed against the outside walls at the back of the temple and along two of its sides.

Reverting to the cubit measurements given in the older versions of the account of the building of Solomon's Temple, the reader discovers that the nethermost chamber was five cubits broad, the middle chamber was six cubits broad, and the third was seven cubits broad. The use of cubit measurements is relevant to the possibility that the *tabnit*, a Hebrew word that can be translated as "shape," "figure," "form," "structure," "likeness," or "design," of Solomon's Temple *was* the outline of a man.

The cubit itself is the distance from the tip of the longest finger to the elbow. It can be converted to about eighteen inches. There is an interesting reference in Ezekiel 43:13 to a variant measurement called a "long" cubit. This was said to be a standard cubit plus the width of a human hand.

Almost all of these ancient measurements were based on the dimensions of the human body, a notion that was very important to proto-Masonic craftsmen such as those engaged in constructing Solomon's Temple. The measurement called the hand was about four and a half inches, and two such hands made a span of approximately nine inches, the distance from the tip of the thumb to the end of the little finger with the hand spread as widely as it could reach. Two of these spans made a cubit.

The problem always was that no two ancient craftsmen were exactly the same size. A tall, slim man with big hands would have different spans and cubits from a shorter, sturdier, more compact, muscular man.

How then was it possible for stonecutters in one area to produce accurate *ashlars* to be assembled by workers in another region? Masonic historians suggest that members of the Craft had a very important secret: *there were standardized Masonic measures that were known to Craft members, but not elsewhere.*

Modern science and technology also recognize the vital importance of having absolute standard measures for important units of length, area, volume, and mass. For example, the original American definition of the metre was exactly 39.37 inches, according to the U.S. Metric Law of 1866. This ruling defined the yard as being 3600/3937 metres and one foot as 1200/3937 metres.

The metre was defined as 1/10,000,000 of the distance from the North Pole to the Equator along the line of longitude passing through Paris. As will be demonstrated in chapter 21, "Masonry in Europe," this Paris Meridian is a line with a great many mysteries of its own, mysteries that form part of the great Masonic reservoir of secret knowledge.

Another of the important proto-Masonic mysteries associated with King Solomon was the location of his semi-legendary gold mines. These mines were said to be in Ophir, but where was that? Some experts believe that Ophir was actually Nejo in Ethiopia, with the Blue Nile to the north. Another theory involves the mysterious ruins of Zimbabwe, only twenty miles from Masvingo. Archaeologists have discovered intricate carvings, ironwork, pottery, and gold among these intriguing ruins.

Some historians believe the Zimbabwe ruins to be the work of the Shona civilization between the thirteenth and fourteenth centuries AD, but other researchers regard the site as far older — contemporary with Solomon and a possible source of his gold. This latter hypothesis is reinforced by the idea that there were Phoenician gold mines in Zimbabwe.

That line of thought is reinforced by considering the strong possibility of Himyaritic conquest all around the Mediterranean and beyond. According to this hypothesis, the Himyarites were a very ancient branch of the Semitic peoples, and the earliest Himyarite roots can be traced to Yemen. They established the Phoenician colonies along the eastern Mediterranean coast and beyond: Carthage, Memphis, Sardinia, Malta, Sicily, and Cyprus.

The Phoenicians sailed as far as Britain for tin, and according to some archaeologists, they seem to have left traces of their nature-based religion in Ireland and Scotland. Were they also responsible for the earliest historical developments in Spain? It has even been supposed that these adventurous, widely travelled Phoenicians left their stone temple designs in Mesoamerica and South America. Zimbabwe would be a very short step for a culture as globalized as theirs was believed to be. Did they carry proto-Masonic secrets on their trading vessels?

A very relevant and interesting reference to the mystery of the Himyarite wealth, their conquests, and their religion can be traced to an article in the *Geographical Journal* dated July 1893. In this article a Dr. Schlichter comments on the character of the ancient religious practices at Zimbabwe as being of a Himyarite nature. So was Zimbabwe the source of Solomon's vast quantities of gold? Was that location known to high-ranking proto-Masons who served Solomon?

Other intriguing research documents refer to a country called Monomotapa as a region near the great Zambezi River. Early Dutch and Portuguese explorers wrote of it, and the word itself seems to have originated in the Bantu language. It may have been loosely translated to mean Land of the Water Elephants. This would have meant a territory in which the hippopotamus was prolific. Is it possible that Monomotapa, which some mainstream historians are now inclined to regard as bordering on the mythical, was very much a real and prosperous kingdom in Solomon's time and was the source of his vast gold supply? Could Monomotapa have been the elusive land of Ophir?

Other equally interesting theories place Solomon's gold-supplying kingdom of Ophir as far away as India. If so, it would almost certainly have been situated along the Malabar coast. Wherever Ophir really was, its location was undoubtedly one of the most important and closely guarded proto-Masonic secrets.

So much then for the Masonic mysteries of Solomon's ancestry, the riddles of his temple, and the enigma of his gold mines. In the next chapter we explore the secrets of the Sadducees, the Pharisees, and other more secretive Jewish groups that flourished contemporaneously with King Herod and his building of the Second Temple. Like the First Temple, it enshrined a number of intriguing proto-Masonic secrets.

Chapter 10

SADDUCEES, PHARISEES, AND THE RIDDLE OF HEROD'S TEMPLE

UNDERSTANDABLY, MASONIC historians have always been keenly interested in the mysteries associated with Solomon's kingdom, his mines, and his temple, but it is equally important to investigate what happened to proto-Masonry when Solomon's long, prosperous reign ended. The Jewish kingdom split after the death of Solomon the Wise. The ten northern tribes separated from the smaller southern kingdom that included Jerusalem and the all-important temple. The rebellious northerners were led by Jeroboam, son of Nebat, who had been biding his time hiding in Egypt. The south remained loyal to Solomon's son, Rehoboam.

In 722–721 BC, the Assyrian emperor, Shalmaneser V, conquered the northern Jewish kingdom and transported many of its captive inhabitants to upper Mesopotamia. What actually became of them has been a matter of historical speculation for almost three millennia. For example, the twelfth-century adventures of the Spanish explorer, Benjamin, son of Jonah of Tudelah, are examined in more detail in chapter 15. Benjamin, who seems to have had proto-Masonic connections, thought he had discovered some of the descendants of the Lost Ten Tribes when he visited Persia and the Arabian Peninsula. In considering Benjamin's pioneering adventures we need to remember that he was a contemporary of the Knights Templar who were traditionally closely associated with medieval Freemasonry. Benjamin also flourished during the heyday of the minstrels, troubadours, and minnesingers, another important secret brotherhood with proto-Masonic and Templar connections. Did Benjamin really locate some descendants of the Lost Ten Tribes, and was their small but fiercely independent religious kingdom, as Benjamin reported it, one of the confused, exaggerated sources for the legends of the mysterious

Kingdom of Prester John? The northerners were carried off into exile by Shalmaneser's army, but what became of the smaller kingdom that contained Jerusalem itself?

In 597 BC, during the reign of the southern king Jehoiachin, the temple was looted and badly damaged, and the first deportation took place. Just over ten years later, during the reign of Zedekiah, Jerusalem was almost completely destroyed and more captives were taken. Finally, according to the account in Jeremiah 52:28–30, there was a *third* deportation from the southern kingdom.

However, once the benign and tolerant Persian emperor, Cyrus the Great, had overwhelmed Babylonia, things improved greatly. He gave the exiled Jews permission to return to Jerusalem in 537 BC.

After the captivity of the Jews, and their return led by Nehemiah and Ezra, Zerubbabel, another outstanding Jewish leader, made an impressive start on the rebuilding of Solomon's devastated temple. Apparently, the Persian emperor had laid down strict instructions concerning the dimensions of this restoration for which Zerubbabel was responsible. This meant that it had to be well short of Solomon's original superb structure, and because of the constant problems the Jews were experiencing from aggressive and hostile neighbours, it resembled a fortified redoubt rather than a place of worship.

The post-exile restorer of the temple, Zerubbabel, is an extremely interesting character as far as Masonic historians are concerned. The name Zerubbabel itself would seem to have Assyrian-Babylonian connotations, and the Persians also knew Zerubbabel as Sheshbazzar. His father was Shealtiel, also rendered Salathiel, and Zerubbabel was the grandson of Jehoiachin, who reigned briefly immediately before Zedekiah, the last ruler of the Southern Kingdom of Judah.

Zerubbabel displayed his innate royal qualities by leading 42,360 Jews back from captivity during the enlightened and benevolent reign of Cyrus the Great. Zerubbabel and Shealtiel are also listed among the ancestors of Joseph the Carpenter of Nazareth, husband of Mary the Mother of Jesus. Being a leader, a warrior, and a skilful builder, Zerubbabel was almost certainly an influential proto-Mason at the time when the Jews came back from their long captivity and exile.

The connection between Zerubbabel and Cyrus is a strong and significant one: the Jewish hero and the benignly magnanimous Persian emperor probably met through their proto-Masonic connections and shared high Masonic ideals, morals, and ethics. Like the larger-than-life Louis XIV of France more than 2,000 years later, Cyrus of Persia was known as the Sun King, and this title, too, has powerful Masonic significance. There are some lodges today that still incorporate solar symbols among their jewels and badges of office.

The career of proto-Masonic Sun King Cyrus was a vivid and colourful one. In 559 BC, Cyrus followed his father, Cambyses, of the ancient Achaemenid Dynasty, as ruler of Ansham, which was then part of the Median Empire. Shortly after Cyrus was born, his grandfather, Astyages, had a strange prophetic dream that this new grandson would eventually overthrow him. Consequently, Astyages ordered his steward, Harpagus, to kill baby Cyrus. Harpagus was a good and honourable man, and his proto-Masonic ethical and moral code would not allow him to kill a helpless infant. Accordingly, he procured the sad little corpse of a stillborn baby boy from elsewhere and convinced Astyages that the dead infant was Cyrus whom he had feared.

Cyrus the Great, Emperor of the Four Sides of the World.

Years later Astyages discovered what Harpagus had done. He had the steward's own son killed and served to his father on a dish. This sick and wanton cruelty was the main cause of Astyages's downfall and the fulfilment of the prophecy. In pursuit of justice, Harpagus went to Cyrus and asked him to rally the Persians against Astyages and his Medes. Cyrus subsequently captured Ecbatana and replaced Astyages as ruler. He then went on to defeat Astyages's allies, the fabulously wealthy Croesus of Lydia together with Nabonidus the Babylonian. Pharaoh Amasis II of Egypt, who also had a treaty with Astyages, had the good sense not to antagonize Cyrus the Sun King, and in return the prudent and tolerant Cyrus left Egypt alone.

The sun symbol in Freemasonry, especially when associated with a great king or emperor, signifies the giving of life, just as the sun itself is essential to earthly plants and animal life. There are reasonable grounds for assuming that both Harpagus and Cyrus were high-ranking proto-Masons, and it was this proto-Masonic strength and wisdom that brought Cyrus to power and informed his liberal and benevolent rule as king of Akkad, Babylon, Sumer, and what were described in his royal decrees as the Four Sides of the World.

The square — the four sides of the world — is also a potent Masonic symbol, and it seems highly unlikely that Cyrus chose that particular title by chance. It almost certainly hinted at the high ethical and moral Masonic principles by which his empire functioned. Returning to the curiosity of Masonic codes and ciphers, the phrase "swift or deft householder," which certainly applied to the wise and prudent government of Cyrus the Great, is an anagram for "the four sides of the world," the area he once governed. Cyrus's territory stretched from the Indus Valley in the east all the way across to Asia Minor and the eastern shore of the Mediterranean.

In 1879 the Cyrus Cylinder was discovered in Babylon by an Iranian archaeologist named Hormuzd Rassam. It provided a great deal of historically important dynastic information. Even more important, it contained what may fittingly be described as an early charter of human rights. Cyrus's magnanimous declaration inscribed on the cylinder is a clear statement of proto-Masonic ethics and morality. His principles are in the highest Masonic tradition, and a practising Freemason from any era and any nation would recognize them immediately as reflecting the highest ethical and moral standards that mean so much to members of the Craft.

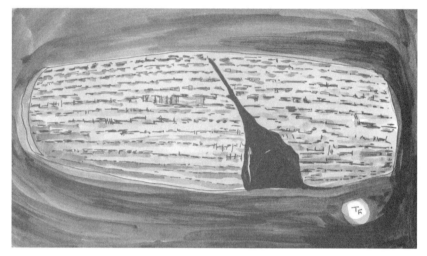

Inscribed cylinder of Cyrus the Great.

Cyrus entered Babylon in 539 BC and was officially crowned at the beginning of spring the next year. The following is what he wrote as conqueror and ruler:

> Members of my large army moved peacefully and without provocation throughout the city of Babylon. I gave them strict orders to harm no one in the countries of Sumer and Akkad. I noted the needs of the Babylonians and did what was necessary to supply those needs. I protected and defended their sanctuaries. Their welfare was important to me. I eased their burdens and ended their misfortunes. I rebuilt and repaired those of their dwellings that were in need of restoration.... I worshipped Marduk, the great god, and he caused the good people of Babylon to love and serve me.... I rebuilt and restored the shrines and sanctuaries

in the cities of Ashur, Susa, and Zamban…. With the aid of Ahura Mazda, it will be my aim to respect and honour the customs, traditions, and styles of worship of all the peoples in my empire. None of my officers shall look down on them or offend them during my lifetime…. I shall not force any kingdom or people to join my empire…. All nations are free to accept or reject my rule…. I will never allow one nation to oppress another. If there is oppression, then I shall intervene and defeat the oppressor…. During my reign, no one shall take away the property of another. As long as I live, I stand against slavery and against religious intolerance. My people are free to live where they like and to work where they choose. Their freedom ends only at the place where it encroaches on the freedom of others. No citizen of my empire shall be made to suffer because one of his relatives has done wrong.

This small sample of the good and generous policies that Cyrus not only proclaimed but also actually carried out to the best of his ability is typical of all that is best in proto-Masonic ethics and morality. Cyrus the Great richly deserves the honour that posterity has bestowed upon him. He not only stands high in the proto-Masonic hall of fame, but he is one of its pillars.

In 19 BC, Herod the Great began expanding, restoring, and refurbishing the temple work that Zerubbabel had done. History has dealt harshly with all of the Herods, deservedly so in view of the unspeakable callousness and cruelty of the Bethlehem children's massacre and the murder of John the Baptist, but Herod the Great (circa 74 to 4 BC) perhaps deserves some small counterbalancing recognition for the effort he put into the Second Temple. Historians sometimes argue over whether it was, in fact, a *Third* Temple that Herod constructed, but he himself always thought of it as the completion of Zerubbabel's labours. Herod's moral and ethical tragedies, and the suffering he caused, stemmed largely from his failure to understand that real religion is concerned with the welfare and happiness of people, not with vast building schemes. His efforts and expenditures in that direction were tainted with the same self-aggrandizement that had characterized the pyramid-building pharaohs.

The Jewish historian Josephus (Flavius Josephus, 37–101 AD) provides details of the 10,000 labourers whom Herod employed, and Masonic historians are especially interested in the distinctions between which parts of the temple the laity could enter and which zones were restricted to priests and Levites, the tribe from which priests were exclusively drawn. Records show that 1,000 Levites were given special training in building, particularly in *stone masonry*. This statistic provides Masonic historians with valuable clues and insights. Those skilled masons who trained the Levites would almost certainly have been members of the Craft brotherhood, and it seems equally likely that they would not have been willing to pass on their precious Craft secrets unless those who received them were themselves initiated into the Masonic fellowship.

These highly skilled Levite builders were now a very special elite. As Levites, they could enter areas of work where the laity, however skilled, were not able to go because of the temple's religious zone prohibitions. Furthermore, as newly initiated members of the Craft, they would have access to skills and knowledge that were unknown outside the Craft. It is also highly likely that they encountered members from the Egyptian, Greek, and Phoenician branches, and learned from them.

Nothing like the amount of work that Herod organized on this Second Temple could have taken place without adequate financial support, and Herod's own ample coffers were generously augmented by the liberal gifts and donations from many wealthy Jews of the Dispersion — those who lived outside Palestine. Work seems to have begun on the area known as the Holy Place, which contained the Holy of Holies. The priests who carried out their religious duties in the temple, and the altar for burnt offerings, were all adjacent to the Holy Place. Beyond them was the Court of the Israelites, with the Court of the Women next to it. Farther beyond those zones was the Court of the Gentiles, with an outer wall surrounding everything. Today's small section of Herod's original outer wall is known as the Wailing Wall, and it has great religious and emotional significance for devout Jews. The temple was connected to the main city lying to the west of it by means of two substantial bridges.

The irony of this great structural enterprise was that after all the work that had gone into the temple (it wasn't finally completed until 63 AD, more than sixty years after Herod's death), it stood only until 70 AD when the Romans destroyed it.

The other great proto-Masonic riddle associated with the temple is its exact and precise location. The first idea, and the one that is probably most widely favoured, puts the temple site a little lower than the Dome of the Rock and places the holy building on the traditional Temple Mount. But that first and most popular theory is not uncontested. Some experts have also suggested the temple was sited either north or south of the Dome of the Rock. In his interesting and thought-provoking book *The Temples That Jerusalem Forgot*, Ernest L. Martin locates the temple over the Ophel water source, the Gihon spring in the old city of David to the south of the Dome of the Rock.

The writings of Josephus supply a great deal of information about the location of the Jerusalem temple. After all, he had intimate knowledge of the city and its culture. On his father's side Josephus belonged to a priestly Jerusalem family, and his mother had proud Maccabean warrior ancestors. Josephus gained firsthand experience of the strict legalistic, puritanical attitude of the Pharisees, but greatly preferred the luxurious freedom and liberality of the licentious Roman aristocracy. He was, for example, a close friend of Nero's notorious wife, Poppaea Sabina.

In addition to the valuable information provided by Josephus, however, there are other important records about the location of the temple. Aristeas reported in 285 BC that the temple was built above a spring that provided copious supplies of water. There are no water sources in Jerusalem other than the Gihon spring. In chapter 38 of his translation, the fourth-century church historian Eusebius maintains that Aristeas, who had seen the temple towards the end of the third century BC, had also commented on a plentiful spring of water that he had seen welling up there.

In his *Histories*, book 5, paragraph 12, the Roman historian Gaius Cornelius Tacitus (circa 56–120 AD) also presents evidence that the temple benefited from a prolific natural supply of water. This makes a great deal of sense in conjunction with the rituals of purification and other priestly functions that required copious water supplies.

Masonic historians are particularly interested in the symbolism behind the total destruction of Jerusalem. Matthew 21:1–2 includes the powerful statement "not one stone here will be left on another." For members of the Craft brotherhood, especially those Herodian Levite Masons and their descendants who loved their temple both for its evidence of their skill as well as for religious reasons, this total destruction of their work was a devastating blow. Josephus witnessed the wholesale, wanton destruction, remarking that if he hadn't seen it happening, he would never have believed that a city had once stood there.

Titus Flavius Vespasianus (39–81 AD), who reigned as Roman emperor from 79 to 81 AD.

Titus, the Roman general responsible for the carnage and destruction in Jerusalem, later became emperor for just over two years. His comments on the ruins of Jerusalem echoed those of Josephus insofar as the *completeness* of the destruction went. With four legions available for the grim task, Titus started the attack on Jerusalem early in 70 AD. In just over three weeks the walls were breached and only the temple and inner city held out. The Romans threw up a siege wall around the city so that starvation became one of their most formidable weapons. By late July or early August, Titus's legions reached the outer court of the temple. The building was burnt down and the last defenders were massacred. The triumphant Roman legionaries then offered sacrifices to their standards in what had once been the temple court. That act was the ultimate sacrilege, degradation, and desecration of the temple.

Masonic historians have shrewdly noted that there were practical, avaricious reasons for the Roman treatment of their Jewish civilian captives after the temple was destroyed and its defenders slaughtered. These Jewish prisoners were forced to dig up and overturn the foundation stones not only as a symbolic gesture of humiliation, but in order that their Roman conquerors could retrieve the gold that had melted when fire destroyed the temple. The same treatment was meted out to the other buildings that the Romans had burnt. Titus's legionaries knew all too well that when war threatened them and their city, prudent Jews concealed their money and golden treasures *within* the stone walls. Once their slaves had dug up and overturned the foundation stones, the Romans simply retrieved the lumps of gold that had melted and run down through the crevices in the burning walls as soon as the temperature passed 1064.18 degrees Celsius, the melting point of the metal.

Once again there are peculiar Masonic anagrams to be found that are germane to this idea of *molten gold under stones*:

- *demons legends turn loot*
- *long lost tremendous end*
- *mould golden rottenness*
- *God! Soon dull resentment*

More evidence that is of particular interest to Masonic historians comes from Eleazar, leader of the stubborn Jewish heroes of Masada who fought on for another three years and finally committed suicide rather than fall into the clutches of General Silva, leader of the Tenth Legion. Eleazar said that the city had been demolished to its very foundations except for "the headquarters of the Romans, the building that still stands upon the ruins of the city." What did Eleazar mean by that description? Was it the Antonia Fortress that Herod the Great, a close friend of Mark Antony, had built for his Roman friends long ago and named after his fallen hero? It was a huge building that could once have accommodated an entire Roman legion if necessary.

Josephus also noted that this immense building had an outcrop of rock *inside* it, so that in some ways its overall design followed the outline of what was to become the familiar Norman-style motte-and-bailey castle a thousand years later. Were the building skills of the Palestinian proto-Masons miraculously and secretly preserved by succeeding generations of craftsmen, to emerge again with the designers and builders of medieval fortresses? The link between the Templars and the Freemasons is a strong, obvious, and enduring one, and it must be remembered that the Templars were superb *builders* as well as superb fighting men.

The mysterious rock outcrop was described by Josephus, and right up until the time of Saladin in the late twelfth century, as the site of the Roman Praetorium. In John 19:13 there is a specific reference to the Pavement (Hebrew *Gabbatha*) — what seems to be a rock platform or lithostrothon. The Church of the Holy Wisdom once stood there, and both its regular worshippers and flocks of visiting pilgrims believed for centuries that it was upon this rock platform that Pontius Pilate passed sentence on Jesus.

Dr. Martin's arguments for the location of the original temple in the Ophel area seem both sound and reasonable, and Masonic historians give them serious consideration. The next question is concerned with the people of those times rather than with the buildings they used for worship. Three main groups require investigation: the Sadducees, the Pharisees, and the mysterious, secretive Essenes.

The Sadducees were powerful and influential during Christ's work in the early part of the first century AD and continued to be so until the downfall of Jerusalem in 70 AD. They date back to the time of Yehoshua Ben Shimon (175 BC), who *bought* the high priesthood, and were supporters of his genealogically disqualified successors. The Sadducees accepted only the written law and were largely dismissive of the oral traditions so greatly loved by their rivals, the Pharisees. Apparently, they did not believe in resurrection, nor in the immortality of the soul and the existence of some sort of spirit world in which souls might continue to live after physical death. Their negative beliefs in these areas, however, may not actually have been quite as grim as they were thought to have been. Sadducees and Pharisees were vehement theological enemies, and in the course of their bitter arguments, the Pharisees may well have represented the Sadducees' position as more extreme than it really was. Although they were numerically fewer than the Pharisees, the Sadducees were wealthy, powerful, and organizationally strong. From the time of Yehoshua Ben-Shimon onwards, the high priest was almost invariably a Sadducee. The Sadducees were fiercely opposed to Jesus and John the Baptist, and they later placed as many obstacles as they could in the way of the young and growing first-century church.

The Pharisees accepted all the restrictive and intricate oral traditions that had grown around the written law like barnacles on a ship, and they held very different views from those of the Sadducees in other areas, as well. For example, the Pharisees believed in the resurrection of the physical body and the immortality of the soul. They thought that a spiritual world existed after physical death and that punishments and rewards in that future world depended on what a person had done during his or her earthly life. They were also inclined, to a limited extent, to entertain ideas about predestination. This belief was theologically and philosophically highly contentious.

If predestination exists, then logically no one can be blamed for his or her moral and ethical failures. Neither can a person be rewarded for choosing goodness and rejecting evil. If we simply run along the loci of our lives like a railway locomotive directed and limited by its tracks, then our imaginary moral and ethical choices degenerate into irrelevant trivia. If Jack the Ripper was *destined* to be a serial killer and Dr. Thomas Barnardo was *destined* to save the lives of scores of underprivileged orphans, neither man had any choice, so neither deserves punishment or merits reward.

Clearly, the highest Masonic ethics and morals soar far above the teachings of the Pharisees. Masonic ethics and morality teach the vital importance of individual freedom, choice, and responsibility. A Mason *chooses* to be a Mason and then *chooses* to follow the highest Masonic standards of behaviour.

Awareness of the ideas of the Sadducees and Pharisees is important, but the most interesting of all these contemporary groups are the mysterious and secretive Essenes. Their history seems to have begun when Antiochus IV Epiphanes (Image of God), a singularly unpleasant Seleucid ruler whose many enemies used a subtle Greek pun and referred to him as Epimanes (Madman), sold the high priesthood to Yehoshua Ben-Shimon in 175 BC. Secret, sacred, Essenian writings frequently refer to a dangerous opponent whom they call the Wicked Priest *(Kohein ha-Resha)*, and this would *seem* to refer to Yehoshua Ben-Shimon, though other interesting theories concerning the identity of the Wicked Priest have been put forward from time to time.

Coin of Antiochus IV Epiphanes bearing the inscription "Antiochus, image of god, bearer of victory."

The Essenes refused to recognize the Second Temple but saw themselves and their community as a living, immaterial, spiritual temple. When the Romans destroyed the temple in 70 AD, the Essenes regarded it as a sure sign that the End of the Age was coming, and they prepared for their equivalent of Armageddon — the Final Battle. The Romans dealt with them ruthlessly and came close to annihilating the sect.

Masonic historians are very interested in what became of the Essene survivors afterwards. Some theories suggest that they amalgamated with the Hillelite Pharisees and so became the founders of rabbinical Judaism. A number of Essene survivors may indeed have done so, but others may equally well have remained separate and secretive for a time before joining an early Judean proto-Masonic fellowship. The Essenes were admired for their truthfulness, piety, and love of justice, all of which are in perfect harmony with Masonic ethics and morality. If this highly probable union of some of the surviving Essenes and the local proto-Masonic brotherhood actually took place, the Craft's influence on its newly acquired Essene members would gradually have moved them away from their vegetarianism and refusal to take part in trade. The rational and practical side of this proto-Masonic influence would have shown their Essene proteges that it was possible to aspire to the highest standards of morality and ethics without refraining from trade or imposing dietary restrictions.

It has also been suggested that Jesus was an Essene before embarking on his public ministry, but one of the difficulties with that hypothesis is that Christ's followers believed in *one* Messiah who would fulfil the tripartite roles of prophet, priest, and king. The Essenes, however, believed in three separate Messiahs — one a prophet, another a priest, and the third a king. On the other hand, the Essenes were enthusiastic about the rite of baptism, and Christ's public ministry began with his baptism by John in the Jordan River.

The other fascinating Essene question concerns their involvement in the mystery of the Dead Sea scrolls. These were discovered between 1947 and 1956 in an area twelve miles east of Jerusalem that lies a surprising 1,300 feet *below* sea level. Of the numerous caves in the vicinity, only eleven have yielded scrolls or fragments. For example, cave number four, which was discovered in 1952, contained a vast number of fragments. Academic experts have identified approximately 900 separate scrolls that fall into two distinct categories: biblical and non-biblical. Some of the most interesting extracts, which could well prove to have proto-Masonic connections, are prophecies credited to Ezekiel, Jeremiah, and Daniel that are *not* found in the biblical versions of their books. The scrolls also contain psalms attributed to David and Joshua that are *not* in the biblical collection of psalms.

All the evidence centring on the scrolls points to their being the work of a sect such as the Essenes, who hid their library in the Qumran caves at the time of the first Jewish uprising against Rome from 66 to 70 AD. Among the other important information contained in the scrolls are the last words of several renowned Jewish patriarchs, including Joseph, Judah, Levi, Naphtali, and Amran, the father of Moses. It would have been proto-Masonic custom to record the final words of wisdom from a revered leader, and the inclusion of these sayings among the Qumran scrolls is a strong hint that some, if not all, of the Hebrew patriarchs were also proto-Masons. Furthermore, the scrolls contain non-biblical details about the lives of Enoch, Abraham, and Noah, all of whom, too, are strong candidates for inclusion in the highest proto-Masonic ranks.

The copper scroll discovered in cave three is probably the most interesting and significant find of all. It provides a list of sixty-four secret subterranean places of concealment in which the treasures from the temple were hidden to protect them from their enemies. The number sixty-four is itself highly significant. The chessboard, as detailed in chapter 3, "The Earliest Origins of Masonry," is comprised of sixty-four black and white squares, and these also form the traditional floor pattern of a typical Masonic lodge.

In this chapter the riddle of Herod's temple and the roles of the Pharisees, Sadducees, and Essenes have been examined and analyzed in conjunction with the development of proto-Masonry. In the next chapter Roman proto-Masonry and the strange secrets of Como will be investigated.

Chapter 11

ROMAN MASONRY AND THE SECRETS OF COMO

ONE OF the major secrets of the long-lasting success of the Roman Empire was that its arts, crafts, skilled trades, and professions were scrupulously and rigorously organized into what their members referred to as *collegia* or guilds. Each of these organizations exercised strict, monopolistic control over its own particular area of work. It would not be an exaggeration to suggest that these *collegia* were modelled on the empire itself and were, as far as they could be, microcosms of it. There were, for example, miniature collegiate "empires" of carpenters, stonemasons, goldsmiths, and armourers.

Tragically, when the macrocosmic Roman Empire fell to the barbarians, these miniature guild empires inevitably collapsed along with it, but not all of them and not entirely. There were remnants and survivors, just as there were remnants and survivors of the Essenes when Rome destroyed Jerusalem and Masada. Istanbul (then Constantinople) was believed to have harboured some of these survivors, as did Rome itself.

A strong and persistent tradition concerning the fate of these high-level professional and trade *collegia* located substantial groups of architects and craftsmen in and around beautiful Lake Como in Lombardy in the north of Italy. The history of Lombardy goes back many centuries. The Lombard people took it from the Eastern Roman Empire in the middle of the sixth century. At a later time it belonged to the dukes of Milan and was at other periods under the control of Spain and Austria.

The Masonic craftsmen who survived in the area made it their centre and headquarters and took their name Comacini from their location. Evidence for their existence dates back at least to the days of the Lombard king, Rotharis, who reigned in the mid-seventh century. The craftsmen, who were referred to then as *magistri Comacini*, were regarded by their contemporaries as master masons and enjoyed numerous important powers and privileges. They were, for instance, fully entitled to make contracts to undertake both private and public building works, and their travel was not restricted. This freedom to enter into contracts and to travel where they wished led to the use of the prefix "free." Masonic historians believe that in addition to the Comacini's outstanding organizational powers, which helped to keep them together in the area, they also preferred the Lombard district around Como because of the excellent stone and marble quarries there to which they had convenient access.

Masonic historians also note with keen interest that when Pope Gregory II authorized the missionary work of Boniface in Germany, it was ordered that stonemasons and architects should be included in the party. Similarly, when Augustine (eventually to become St. Augustine, the first archbishop of Canterbury) was sent to Britain at the end of the sixth century, he, too, was accompanied by stonemasons. It is also recorded that because Augustine was so successful he sent back to Rome for additional masons to construct even more religious buildings than he had originally hoped would prove necessary as the result of his missionary activities. It is believed that many of these highly skilled masons were Comacini and came originally from the Como area.

When a careful study is made of the building techniques and architectural styles typical of the period, many similar points of workmanship can be observed. Careful scrutiny of these points leads to the strong possibility that Comacini masons and architects were at work over large areas of Italy, Sicily, and Normandy during these centuries of prolific church, cathedral, and abbey building.

There can be little doubt that when the barbarians overran the Roman Empire, the professional and trade *collegia* suffered badly and many were destroyed. Fortunately, the most senior, the most skilful, and the most learned members of the Architectural College of Rome, who were almost certainly high-ranking proto-Masons, made their way to the Como district of Lombardy while these disasters were happening.

During medieval times, the Comacini Masters were widely recognized and greatly respected as one of the foremost Masonic fraternities in the whole of Europe. Masonic historians who have analyzed their working customs and practices in detail have expressed the view that their work had a decidedly Roman flavour. These theorists believe that there was every likelihood that the Comacini had somehow survived the overthrow of the original city and empire and had taken their precious Masonic skills and secrets much farther afield.

There is also a substantial body of evidence to suggest that Masonic monks were quite frequently encountered in medieval times, and there are good reasons to believe that many of them had Comacini connections. The Venerable Bede's accounts are generally accurate, factual, and reliable, and from what he wrote of Augustine's religious travels and adventures, it seems that Augustine had Masonic architects and builders accompanying his missionary expeditions. It is also probable that Gregory would have selected architects and masons who followed the most pure and ancient Roman traditions in preference to the styles that had blossomed in Constantinople.

One of the many strange stone animals on the wall of Cardiff Castle. Did the marquis of Bute deliberately copy the Comacini style?

Saxon styles and Comacini styles were both rich in stone representations of animals, and when the marquis of Bute restored and refurbished the ancient castle of Cardiff in Wales, the animals he placed around its walls bore a remarkable resemblance to those that were characteristic of these most ancient proto-Masonic types. Was the marquis speaking quietly and secretly to those who understood the significance of his stone beasts that were reminiscent of the Comacini carvings? Cardiff was, after all, originally a *Roman* castle.

This beautiful symbolic Masonic eagle adorns the wall of Cardiff Castle. What secret messages did the marquis of Bute hide in these stone creatures?

In addition to the trustworthy and accurate evidence provided by the Venerable Bede, Richard the Prior of Hagustald (now known as Hexham in Northumbria, England) had some interesting evidence to offer. He recorded that St. Wilfred brought masons and architects from Rome during the seventh century in order to build a church in honour of St. Andrew. Some historians believe that they have detected extracts from the writings of King Rotharis and King Luitprand.

Luitprand was responsible for restoring the Basilica of St. Peter of the Golden Ceiling in Pavia during the early years of the eighth century AD. He later arranged for the body of St. Augustine of Hippo to be interred there. Undoubtedly, proto-Masonic Comacini craftsmen carried out the important architectural designs and plans for the refurbishment of this basilica, as well as the actual building work itself.

Rotharis is also a singularly interesting character as far as proto-Masonic history is concerned, and in order to understand his significance in early Freemasonry, it is necessary to return briefly to the history of the Lombards in the Lake Como area. Columban, a missionary from Ireland, established a monastery there in 614 AD.

In their earliest days the Lombard invaders were an interesting mixture of Arian Christians and barbarian, pagan warriors. One of their sixth-century leaders, Agilulph, married a beautiful and highly intelligent girl named Theodelinda in 590 AD. She was a devout Christian who exerted a strong, positive influence over him. Together she and Columban converted Agilulph, and he gave Columban a ruined church to restore in Ebovium. Proto-Masonic craftsmen were undoubtedly employed in this work. It was here in Ebovium, too, that Columban and his followers created one of the most important Italian libraries of their time. As well as devotional books, it very probably contained a great many examples of seventh-century proto-Masonic wisdom.

Under the Arian Lombard ruler Rotharis (636–652 AD) there was vehement conflict between the opposing theologians and clerics. After Columban's death, Attala and Bertulf, who were equally erudite and scholarly, succeeded him. Their wisdom almost certainly included the benign and positive proto-Masonic ethics and morality that were so pervasive in the area then.

The Arian doctrine that Rotharis followed was frequently denounced as heresy by its theological and philosophical opponents. The teachings were the brainchild of a Christian priest named Arius, who had lived and worked in Alexandria, Egypt, during the early part of the fourth century AD, where he would certainly have encountered early Egyptian proto-Masons. In Arius's view, Jesus, unlike God the Father, had not always existed but was a *creation* of God the Father. Arius felt that at some point during the infinite timelessness of God the Father, Jesus had come into being as a divine entity. Arius never denied that the pre-existent Jesus was a truly divine being, but for him God the Father had existed *before* Jesus was created.

The tragedy of the early church was its rigorous insistence on trivial matters of dogma and inconsequential religious minutiae, which all too frequently got an opponent killed. In any case, the finest minds of the most erudite theologians on both sides of these inconsequential arguments could never hope to resolve any of them satisfactorily. None of the church fathers was a fly on the wall in heaven prior to Christ's incarnation; none stood stopwatch in hand to mark the precise second at which Christ came into being or, conversely, to observe that Jesus had always been there as the Logos or Word of God in the sense that St. John meant it in his gospel.

Tragedy and schism could all have been so easily avoided if only the theologians had had the sense to agree to differ and to be tolerant and understanding of one another's points of view in the true spirit of Christian love. It is in this breadth of tolerance and understanding that so much Masonic intellectual strength is to be found. The primal morality and ethics of Masonic teaching are absolute. Masonic belief in the existence of a divine being, by whatever name that being is known and revered, leads to an unfailing Masonic determination to treat all of creation with love and respect. Christ's words — "In as much as you have done it to the least of my brethren, you have done it unto me" — are the perfect summation of all that is highest and best in Masonic morality and ethics. What matters to a Masonic theologian is not some unprovable speculation about the precise nature of God, or Trinitarianism versus Arianism, but rather the manifestation of faith in a Supreme Being via actions of kindness and generosity to those of his children who are in greatest need.

Arianism held sway at the time of Constantine and influenced him and his family. When Ulfilas, another Arian, preached to the Goths, Ostrogoths, and Visigoths, it was naturally to Arian Christianity that they were converted.

Yet again it becomes impossible to separate Masonic mysteries and secrets from the mysteries and secrets of Rennes-le-Château close to Carcassonne in southwestern France, the colourful, historic area that is also known as Languedoc. Bérenger Saunière, who began his working life as an impoverished parish priest there in the late nineteenth century, inexplicably became the richest man in the south of France after his enigmatic discoveries in 1885. The precise nature of the source of his very considerable wealth remains an unsolved riddle, but Rennes-le-Château was once a powerful Visigothic kingdom. The Visigothic Christian rulers had an Arian Christian heritage. Was it some strange Visigothic secret or the enigmatic location of a treasure hoard lying hidden in a concealed vault beside the body of an ancient Arian Visigothic king that made Father Saunière so unexpectedly and unaccountably wealthy?

There were other so-called religious "heretics" living in and around Rennes in medieval times. These were the Albigensians, also called the Cathars. They were believed to have guarded a mysterious religious treasure — the Ark of the Covenant perhaps or the Holy Grail? What were the mysterious secrets that meant more to the besieged Cathars of Montségur than their own lives when the implacable forces of Christian orthodoxy overwhelmed them in 1244? Could they have been connected in any way with the ancient proto-Masonic secrets known to the craftsmen of Como?

When the forces of orthodox Catholic religion were launched against the almost impregnable Cathar fortress of Montségur in 1244, the Cathars were offered extremely generous surrender terms provided that no one left the fortress before the actual surrender took place. However, if anyone attempted to leave with *anything* before the gates were opened to their triumphant Catholic enemies, the generous surrender terms would be withdrawn and the Cathars would be burnt alive.

Despite those conditions, four fearless Cathar mountaineers descended under cover of darkness and escaped, carrying with them what were described as "the treasures of their faith." Perhaps these were ancient books full of secrets; perhaps they were priceless religious artifacts.

Co-author Patricia at the Cathar fortress of Montségur.

There is a tradition that the four desperate Cathar mountaineers reached Ussat-les-Bains and the mysterious Caves of Savarthez, or Savarthes, in the valley of the Ariège River. If anything of significance was once hidden in those mysterious caves, it would almost certainly have been known to the proto-Masons of thirteenth-century Languedoc.

In one Latin record left by the Inquisition, the Cathar treasures were supposed to be *pecuniam infinitam*, literally "unlimited money." It is far from likely that medieval alchemists had mastered the art of turning base metals into gold, but what else could be described as *unlimited* money? The Cathars operated close to Rennes-le-Château where Saunière became immensely rich more than six centuries after the fall of

Montségur. Inside Saunière's church, which is dedicated to Mary Magdalene, there is a curious group of statuary that seems to hint at alchemy and the four-element theory of earth, air, fire, and water.

Co-author Lionel in the pulpit of Bérenger Saunière's church of St. Mary Magdalene in Rennes-le-Château.

The Cathars shared some ideas with Arius, but in most respects differed widely from his teachings. Their name came from the Greek word for *pure*. They seem to have developed from another, earlier, heretical sect known as the Bulgars, or Bogomils, who were theologically a mixture of Adoptionists and Manichaeans. Adoptionism was condemned as a heresy by Pope Victor (190–198 AD) but was revived in Spain by Archbishop Elipandus of Toledo and Felix, bishop of Urgel. Pope Leo III finally endorsed Victor's denunciation of Adoptionism as a heresy in 798. The central point of Adoptionism was that Jesus had been *adopted* as God's firstborn son after he emerged from the Jordan where he was baptized by John.

Manichaeism was founded by a religious teacher named Mani who came from Persia and flourished from approximately 210 to 276 AD. He himself seems to have been influenced by the Mandaeans, who were very strict dualists theologically, more so even than the Gnostics. They divided the universe into the opposing spheres of light and darkness, the latter being ruled by Ptahil, the equivalent of the Gnostic demiurge. They admired John the Baptist above all other religious teachers and believed that Adam and Eve in Genesis had actually worshipped along Mandaean lines. The most prominent of the Mandaeans' numerous religious writings is called *Ginza Rba*. Their language, known as

Mandaic, is similar to Aramaic. It can readily be seen, therefore, that a combination of Adoptionism and Manichaeism is a theologically volatile mixture.

The Paulicians were another early heretical sect from which the Cathars eventually developed. They seem to have originated in Armenia during the sixth century and based their ideas on the teachings of Marcion and Paul of Samosata. Marcion rejected the God of the Old Testament and taught instead that Jesus was the Son of the Good God who opposed the God of the Ancient Covenant. Paul of Samosata was active during the second half of the third century AD. He was anti-Trinitarian and held Monarchianistic views theologically. As far as Paul of Samosata was concerned, God the Father was an all-powerful and sole ruler to whom both Jesus and the Holy Spirit were subordinate. Paul of Samosata may well have been the tutor of Arius at one time, and so further links are established between these ancient heretical leaders and the wisdom of their contemporary proto-Masons.

The question arises as to *why* these prominent heretical religious leaders thought as they did. What secrets did they share with the wise old proto-Masons? The spoor of that ancient but vitally important secret proto-Masonic wisdom and truth is not easy to follow, yet the track *is* there.

If we revert to the first awesome possibility, the daring hypothesis that the very earliest proto-Masons, the secret guides and guardians of our earliest ancestors, may have had an extraterrestrial origin, then we must also remember that the core of Freemasonry is veiled in allegory. If we dare to suppose that not one but *two* extraterrestrial groups were involved with our remotest ancestors, and that this was one of the most closely guarded proto-Masonic secrets, then we have the strong possibility of rivalry and competition between these visiting aliens.

As has already been surmised, one group is benign, moral, and ethical, planning nothing but good for the developing human race whom they are protecting, educating, and nurturing. The other group is evil, exploitative, intent only on using us and our planet's resources for their own greedy and selfish ends. To paraphrase the immortal words of C.S. Lewis: *The powers of evil want to enslave human beings as cattle who will become food — the powers of goodness want human beings as well-treated students who will become free and independent sons and daughters.*

The allegories enshrined in Mandaeanism, Manichaeism, Paulicianism, Bogomilism, Catharism, and all the other varieties and subcategories of Gnostic Dualism finally make sense. By teaching via the allegory of a good god in conflict with an evil god, the proto-Masons are sounding a clear warning that although they are very much on our side, *there are other extremely powerful nonhuman entities who are not.*

How now does the heretical concept of an anti-Trinitarian, Monarchianistic God fit alongside the dualistic allegories of the various forms of Gnosticism? What is it that the proto-Masonic guides and advisers were teaching via their Monarchianistic allegories? They needed to make it clear that life on Earth was not free of hazards. They needed to warn our ancestors to be on their guard against the sinister negative forces that were attempting to harm them, whereas they, the proto-Masonic teachers, were doing all they could to protect, develop, and guard humanity.

Being extraterrestrials with vastly superior knowledge and technology did not make them atheists or even agnostics — far from it. They were well aware that the wider universe as they understood it was the work of an infinitely powerful benign being whom they variously described as the Great Architect or Great Geometrician. In the Monarchianistic "heresy" they were adding a further layer to the allegory. They were declaring that although two closely matched superhuman powers — theirs and their rivals' (one being good and the other being evil) — were in conflict, there was a supreme benign being whose powers were infinitely greater than theirs. The apparent theological and philosophical paradox of trying to reconcile Dualism with Monarchianism was resolved.

In this chapter we have examined the mysteries of Roman proto-Masonry and the way that it survived the downfall of the Roman Empire in the Como district, spreading from there throughout medieval Europe, taking with it in the form of allegory those vital truths concerning all that is best in Masonic ethics and morality.

Chapter 12

MASONIC MYSTERIES OF THE CELTS AND DRUIDS

WHEN WE scrutinize the Masonic mysteries associated with Celts and Druids, once again the trail leads back inevitably to the enigma of Rennes-le-Château, largely because Celtic Tectosages were among its earliest inhabitants. The name Tectosages can be traced back to root words meaning "wise," "skilful," or "clever," plus the idea of "building," "constructing," or "making." The Tectosages, therefore, were the Wise Builders. There can be no better synonym than that for Freemasonry.

The Tectosages were part of a larger Celtic nation known as the Volcae, who were extremely powerful, free, and independent in the second century BC. They lived principally in the area bounded by the Garonne and Rhône rivers and the Cévennes —the area later known as Languedoc — where they enjoyed their own laws. The other group of Volcae were the Arecomici; they occupied the eastern zone, while the Tectosages held the west with their capital city at Toulouse, not far from Rennes-le-Château. The Volcae were incorporated into the Roman Empire as part of the province of Gallia Aquitania after Julius Caesar's conquest of Gaul in the first century BC.

It seems highly likely that Roman proto-Masons were in touch with their Tectosages brethren over several centuries, and that after the fall of the Roman Empire and the survival of the proto-Masonic *collegia* in the Como district of Italy, this fraternal contact would have continued. In times of political, military, and social uncertainties, such as those that followed the collapse of the Roman Empire, mutual help and support are more important than ever.

In the village of Rennes-les-Bains, near Rennes-le-Château, a priest named Henri Jean-Jacques Boudet was a contemporary of the enigmatic Bérenger Saunière. Rennes-les-Bains is also of significance to Masonic historians because of its Roman spa baths and other ancient buildings.

Just as Saunière probably took the living at Rennes-le-Château in order to look for its legendary treasure, so it seems equally probable that Boudet deliberately sought the living at Rennes-les-Bains in order to delve into the mysteries associated with the Tectosages and the intriguing old cromlech nearby, both of which were potentially saturated with proto-Masonic mysteries and secrets.

Henri Jean-Jacques Boudet was born on November 16, 1837, in the village of Quillan. Although Boudet's own family members were poor, a generous local priest paid for his education — a typically Masonic act. Ordained in 1861, when he was twenty-four years old, Boudet was appointed to the living of Rennes-les-Bains in 1872, several years before Saunière obtained the living at Rennes-le-Château.

Both men enjoyed long walks in the historic countryside in which their respective parishes were situated, and Boudet was once heard to remark to another neighbouring priest that he preferred walking in winter when the leafless trees *did not hide the stones*. That declaration raises the intriguing question of what the two men might have been looking for in the way of special landmarks and pointers in the landscape.

Henri Jean-Jacques Boudet's memorial commemorating his years as priest of Rennes-les-Bains.

Boudet's death was as mysterious as it was tragic. In 1914, at the age of 77, Boudet was gravely ill with intestinal cancer. The harsh and unfeeling Bishop Beauséjour, who also did his best to make things difficult for Saunière, deprived the sick old man of his parish. Boudet's mother, sister, and brother had all predeceased him by some years, and his final months must have been a mixture of pain and loneliness after he retired to the old family home in Axat. Although such details are difficult to substantiate after almost a century, there were strong rumours at the time that Boudet, sick as he was, did not die of natural causes. Mysterious visitors apparently left him dying in agony after they went.

When we visited Boudet's grave and photographed it, the most notable feature was a carved representation of a book. Was it simply meant to be a Bible or New Testament, appropriate enough for a priest's grave, or was it meant to be the very mysterious book that the scholarly old priest had written? The lettering looked as if it had been interfered with. Was it simply the Greek word for *fish*, an early Christian code word? Or was it a clue to page 310 or 311 of Boudet's enigmatic book?

The riddle of the stone book on Boudet's grave: is it a reference to his own book, to the Bible, or to something entirely different and unsuspected? Could it even be a reference to the mysterious Priory of Sion?

Having investigated the mystery of the Rennes treasure since their first research visit in 1975, when Lionel was lecturing on unsolved mysteries for Cambridge University's Board of Extra-Mural Studies, the authors are inclined to agree with those investigators who surmise that the older, more intelligent Boudet was the brains of a two-man team in which Saunière was the resolute, powerful, muscular, and occasionally *ruthless* limbs.

Some of the light that Boudet sheds on the proto-Masonic mysteries involving the Tectosages is to be found in his enigmatic book *La Vraie Langue Celtique et le Cromleck de Rennes-les-Bains*. The title alone may contain some very curious, coded anagrams. *La Vraie Langue Celtique*, for example, produces: "Alive, angelic, true equal," "Give an equilateral clue," "Equal guile alert in cave," and "Quite real angelic value." *Le Cromleck de Rennes-les-Bains* furnishes: "Ensnared bee; sins; rock cell; elm." This last anagram has fascinating connotations that will be explored in depth later, and it must be borne in mind that the highly intelligent and academic Boudet was an expert linguist.

One of the controversial theories centring on Rennes-le-Château concerns the possibility that Jesus was married to Mary Magdalene and that she brought their children to the safety of Languedoc. Those who subscribe to this theory further speculate that one of those children later married into the Merovingian dynasty (457–750 AD) that ruled France prior to the coming of the Carolingians (750–887 AD). The anagram "Alive, angelic, true equal" could refer to this Mary Magdalene theory. The second anagram, "Give an equilateral clue," could refer to the enigmatic landmarks occurring all over the Rennes area. The mysterious Tomb of Arques, for example, could well be one of the vital points on such a triangle, and the ruined Château Blanchefort along with neighbouring Château Hautpoul situated next to Saunière's old church, which is dedicated to Mary Magdalene, might perhaps be the other two points. Triangles, it must be remembered, are significant Masonic symbols.

Another of the mysterious theories associated with the Rennes treasure riddle is that whatever valuables are concealed there, they are in some way connected with the entombed corpse of King Dagobert II. This theory incorporates the idea of a curse that protects the treasure, whatever form it takes. When one of the rather dubious "coded manuscripts" *supposedly* found at Rennes is "decoded," it *allegedly* contains the phrase *et il est la mort.*

This ambiguity can be interpreted either as "and he is there dead," or more sinisterly as "and it is death." The treasure hunter can interpret the phrase to mean that the wealth is buried beside Dagobert II, or that whoever disturbs it will be activating a fatal curse. This makes sense of the third anagram, "Equal guile alert in cave." The film *Raiders of the Lost Ark* featured a series of booby traps designed to deal with tomb raiders, and it is possible that the famous Oak Island Money Pit in Mahone Bay, Nova Scotia, might be a protected grave rather than a treasure cache, although like Dagobert's tomb, it may serve a dual purpose and protect both a corpse and a treasure. Anyone seeking the mysterious Rennes treasure in one of the many caves in the area is well advised to explore it prudently and cautiously. Prudence and caution are integral parts of wise Masonic teaching about lifemanship in general.

The fourth anagram is "Quite real angelic value." Does this one carry the secret coded message from Boudet that the treasure of Rennes is neither mythical nor legendary, but that it is some sort of priceless religious artifact? Another theory devised to explain the source of Saunière's wealth suggests that he found such an object — so valuable that it could not be sold — and passed it to the Habsburg family (who then controlled the Austro-Hungarian Empire) in return for a very large pension.

Turning to the second part of Boudet's book title, *Le Cromleck de Rennes-les-Bains*, produces the enigmatic anagram "Ensnared bee; sins; rock cell; elm." This one is really strange. The bee was a very significant symbol throughout history and is revered in Masonic symbolism as an emblem of working together for the good of the whole organization.

Bee working on flowers.

Bees also signify resurrection and immortality. Napoleon used bees as part of his heraldic symbolism in order to link his imperial dynasty with the Merovingians. He is known to have been a member of a military Masonic lodge observing the Ecossais Primitive Rite of Narbonne during the 1790s. We need to remember that Napoleon was fascinated by ancient Egypt and its wisdom and secret knowledge, much of which was the work of the ancient Egyptian proto-Masons. This knowledge must have had a profound influence on him, since bees were very important in the Egyptian symbolism that he studied. It is also significant that golden bees were discovered at Tournai in 1653 in the tomb of Childeric I, who was the founder of the Merovingian dynasty in 457.

After Bérenger Saunière died in suspicious circumstances in 1917, his faithful housekeeper and partner, Marie Dénarnaud, who also shared his secret knowledge of the Rennes treasure mystery, arranged for his body to be seated in state and wrapped in a mantle with multiple tassels that looked remarkably like *bees*. His faithful villagers filed past him to pay their respects and each took one of the tassels as a souvenir. This ceremony would have been especially meaningful for any Freemasons in Rennes.

As far as the ancient Egyptians were concerned, bees were the living tears of their sun god Ra and were also frequently depicted on Egyptian tombs as symbols of resurrection and eternal life. The bee is associated with Greek and Roman gods, too, including Cupid and Aphrodite, which gave rise to the concept of honey as an aphrodisiac.

There is an interesting proto-Masonic allegory with a rich moral teaching inside it concerning bees and the highly skilled architect brothers, Trophonius and Agamedes, from Lebadia. They were commissioned to build a treasure vault for one of their rich clients, but yielding to temptation they left one stone unsecured as a secret doorway through which they could enter and steal the treasure they had been employed to protect. As the old adage warns, "The corruption of the best is the worst."

The owner of the vault suspected that something was amiss and set a trap accordingly. Agamedes was caught in it, and descending from theft to fratricide, Trophonius cut his brother's head off and fled for his life. He reached the Grove of Lebadia and attempted to hide there, but a chasm opened beneath his feet and he fell into its Stygian depths.

Forever afterwards, it was said that the restless spirit of Trophonius gave oracular prophecies from the depths of the subterranean caverns into which he had descended after murdering his brother.

Bees filled the Grove of Lebadia and were held to be sacred because they had been instrumental in leading a party of high-ranking visitors from Boetia to the place where the doomed Trophonius uttered his strange, subterranean prophecies. The ethical and moral messages of this allegory clearly warn of the dangers of departure from the high Masonic principles of virtue, fidelity, and honesty.

The bee is also highly regarded in Ireland, and ancient laws were passed to protect it there, especially since honey was the basic ingredient of mead, traditionally the drink of passionate lovers and the immortal Irish gods. Ireland is also connected with Dagobert II, the Merovingian king.

Symbolic golden bees from ancient Crete.

Slane in Ireland is an extremely ancient and important site. Its history goes back to the Stone Age, and it is probable that the Celts of Ireland had contact with their Tectosages cousins in the Rennes-le-Château district. The Irish Fir Bolg King Sláine is said to be buried on or near the great Hill of Slane. Another of the Slane legends concerns a healing well in the vicinity that was used by the Tuatha De Danann to heal any wounds they sustained in battle. It was to Slane that young Dagobert II was brought for safety after the death of his father. He was well cared for and was invited to the court of the high king of Ireland in Tara. While in Slane he married the beautiful and courageous Celtic princess Mechtilde.

Having returned to assume his throne at Rennes-le-Château in what was then the Merovingian Kingdom of Austrasia, Dagobert II died in an ambush. There are various accounts of what happened next.

The seventh-century Dalle des Chevaliers found below the church floor at Rennes-le-Château during Bérenger Saunière's time there as parish priest.

The enigmatical seventh-century Merovingian tombstone found below the floor of Saunière's church in the late nineteenth century provides important clues. Was it carved by a proto-Masonic craftsman who knew the truth about what happened to Dagobert II? It shows what looks like two people on one horse, and a version of the legend of the fatal ambush in which Dagobert II was killed suggests that he held off the enemy while his faithful wife escaped to safety with his infant son.

In one unproven version of Dagobert II's grim and tragic story, his beautiful Celtic bride died before he did and he subsequently remarried. It may well be, however, that this account of his second marriage, reputedly to Giselle, daughter of the count of Razès, was purely a political and dynastic fabrication intended to link Dagobert II with the bloodline of the counts of Razès.

Nothing is certain, but another, more probable version of the ambush story is that Dagobert II was accompanied by his fiery Celtic queen, Mechtilde, and their infant son, Sigebert, when the treacherous attackers sprang upon them. Trained as a swordsman in the Irish high king's court at Tara, Dagobert II was no easy target. Urging Mechtilde to take their son and ride for their lives, the Merovingian king blocked the pass and fought valiantly to the death, by which time Mechtilde and Sigebert were out of sight. Knowing the mortal danger they would both be in if they stayed in Austrasia, the fearless Celtic girl and her son made it safely back to Ireland where her Celtic kinsman protected and cared for both of them.

So proto-Masonry would seem to have strong links with the Tectosages of Rennes and the high-spirited warrior Celts of Ireland. But what about the *rest* of the strange anagram — "Ensnared bee; sins; rock cell; elm" — based on the second half of the title of Boudet's cryptic book? The "ensnared bee" could relate to the end of the Merovingians when the Carolingians replaced their dynasty, to the fate of Emperor Napoleon (who was probably poisoned), or to the unenviable destiny of Trophonius, the architect whose gloomy oracle at Lebadia was associated with sacred bees. Or might it have referred to Dagobert II (another Merovingian bee king) ensnared in the fatal ambush from which his beloved Celtic wife and infant son escaped?

What are the *sins* that are referred to? Were they the sins that Boudet and Saunière were committing in the course of their treasure hunt? Did the word refer to the sins of the Carolingians in usurping the Merovingian throne? Were they the sins of the fratricidal Trophonius? Or were they the far deeper and more damaging sins of lies and deliberate concealment of ancient truth of which Saunière and

Boudet felt that the Church itself was guilty? If they were adherents of one of the old heresies involving Gnostic Dualism, they may well have regarded the massacre of the hapless Cathars of Montségur as a gross and terrible sin committed by the orthodox Catholic Church. Or was it the sin of Philip le Bel and Pope Clement V when they destroyed the good, honest, innocent, and noble Order of the Knights Templar in 1307?

The "rock cell" could relate to any of the caves and labyrinths in and around Rennes, or even to the riddle of the Tomb of Arques. There is also a curious story about a lost Roman gold mine in the vicinity, within which a shepherd boy named Ignace Paris discovered skeletons and treasure during the Middle Ages. The local lord of the manor promptly accused him of theft and hanged him before he could reveal its exact location.

The "elm" almost certainly refers to the supposed cutting down of the huge old elm at Gisors in France in 1188. This felling of the symbolic tree allegedly separated the Templars from the Priory of Sion that had supposedly been associated with them previously. Indeed, there are researchers who believe that the Priory of Sion was an extremely old proto-Masonic organization and that the Templars were its armed might. Just as with Boudet and Saunière, one was the mind, the other the muscle.

The mysteries of Celtic proto-Masonry involve the Tectosages of Rennes-le-Château and their possible link via Dagobert II with the warrior Celts of Ireland. Druidism and Freemasonry also have a great deal in common in the area of allegory, ethics, and morality. The central point of both sets of teaching — Masonic and Druidic — is faith in the existence of a supreme divine being (by whatever name that being is known) and a determination to treat all human beings as sisters and brothers because that supreme benign being is the parent of all of us.

Much as the history of proto-Masonry can be traced back through many millennia, so can the history of Druidism. Expert historians of Druidism are very interested in the caves of Lascaux in France and Altamira in Spain, just as Masonic historians are. It seems highly likely that the early proto-Masonic initiates went deep into the cave (symbolizing darkness and death) and then emerged again into the light (symbolizing rebirth). Early Druidic rituals would have proceeded along very similar lines, suggesting that the earliest members of both great organizations could have belonged to one or the other — or *both*.

The deep wisdom and knowledge of the Druids and proto-Masons were entirely ecumenical, because the leaders of both groups realized that ecumenism was the hope of the world. Judgemental exclusivity and intolerance have probably led to more pain, suffering, and death than the worst natural disasters, starvation, and plague. Masonry and Druidism are both tolerant, loving, and inclusive faiths. Whoever the very first proto-Mason Druids were, and wherever they came from, they knew that humanity had to learn to live by that vital, central truth.

Five thousand years ago, it seems that the Druids and proto-Masons, especially among the perceptive Irish Celts at Newgrange, were creating special artificial mounds through which these symbolic death and rebirth ceremonies could be dramatically enacted. It is possible to enter into the dramatic feelings of the initiate sitting in the Stygian darkness at the centre of the mound waiting for the first rays of the winter solstice to shine down the carefully oriented shaft and ceremonially bring him back to life.

In addition to the religious symbolism of these Druidic ceremonies, there was a deep knowledge of the psychology of creativity. Sixteenth-century references to Druidic training tell how the candidate was instructed to remain inactive in the dark for long periods, then suddenly emerge into the inspiring brightness of the light. This process appears to have triggered something important in the subconscious and inspired poetry and music of high bardic quality.

In order to put Druidism into perspective alongside ancient Freemasonry, it is helpful to be aware of the four great historical epochs of Druidism. The first era may be said to have begun as the glaciers of the last ice age retreated and people began to build stone circles. They also raised mysterious cromlechs like the one at Rennes-les-Bains that so fascinated Father Boudet. These people were truly intelligent and practised mathematics, astronomy, and engineering to a remarkable degree, strongly suggesting they were helped and inspired by extraordinary leaders.

The second era of Druidism recognized three orders: teachers, philosophers, and judges, categories quite similar to Plato's idealized philosopher-kings, healers, and prophets, referred to as ovates. Augmenting these three Druidic orders were the bards who knew all the songs and stories through which Masonic-style morals and ethics were taught allegorically. Writers, including Julius Caesar himself, commented on Druidism during this period, and there was much interchange of culture, skill, and knowledge among the Celts, Greeks, and Egyptians while the Roman Empire kept peace in the ancient Mediterranean world.

The third era of Druidism coincided with the arrival of Christianity. Tolerant and inclusive Christianized Druids continued to teach, heal, write poetry, and sing songs. Several Christian priests took a commendable, scholarly interest in Druidism and wrote down what they could discover of the old Druidic teachings, songs, and stories. No less a Christian leader than St. Patrick of Ireland recorded many Druidic laws and some of their other writings.

The fourth era of Druidism is what might best be described as the period of rediscovery, which has been going on for the past five or six centuries and shows every sign of continuing to do so. The wisdom and knowledge of Druidic teaching marches alongside the high moral and ethical principles of Freemasonry, and both offer great benefits to society throughout the world.

It would not be possible for authors living in Cardiff, the capital of Wales, to complete this examination of Druidism without commenting warmly on the life and work of Iolo Morganwg (also spelled Morgannwg). Co-author Lionel's widely acclaimed recent television series *Talking Stones* investigated the lives of prominent Welsh men and women of the past. Each episode included a visit to the graves of such outstanding characters as actor Richard Burton and Iolo Morganwg and the retelling of their life stories.

Morganwg's real name was Edward Williams and he came from Llancarfan. Born in 1747, he was a professional stonemason and must certainly have been a member of the Craft. From ancient documents that Iolo discovered, for he was an antiquarian as well as a skilled professional mason, he reconstructed a number of interesting bardic rituals. Detractors have accused Iolo of forgery, but even if his imagination made some contributions to his reconstructions of ancient Druidry, there is much in his work that is scholarly and praiseworthy.

Iolo was the author of the impressive *Druid's Prayer*, which is also called the *Gorsedd Prayer*, and organized a Druidic ceremony at Primrose Hill in London in 1792. His teachings included the theory of concentric circles of being, starting with Annwn, a kind of "other world," and going on from there to what Christians would describe as heaven. Iolo called heaven Gwynfyd. His death in 1826 left a rich legacy for contemporary Druids to enjoy.

John Renie, a craftsman housepainter and a founder member of the Oddfellows Friendly Society, was a contemporary of Iolo's. In 1832, when he was thirty-three, Renie died in Monmouth, not many miles from Iolo's beloved Glamorgan in South Wales. His unique grave carries the inscription "Here lies John Renie," which is a very curious acrostic of a type that would have been familiar to proto-Masonic code makers. Acrostics are word puzzles that have been known since classical Greek and Roman times. The anagram of "Here lies John Renie" is "Rejoin Helene's heir." Was Renie a young Masonic friend and brother of Iolo the Druid? Did both of them acknowledge the wisdom of the great Greek and Roman proto-Masons? And did the dying Renie, who seems to have devised his own strange tombstone, regard himself as one of the heirs of the Hellenes, the Greek proto-Masons he was soon going to rejoin?

Chapter 13

MASONIC LIGHT DURING THE DARK AGES

DESPITE ALL the Masonic foundations that were laid in ancient times, the Dark Ages slowed down human development, culture, and technology, yet not everything then was dark. After the fall of the Roman Empire and the withdrawal of the legions from Britain, the Romanized Britons still did what they could for a time to maintain the Roman-style *collegia* of architects, stonemasons, and other wise and skilled craftsmen.

There are Arthurian researchers who believe that the exploits attributed to the noble Arthur and his chivalrous Knights of the Round Table actually belonged historically to a Romano-British armoured cavalry detachment led by a warlord named Arturus. If those suppositions are right, then the years during which Arturus and his cavalry defended as much as they could of Romanized Britain from the invading Saxons would have been years during which architects and stonemasons could have got on with their work in comparative safety. Even after the Saxon invasions became a serious threat to the Romano-Britons, Saxon culture indicated a greater interest in agricultural land than in cities, and so, rather surprisingly, the *collegia* were not under as much pressure as might have been expected.

Because the monastic communities during the Dark Ages were also centres where culture and learning were preserved, there seems to have been an inevitable cross-pollination between the learned and skilful proto-Masonic architects and stonemasons on the one hand and the religious monastic scholars on the other. Neither was the gap between them a wide one. Masonic tolerance of *all* religions on one hand and generous, monkish hospitality on the other were further reinforced and integrated by the strong beliefs of both sides that brotherly love and help for the needy formed the essential core of true morality and genuine ethics. Monks and stonemasons, therefore, had a great deal of mutual respect and friendship during the Dark Ages.

The beautiful, picturesque island of Arranmore, off the coast of Donegal in Ireland, has a very long and colourful history. One of the ancient fortresses there is almost certainly the work of highly skilled proto-Masonic architects and stonemasons. Its walls were over 200 feet long and in the region of twenty feet high. Their massive strength lay in a thickness that matched their height. Well defended by spirited Irish Celtic warriors, the fortress must have been impregnable on the sheer cliffs rising hundreds of feet out of the sea. To build such a fortress on such a site was a feat requiring the greatest architectural and stone-cutting skills. The very existence of such a site is a significant clue to the survival of the collegiate proto-Masons during the Dark Ages.

Another indication of the nexus between Dark Age proto-Masons and church personnel was the existence of clergy who were also skilled architects and builders. They could never have achieved those levels of skill unless they had also been members of the Craft, a situation very similar to that of the Levites who helped with the reconstruction of the Jerusalem temple.

By the time the Saxons became a prominent power in Britain, the Romans had left impressive structures over a wide area of the country. Chichester, London, York, and Newcastle all contained evidence of Roman occupation on a major scale. Before 80 AD the Romans had a bridge (Pons Aelii) over the Tyne River connecting their military head-quarters with Gateshead on the other bank. According to local tradition, the great Cathedral Church of St. Nicholas on the corner of Mosley Street and the Groat Market in Newcastle was built over the site of what had once been a Roman temple.

Alfred the Great's grandson, Athelstan (895–939), was the first king of the whole of England, which he ruled from 925 until his untimely death in Gloucester on October 27, 939. His tomb stands in Malmesbury Abbey, but his remains went missing during Henry VIII's dissolution of the monasteries. Athelstan's body might have been hidden by pious monks (and might yet be rediscovered) or Henry's commissioners might have destroyed it.

Several of Alfred's genes must have made Athelstan the outstanding warrior that he was. His military campaigns were highly successful, and he won impressive victories against the Welsh, Cornish, Scots, and Danes, the last of whom he took York from in 927. Athelstan was a thoughtful maker and upholder of laws and did a great deal to regulate trade and commerce and to prevent fraud and injustice in business transactions. Apart from his military prowess and well-ordered civil government, Athelstan was an avid collector of religious relics and works of art. In almost every respect, therefore, he displayed many of the traditional Masonic virtues.

King Athelstan lived between 895 and 939 AD, reigning England from 925 to 939 AD.

Traditionally, Athelstan was said to have established York Rite Masonry in 926 AD by presiding over the group's meeting and granting it a royal charter. This charter entitled Masons to meet annually and was the starting point of much important construction work that included several castles, fortresses abbeys, and other religious buildings. The Regius and Matthew Cooke manuscripts both refer to Athelstan's help and support for Masons. It seems very likely that he himself held the highest rank among the Craft members, and his brother, Edwin, was said to have been their grand master. According to tradition, the rules that Athelstan and Edwin laid down for their Masonic brethren were based on old manuscripts written in Greek, Latin, and other ancient languages, thus reinforcing the idea that the Craft was well established both in classical Greece and throughout the Roman Empire, including its survival via the Comacini after the empire collapsed.

Masonic historians have suggested that the crypt of York Minster provides evidence of the interesting ways in which British Masonry grew and developed from the Romano-British era into Saxon times. The crypt's blue-and-white mosaic floor is suggestive of the floor of a modern Masonic temple, and traces of triple altars, which seem to copy the old Egyptian custom, are still visible. Tradition records that these old stone altars provided the seats for the master and his two wardens when they met in secret in the crypt, just as the ancient Egyptian, proto-Masonic priests had met in sacred, secret sanctuaries.

The Cooke manuscript is noted in the British Museum records as *Additional M.S.23,198*. Experts, including the scholarly Worshipful Brother William James Hughan (1841–1911) of St. Aubyn Lodge 954 in Devonport, agree that the manuscript was written during the mid-fifteenth century and appears to be a transcription of a much older document. It was published by Spencer of London in the second half of the nineteenth century and was named after Matthew Cooke, who did the editing.

The older Regius manuscript seems to date from the late fourteenth century, and James Halliwell published a version of it in the first half of the nineteenth century. It was once part of John Theyer's library and is included in his library catalogue of 1670. The Theyer books and manuscripts went to Robert Scott in 1678, and from him they were passed on to the Royal Library, where the Masonic manuscript acquired its name Regius. The manuscript remained there until King George II gave it to the British Museum in 1757.

From a Masonic historian's point of view, the manuscript's main significance is its discussion of Euclid, the great mathematician, as being a Masonic founding father, and its reference to the work of King Athelstan in tenth-century England. The following seven extracts from the fifteen articles the Regius manuscript contains are also worth noting, since they highlight Masonic ethics and moral standards.

- A Mason must be worthy of the confidence that his employers place in him.
- The master mason shall pay his fellow workers a fair and just wage.
- The master mason shall employ and teach his apprentice for no less than seven years and shall provide him with good food and lodgings during those years.
- The master mason shall not employ any thieves or murderers.
- The master mason must be certain that the foundations of the structure he works on are securely made.
- The master mason must never take on or interfere with the work of any other master mason.
- The master mason may do no work at night, but he may study at night.

In addition to the careful thought underlying the fifteen articles, the Regius manuscript contains fifteen points. The seven examples that follow also shed light on Masonic morality and ethics during the Dark Ages.

- All members of the Craft must love God and his Church and serve their fellow men.
- Masons must settle their disagreements in a friendly and tolerant way.

- If a brother's work is seen to be at fault, a wiser and more skilful Mason shall teach and help him to improve it, but always in a kind and friendly way.
- A Mason must not sleep with another Mason's wife or mistress.
- A Mason shall never steal, nor shall he ever assist or help a thief in his crimes.
- Masons take turns at serving their brothers at table.
- Masons are true to their master, their brother Masons, and their king.

By the standards of the first millennium AD, these Masonic moral and ethical teachings were very enlightened indeed.

The Regius manuscript also contains interesting references to Severius, Severian, Carpophorus, Victorian, Claudius, Castor, Symphorian, Nicostratos, and Simplicius, the Nine Masonic Martyrs. The spellings of their names can vary from one ancient account to another. Their persecutor was Diocletian (Gaius Aurelius Valerius Diocletianus, 245–312 AD). He was the Roman emperor from November 20, 284, until May 1, 305. When Diocletian visited the quarries in Pannonia, he greatly admired the work of four or five highly skilled stonemasons who were squaring the stone to perfection. The emperor ordered them to carve a statue of the pagan god of healing, Asculapius, also known as Asclepius. (In classical mythology this god was the son of Apollo, who had been educated by Chiron the centaur.)

The Masonic brethren refused to carve the statue because they were secretly Christians. Years later other secret Christians refused to bow to an image of Asculapius and were also martyred. Accounts of the grue-some details of their martyrdom vary between being beaten to death with lead rods and being sealed inside lead-covered barrels and thrown into the sea — or both. Their "offences," according to Diocletian, were a refusal to carve a statue of a pagan god and refusing to pay homage to a pagan god. The irony of the tragic situation is that the valiant and faithful Christian Masons of Pannonia were the kind of good and charitable men who would gladly pay a healer to help the sick and injured — in accordance with their high proto-Masonic ethical and moral principles.

The Roman emperor Diocletian, who killed the Masonic Martyrs.

These events occurred in 287 AD, and the Nine Masonic Martyrs are remembered on November 8, which is officially known as the Feast of the Four Crowned Martyrs (Quatuor Coronati), though in reality there were nine of them. Saints and martyrs usually have special symbols associated with them, like St. Peter's keys. In the case of the brave and honourable Masonic Martyrs, the symbols are the square and compasses, the saw, and the mallet.

The story of the Nine Masonic Martyrs also contains a number of concealed symbols and may be thought of as having an allegorical as well as a historical dimension. Nine, for example, is a very significant number to members of the Craft, to whom three is an important symbol. Being *on the square* in the Masonic sense endows nine with special significance because it is the *square* of three. Masonic courage and honesty are also embodied in the episode: these men preferred death to compromising their principles. The sealing into leaden barrels is reminiscent of the Masonic concepts of death and rebirth. From the Stygian darkness inside the lead-cased barrels, the concept of emerging after death into the bright, eternal light of heaven is clearly an important part of Masonic teaching.

It must also be remembered that during the Dark Ages and early Middle Ages, Masonic groups operated across national boundaries. French Masons (members of the Compagnnonage) worked in Scotland and Hungary; German members of the Craft, known as Steinmetzen, built structures in Italy; and British Masons plied their skills in various parts of Europe.

Some Masonic historians suggest that these various groups arose independently and more or less spontaneously, and that they found out about one another and came together to form worldwide Masonry many years later. It seems much more likely, however, that they were branches of the same great proto-Masonic tree that had existed for millennia, rather than that they were disparate groups that generated simultaneously in ignorance of one another's existence. The fact that the French Compagnnonage and the German Steinmetzen benefited France and Germany respectively in such similar ways possibly indicates a nexus between those two admirable groups.

Brethren from these early periods were often able to identify themselves by the way they *dressed*, and these early trade costumes almost certainly led to the wearing of Masonic uniforms and regalia in later lodges. When they travelled from one working site to another, these early Masons probably wore short grey or black tunics with side openings. A cowl, hood, or gorget was also worn. The gorget is particularly interesting. It was originally a type of armour designed to protect the neck against blows from swords or axes. Gorgets could also be simple neck protectors worn under a soldier's back plate and breastplate. They served an additional purpose insofar as they took the weight of the armour and were often equipped with shoulder straps and other fastenings to which armour could be attached. By the Renaissance, gorgets became largely decorative and symbolic and were frequently exquisitely and expensively embellished.

The travelling Masons of the Dark Ages wore strong leather girdles and carried short, heavy swords of the old Roman pattern. Centuries of warfare against barbarian hordes had proved the superiority of this type of weapon in the hands of a strong Roman legionary, and stonemasons were even stronger than blacksmiths by virtue of the physically demanding nature of their work. The girdle also supported the Mason's leather satchel, which seems to have developed into the ceremonial aprons worn by modern speculative (as opposed to operative) Masons. On top of this tunic a travelling Mason wore a black scapulary (a long, wide cloth with a hole for the head), which was tucked up into the girdle while he was working. Travelling Masons also wore wide-brimmed hats if the weather required them during their trips. Snug-fitting leather breeches that were tucked into their sturdy leather boots completed their attire.

In this chapter we have examined some of the ways in which early Masons endeavoured to make the sinister and hazardous worlds of the Dark and Middle Ages safer, fairer, and happier to inhabit, not only for themselves but for all who benefited from the time-defying fortifications and places of worship they built. In the next chapter we shall investigate the lives of some magicians, wizards, and alchemists who were suspected of harbouring Masonic connections, or to have stolen ancient Masonic secrets.

King Arthur's Merlin was filled with proto-Masonic Celtic wisdom and skill.

Chapter 14

MASONIC MAGICIANS, WIZARDS, AND ALCHEMISTS

DURING THE Middle Ages, and for several centuries afterwards, science that was not fully understood was frequently condemned as magic. Technology that was too far ahead of its time was called wizardry and aroused great fear and suspicion. Opposition to cloning, genetic engineering, and life-saving stem-cell research today reveals that negative attitudes still persist among some people even in the enlightened, scientific, and technologically advanced twenty-first century.

Freemasons throughout history have always been more open-minded and less fearful than their timid and superstitious contemporaries. There is reason to suspect a strong connection between the intellectual giants of what became known as the Western Hermetic school of thought and the leaders of European proto-Masonry as the Renaissance got underway. The line of such mystical thinkers can be traced without too much difficulty despite the secrecy in which they often had to live and work due to the dangerous narrow-mindedness of strict religious traditionalists and fundamentalists.

Before examining these Renaissance figures, however, it is essential to mention the most famous wizard of all. The fabled figure of King Arthur's Merlin, despite being historically somewhat shadowy, is nevertheless a strong claimant for inclusion in the ranks of Masonic magicians. Moral and ethical, as well as wise and powerful, the Merlin of legend has all the necessary proto-Masonic attributes. The likeliest of the historical theories of the real man behind the Arthurian saga is that Merlin was Welsh-Celtic and accordingly had access to the proto-Masonic mysteries of the Celtic Tectosages from southwestern France. His magic was always entirely benign. He used his spells to rescue those in distress and to defend the weak and helpless.

Moving on almost a thousand years into the immediate pre-Renaissance period, we encounter a proto-Masonic magician to equal the great Merlin. His name was Nicholas Flamel and he lived from 1330 until 1418, though there are those who argue that his empty tomb was not so much the result of a visit by grave robbers in search of his alchemical secrets as of his own legendary magical skills. There were rumours that he and his beloved wife and partner in magic, Perenelle, discovered the Elixir of Life and are still with us today! His old house, built in 1407, still stands at 51 Rue de Montmorency and is now a restaurant. Do Nicholas and Perenelle still call there incognito to enjoy an occasional meal and reminisce about the old days?

Flamel acquired a priceless book, allegedly written by a Hebrew magician known as Abraham the Jew. He set off for Spain to try to find someone who could translate the strange, old copper-and-bark volume and eventually mastered some of the book's secrets and became extremely wealthy.

There is a curious parallel here between the wealth that Flamel acquired from his enigmatic book and the riches that Bérenger Saunière accumulated at Rennes-le-Château. When the Cathar mountaineers escaped from the siege of Montségur in 1244, they were believed to have taken with them a book containing strange secrets. Did Saunière discover and use those secrets to amass his vast wealth five centuries after Flamel's time? This good and brilliantly intelligent man was almost certainly a high-ranking proto-Masonic magician.

Shortly after Flamel's supposed death, another potent magician came on the scene. This man was Marsilio Ficino (1433–1499), who was part of the establishment set up by Cosimo de Medici. Ficino translated ancient texts linked with the wisdom of Hermes Trismegistus of Emerald Tablets fame and did all he could to organize and systemize what was generally thought of as magic, occultism, and mysticism during his era. He was interested in astrology and the use of talismans for purposes of healing and protection. Like the other thinkers who were links in this Masonic chain, Ficino had a very powerful mind, but there was a scarcity of adequate data for it to work on. Nevertheless, *some* of the ancient proto-Masonic secrets from Egypt, Greece, and Rome had been preserved, and their high ethical systems were vital for the improvement of the turbulent and dangerous Renaissance society.

Giovanni Pico, of the family that had long owned the castle of Mirandola, lived from 1463 to 1494 and was one of Ficino's most amazing and able students. Pico gave his share of the castle and its estates to his brothers so that he could devote his entire life to study. In consequence, his brilliant *Oration on the Dignity of Man*, written in 1486, became the manifesto of Renaissance thinkers. Pico is very close, indeed, to Masonic thinking when he argues for the vital importance of humanity's quest for knowledge. In Pico's mind God had created human beings *outside* the rest of the order of creation. For Pico every vacancy in that order had been filled — from the simplest earthworms all the way up to the mightiest archangels.

As far as Pico could ascertain humanity's role in creation, God had wanted to create thinking, self-aware beings with the capacity to appreciate and understand all that had been made. But the *chain of being*, as it was conceived in Pico's time, was already full. Humanity had no set place in it. Thinking human beings were, therefore, peripatetic — intellectual nomads with the capacity to move up or down the chain of life depending on what they *chose* to do with their minds. According to Pico (who had more or less successfully blended Hermeticism with Neoplatonism and Gnosticism at least to his own satisfaction), human beings were intellectual shape-shifters, protean entities who could learn from, and even imitate, any other link in the chain. Inventors, scholars, philanthropists, and philosophers ascended the chain in the direction of God and the angels, while those who chose not to think descended among the so-called lower orders. To Pico, whether a person became a companion of the angels or a slug was entirely up to that person. (It cannot have entirely escaped Pico's attention that he himself was a renowned philosopher!)

What Pico said about the importance of thought, and its ability to change the status of a thinking human being, gave sense and meaning to life for many of his disciples and others who read his works or listened to him. It is no exaggeration to say that he was one of the far-seeing admirals aboard the flagship of the Renaissance. It was due to Pico's influence that the attitude of society towards artists and craftsmen changed so dramatically. Before the Renaissance they were in much the same category as all other workers; after Pico's arguments became widely understood and accepted, artists and sculptors were recognized as geniuses. This was very much in line with Masonic thinking that had always recognized the importance of craftsmen and women and their positive contributions to society. Pico was among the most important proto-Masonic leaders of his age. Sadly, but not surprisingly, the conservative forces of medieval, orthodox religion and traditionalism vehemently opposed him and his ideas.

Johann Reuchlin (1455–1522) was another proto-Masonic scholar-magician of the time. A brilliant linguist, he worked on the theory that Hebrew letters had numerical values and linked this notion with his interest in Pythagorean mathematics.

Another of the great proto-Masonic scholar-magicians was Heinrich Cornelius Agrippa von Nettesheim (1486–1535). His most surprising work, and arguably his most important, was an enlightened treatise entitled *Declamation on the Nobility and Pre-eminence of the Female Sex*. There is a real sense in which this highly moral and ethical man was a pioneer feminist. His other academic works were mainly on magic, and he was known to have consulted in depth with Trithemius, another contemporary intellectual giant.

Trithemius (1462–1516), author of *De Septem Secundeis* (which translates roughly as *The Seven Secondary Minds*), was a brilliant experimental cryptographer and almost certainly a leading member of the Craft. His early theories, as expressed in his intriguing book, suggest that world history was influenced by superhuman, paranormal entities — angelic beings perhaps *or* proto-Masons from elsewhere. In some of the amazing codes and ciphers that Trithemius used, entire words could stand for single letters. In fact, a few of the anagrams that can be formed from his name would have given him a delighted smile: "this humane," "iron jest," "he joins this true man," "in this just hero, amen!"

Another of Trithemius's intricate and sophisticated coded works was called *Steganographia*, broadly meaning "hidden" or "secret writing." The book had to be read on two or three distinct levels, and one of these purports to be a learned treatise on epistemology, mnemonics, magic, linguistics, and techniques for transmitting and receiving messages by what appeared to be inexplicable means. The work generated so much awe and trepidation when shared with other members of Trithemius's academic circle that he modified the most challenging parts of it and decided never to publish the rest. Despite his wishes, however, the book did reach print in 1606, ninety years after his death.

The third part of the *Steganographia* was a maze of numerical tables to which signs of the zodiac and symbols representing planets were added. The treatise *could* be entirely valueless, but if Trithemius really *had* discovered some amazing method to transmit and receive information without either symbols or trustworthy messengers with good memories, the book would be priceless!

Trithemius was very interested in the way the human mind worked: is there a million-to-one chance that he found a way to make telepathy work accurately and systematically? Perhaps he hadn't so much *discovered* telepathy as had it *revealed* to him by what he described as the angelic powers (the original extraterrestrial, proto-Masons perhaps?) that he believed in so ardently.

Using an allegory, in the surest proto-Masonic tradition, Trithemius "explained" this technique by saying that the message had to be sent to the appropriate angel. The person for whom it was intended would then contact that same angel and receive the message from him or her. In the highly technological twenty-first century, does this sound just a *little* like an allegorical description of satellite technology, mobile phones, and the Internet?

Who exactly *was* this remarkable proto-Masonic magician? Whatever mysterious researches into obscure areas of knowledge Trithemius might have undertaken, he was, above all, a good, moral, and ethical man in the best Masonic tradition. Some of his deep, philosophical teachings can be summed up and paraphrased as:

- Application to learning and study brings knowledge.
- Knowledge teaches us that love is the greatest good.
- Love induces virtue, kindness, and generosity.

- Virtue is the source of dignity and power.
- Those who have acquired power can work miracles.

Trithemius was born in Trittenheim on the Mosel River. His baptismal name was Johann (spellings vary and sometimes his given name is rendered as Johan) and his surname was Heidenberg. He left Trittenheim to study at the University of Heidelberg.

The smallest incidents can change the entire course of a man's life. Trithemius was caught in a severe blizzard and ran for shelter to the nearby Benedictine abbey of Sponheim. The life appealed to him and he stayed there. It was a wise decision for him: when he was only twenty-one, Trithemius was elected abbot of the abbey. This position gave him the opportunity to create a vast library, to study assiduously, and to write his own amazing books. In 1506 he moved on to become the abbot of St. Jacob's in Wurzburg, where he died ten years later. Abbots were extremely powerful and influential men in Trithemius's day. They also frequently required the services of members of the Craft for work on their abbeys, monasteries, and other ecclesiastical buildings.

The most famous contemporary of men like Pico and Trithemius was undoubtedly Michel de Nostredame, known to history as Nostradamus. He was born in St. Rémy, Provence, France, in 1503. His family members were prosperous and well-educated Jews who were reputable, honest, and well-established corn traders. They had, however, converted to Catholicism, and this gave young Michel an opportunity to study both biblical prophecy and the mysteries of the Cabala.

Nostradamus was a highly intelligent youth who mastered Hebrew, Greek, and Latin while studying at home before going on to the University at Montpellier when he was nineteen. He became a doctor of medicine and practised with the normal sixteenth-century mixture of pharmacy and alchemy. In Agen he married and was blissfully happy for a few years with a loving wife and two children. Tragically, all three of them died in a plague epidemic in 1538. The heartbroken Nostradamus became a wanderer, learning all he could about medicine — both orthodox and unorthodox varieties — during his long years of travel. Predictably, the Inquisition thrust its malicious nose into his work and accused him of heresy.

Co-author Lionel beside a waxwork of Nostradamus in the
Nostradamus Museum in Salon, Provence, France.

Years ahead of his time Nostradamus realized that cleanliness and good sanitation could help prevent disease. This idea brought him medical success and enhanced his reputation as a physician. In 1547 he met and married Anne Ponsart Gemelle, a rich and attractive young widow, and they moved to Salon, not far from Aix in Provence. It was there that he found peace and happiness once more after the trauma of losing the first family that he had loved so much during their years in Agen.

In Salon, Nostradamus began to write his famous prophecies. They are, naturally controversial, but some of them are difficult, if not impossible, to explain away as mere coincidences, mistranslations, anachronisms, or ambiguous renderings. Nostradamus may have used narcotic herbs to help him focus on the bowl of scrying water resting on its tripod in front of him. (Scrying is a paranormal technique of looking into a crystal, a globe, a mirror, or a bowl of water in an attempt to see the future.)

How are the seemingly accurate prophecies to be understood? The future cannot be fixed and immutable — that does away with all ideas of human choice and free will. It also disposes of morality and ethics. If saints on one hand and psychotic serial killers on the other are merely following their inescapable, predestined tracks, then there are no moral choices for which they can be praised or blamed. All that Nostradamus could have seen during his scrying sessions would have been *possible* futures, probability tracks, the Worlds of If.

Nostradamus died on July 2, 1566. Originally buried in the wall of the Cordeliers Church in Salon, his remains were transferred to the Church of St. Laurent in the same town. When co-author Lionel was filming the television documentary *The Real Nostradamus*, there was a rather curious episode beside Nostradamus's wall tomb. A spotlight was designed to illuminate the stone as visitors entered the chapel or went out as they left. When the film crew entered for Lionel's piece-to-camera beside the tomb, this spotlight went stroboscopic, flickering rapidly on and off in a way that made filming impossible. The crew tried everything, but the light stubbornly refused either to come on steadily or to go out. Finally, the cameraman said to Lionel, "You're an ordained priest as well as a professional actor and presenter, please say a prayer for Nostradamus, just in case it's him!"

Lionel blessed Nostradamus's tomb as his friend had asked, finishing with "Nostradamus, *requiescat in pace*. Amen." As he said "Amen," the light went out and the filming was satisfactorily concluded. It might have been nothing more than simple coincidence, or it might have been that kind, proto-Mason Michel of Nostredame was obliging a brother in the Craft!

Co-author Lionel at the tomb of Nostradamus in the Church of St. Laurent in Salon, Provence, France.

A younger contemporary of Nostradamus was the celebrated Dr. John Dee (1527–1609), who had the same massive intellect possessed by Nostradamus, Pico, Trithemius, Reuchlin, and Agrippa. The profound secret knowledge and wisdom that these enigmatic men shared contained much that was proto-Masonic. Dee was fascinated by Hermetic philosophy, divination, alchemy, astrology and astronomy, geography, and mathematics. The combination of mathematics, astronomy, and geography enabled him to become an expert navigator, and it is no exaggeration to claim that it was Dee's navigational teaching that enabled the daring sixteenth-century sailors to succeed.

Just as Trithemius had been fascinated by theories of angel magic, so, too, was Dee. Part of the proto-Masonic wisdom and knowledge that bound these great minds together was a refusal to separate hard science and mathematics from philosophy, theology, mysticism, and magic. For them the entire universe was God's universe, and there was plenty of room within it for magic as well as for the scientific method. Knowledge could come from *any* direction — from a laboratory, a telescope, a magician's cauldron, an alchemist's furnace, or from communication with an angel.

Dee was originally from a Welsh family that had moved to London. Their Welsh surname Du meant "black," which some of Dee's opponents saw as sinister. The Welsh background, however, was full of timeless Celtic wisdom like that of the mysterious proto-Masonic Celtic Tectosages from the Carcassonne and Rennes-le-Château areas of France.

Starting his education at Chelmsford Chantry School, Dee then went to St. John's College in Cambridge, and from there to a founding fellowship at Trinity College. His European travels included lecturing in Paris where his special subject was Euclid — Masonry and mathematics once again seen as inseparable. Co-author Lionel's mathematics and Masonry provide a twenty-first-century example. As a math tutor, his three famous mathematical shortcuts for students are:

- The square root of two multiplied by the length of the side of a square gives the length of the diagonal of that square.

- The square root of three-quarters or 0.75 multiplied by the side of an equilateral triangle gives the vertical height of that triangle.
- The square root of three multiplied by the side of a cube produces the length of the diagonal of that cube.

Dee's knowledge of much ancient and mysterious wisdom, some of which dated back millennia, led to his creation of an extremely mysterious symbol or glyph. He wrote about the figure at length and in great depth in *Monas Hieroglyphica*.

An artist's impression of Dr. John Dee's strange symbol or glyph.

Enlargement of the photograph of one of the strange, unknown characters from Roswell, New Mexico. This is the eighth figure from the line shown below.

Bizarre symbols from the Roswell, New Mexico, I-beam. Note the strange similarities between Dr. John Dee's sixteenth-century glyph and the eighth symbol in this line.

When we consider once more the theory that the first proto-Masonic guardians and guides may have been extraterrestrial visitors to Earth millennia ago, the strange similarity between Dee's glyph and the enigmatic characters on the Roswell, New Mexico, I-beam becomes intriguing. What if the seemingly impossible were true? Were what Dee thought of as angelic messengers really benign extraterrestrials with paranormal powers?

Dee used the whole of *Monas Hieroglyphica* to explain his curious glyph as the symbol of the mystical unity of the whole of creation, but there are numerous significant points that can be taken from the book in summary form:

- The crescent-shaped curve at the top symbolizes the moon, with connotations of lunar goddesses such as Astarte or Ashtoreth. It also symbolizes a possible moon base from which extraterrestrial aliens found it convenient to shuttle back and forth to Earth. There is the additional idea of bull's horns. The crescent can also indicate a ship — the ship of the dead — sailing from one world to another.

- The large circle is the Earth, or even the entire universe. It can also represent the sun. Additionally, it signifies the environment, the biosphere that surrounds us, and of which we are also a part. Furthermore, it indicates the cycle of life and the seasons. The great circle indicates eternity and immortality. There is no beginning and no end.

- The central dot represents the origin of the circle — the location from which every point on the circumference is equidistant. The central dot is also a microcosm of the universal circle. It could represent Earth as a planet judged against the vastness of the large circle — the sun or the universe. It is the Rosicrucian teaching of "As above, so below."

- The cross below the circle has deep religious significance for Christians. Great thinkers like John Dee and his contemporary Masonic magicians managed to amalgamate and integrate the ethical and moral teachings of Christianity,

Hermeticism, Neoplatonism, and Gnosticism. The cross can also be seen as the torso and arms of a person of which the circle with the dot at its centre is the head. The dot then stands for the third eye, the psychic eye, enabling the human being to see beyond the physical universe and into the spiritual one.

- The curved mounds at the foot of the glyph can represent an archer's bow, pulled back and full of potential power. It represents the potential power within a person, which can be liberated only when that man or woman has studied proto-Masonic wisdom and knowledge. The curves can also be said to represent the wings of a bird, like the sacred Masonic owl, the symbol of wisdom. It is wisdom that enables flight, helping the person to soar metaphorically to new heights of knowledge and achievement.

John Dee filled an entire book with a complicated analysis of his intriguing, thought-provoking glyph. The above summary suggests only what *some* of the proto-Masonic meanings behind it *could* be.

In 1582 Dee met with Edward Kelley, an encounter that proved to be a turning point in the learned doctor's life, but not a particularly helpful one for him. Never the most patient of men, Dee wanted to speed up his learning processes by making better and more frequent contacts with the spirit world, especially the realm of what he described as angel magic. If Kelley was *genuine*, then the material he gave Dee as the result of his scrying (along the lines that Nostradamus had favoured) could repay the years of closely applied study that it would require. If Kelley was merely a cynical exploiter of Dee's credulity, his work means nothing. The third possibility is that Kelley was an honest but unsophisticated and misguided man who was simply self-deluded by the strange ideas that sprang from his own creative subconscious.

Another significant turning point in Dee's life was when he met Albert Laski, a member of the old Polish aristocracy, who invited Dee and Kelley to come to Poland with him. Unfortunately for Dee's continental adventures, Laski was not influential with the Polish establishment, and he had no money. Nevertheless, Dee was able to enjoy audiences with King Stephen of Poland and Emperor Rudolf II. The suspiciously dubious Kelley had established a reputation as an alchemist during their continental journeyings and was beginning to eclipse Dee. It also seemed that Kelley had taken a fancy to Dee's attractive young wife and told Dee that a message he had just received from the angel Uriel ordered them to share their partners. That was the end of Dee's association with Kelley! The doctor returned to Britain in 1589, a sadder, wiser man.

Dee died in 1609, and a few years later Robert Cotton, a scholarly antiquarian, bought land adjacent to the doctor's old home and began to excavate it. He unearthed a number of Dee's manuscripts referring to what Dee had believed were angelic communications.

There is some evidence to suggest that Dee was involved with the Rosicrucians and that he might well have been a distinguished proto-Mason. There are also a number of very interesting pieces of Dee memorabilia in the British Museum. The most significant exhibit is his "mirror," which is actually of Aztec origin and reached Europe in the early sixteenth century. The object is a piece of obsidian shaped like a conventional hand mirror.

Dee was only a teenager when Paracelsus died, but it is more than possible that he was familiar with Paracelsus's work. Born in 1493, barely a year after Christopher Columbus reached America, Paracelsus was a combination of doctor of medicine, alchemist, and astrologer. His real name was Theophrastus Bombastus von Hohenheim, and a proto-Masonic anagram for that full name, which would have both flattered and pleased him, is "The robust, humane, smooth-shaven bishop."

Paracelsus was born in Einsiedeln, Switzerland, to a Swiss mother. His father was a Swabian chemist, and young Theophrastus qualified in medicine in Vienna in 1510 at the age of seventeen. Centuries ahead of his time as far as toxicology was concerned, Paracelsus maintained that it was the dosage that decided whether a substance was toxic or not. However, there is much in the man's life that is confusing. There are other accounts of his medical qualifications that placed him at Ferrara in 1516, but perhaps that apparent problem can be resolved by suggesting that he took a *second* medical qualification there.

What proto-Masonic secrets did wise old Paracelsus use?

Most of the wise proto-Masons of the era were great travellers, and Paracelsus was no exception. Travel was the way to acquire wider knowledge. He served as a military surgeon in Italy and in Holland, and one of his Russian adventures ended with his being taken prisoner by the Tartars. Were his magical skills responsible for his escape from such fierce and awesome captors, or was he able to call on the services of proto-Masonic brethren to regain his freedom? His other, later journeys took him to Palestine, Egypt, Arabia, and Constantinople, where he continued his learning process. By one route or another, this Masonic magician explored most of the known world, not only learning as he went, but sharing his proto-Masonic medical wisdom with all who had the good sense to listen to him.

Paracelsus's greatest and wisest contribution to knowledge — in the finest proto-Masonic tradition — was to write: "Resolute imagination is the beginning of all magical operations. Because men do not perfectly believe and imagine, the result is that arts are uncertain when they might be wholly certain." What Paracelsus is hinting at here is that the power of the mind is far greater than most people imagine, and if only that power could be better understood and harnessed, human achievement would be vastly enhanced. An amazing man much closer to our own century than Paracelsus seems to have put that near-magical, proto-Masonic mind power into effect with tremendous success.

Harry Houdini, the great illusionist and escape artist, was born Eric (or Ehrich) Weiss on March 24, 1874, in Budapest. His family left Europe to start a new life in the United States, possibly because of anti-Semitism. Eric's father's Hungarian friends in Appleton, Wisconsin, helped the father to obtain a position there as a rabbi, but the man's old, traditionalist, European ideas differed significantly from the enlightened liberal understanding then prevalent in much of the United States. As a result, the Weiss family travelled to Milwaukee and then moved on to New York City.

By the time he was seventeen or eighteen, young Eric had studied the work of Jean Eugene Robert-Houdin, one of the greatest French magicians, illusionists, and builders of ingenious automata. Magicians and automata go together like strawberries and cream, and in the century before Robert-Houdin's superb work that young Eric Weiss thought of so highly, Wolfgang von Kempelen (1734–1804) had created a mysterious model that apparently played chess to a very high standard. Known as the Turk, it was built by Kempelen in 1769 and supposedly defeated not only Benjamin Franklin but the Emperor Napoleon, as well.

The structure of the automaton consisted of a maple wood cabinet about three feet in depth, with rectangular sides measuring about four feet by a bit more than two feet. At one side of the chessboard on top of

Jean Eugene Robert-Houdin was famous for his astounding automata as well as for his conjuring and illusions. These amazing "monsters" in the Robert-Houdin tradition can still be seen working in Blois, France.

the cabinet sat a model of a Turk wearing a cloak and turban. What appeared to happen was that the Turk automaton moved the pieces in response to the moves of his opponents — and beat them more often than not! When the sides of the maple wood cabinet were opened, they appeared to be filled with a mass of complex machinery to such an extent that no human chess player could possibly have been concealed inside to work the Turk. The secret, however, was that the interior of the cabinet could be folded back on itself and so leave more than enough space for a human chess player of normal size to be hidden.

Kempelen died in 1804, and the mysterious chess-playing automaton eventually passed into the hands of Johann Maelzel. He had a trusted friend named William Schlumberger, who was also his confidential secretary and an expert chess player. Under Maelzel's ownership of the automaton, it was almost certainly Schlumberger who was hidden inside the cabinet to operate the model Turk. While the show was touring Cuba, Schlumberger died, and shortly afterwards Maelzel went bankrupt. He was found dead in his cabin while returning disconsolately to the United States and was buried at sea.

In 1854 the Turk was destroyed in the fire that wiped out the Philadelphia museum to which it had been donated. It is only fair to say that Kempelen was an outstanding craftsman, even if his Turk wasn't a true automaton. However, in 1890 another exceptional craftsman, Luis Torres y Quevedo, created a *genuine* chess-playing mechanism called El Adjedristica. This one only played king and rook endings against a lone king, but it was a true and honest automaton. Kempelen may not have had the high moral and ethical principles of a Freemason, but Luis Torres did. Did the skill and knowledge that enabled the Spaniard to create El Adjedristica come from the long history of chess and craftsmanship that form an integral part of the true Masonic heritage, as exemplified in the black and white squares of a typical lodge floor? Did part of that ancient, secret, proto-Masonic knowledge also reach Robert-Houdin?

Eric Weiss certainly admired his French idol — so much so that he decided to take the stage name of Harry Houdini (the Harry part was for the benefit of alliteration). Houdini's ultimately successful show business career was very hard work at first. Physically, he was shorter than average, but he developed an amazing power-weight ratio that was invaluable in his many escapes and stunts. His muscles matched his mind and his unconquerable Paracelsus-like determination to succeed. This in itself was a clear indication of his membership in the Craft.

Houdini married his beloved Bess (whose real name was Wilhelmina Beatrice Rahner) on June 22, 1894, when he was twenty years old, and their marriage endured until his tragic and untimely death in 1926. Bess worked in the act with Houdini, but despite her valuable extra input, success still eluded them for a few more years.

It was when he started adding escapology to his other stock numbers that his career improved dramatically. He studied the skills of the locksmith's craft, and in time became an absolute master of the profession. That, alongside his vast physical and mental strength, made some of his escapes seem so difficult that there were serious suggestions that he really did have magical powers. Arthur Conan Doyle of Sherlock Holmes fame suspected that Houdini really could dematerialize in one place and reappear later in another.

The Masonic side of Brother Eric Weiss was clearly evident in his unstinting generosity. Once he had achieved the fame and prosperity that his ability and hard work so richly merited, he provided food, lodgings, and all kinds of help to those in need, especially show business people who had fallen on hard times. He gave his time over and over again to hospitals, homes, and orphanages.

One of the few "prisons" Houdini couldn't escape from was the ridiculous social nonsense of ageism. This incredibly fit and brilliantly intelligent man was turned down when he volunteered to serve in World War I *because* he was forty-three years old in 1917 when the United States entered the conflict. Prevented from taking part in active service due to the crass stupidity of ageism, Houdini visited American military training camps and bases as an entertainer, frequently asking no fees and meeting all his own expenses. He also raised vast sums of money for Liberty Bonds to help finance the war effort.

Masonic records show that Brother Eric Weiss (Houdini) was initiated into St. Cecile Lodge in New York City on July 17, 1923, becoming a master mason on August 21. Following a tragic accident, however, this great and good brother died of peritonitis on Halloween Day, October 31, 1926, leaving the world a poorer, emptier place because of his passing.

Houdini was one of an impressive band of modern Masonic magicians, conjurors, and illusionists. Brother Harry Keller (1849–1922) was a contemporary of Houdini's and was the second of the founding fathers of the Dynasty of American Magicians, having been awarded the proud mantle of Greatest American Magician from Herrmann the Great (real name Alexander Herrmann) in 1896.

It was customary for one particularly admirable and expert performer to be honoured with the title of Greatest American Magician. Keller (some records spell his name Kellar) passed on the title to the very high-ranking Freemason and holder of the thirty-second degree, Howard Thurston (1869–1936). One of Thurston's great pieces of stage magic was to make it appear that a duck and a rooster had magically changed places when he uttered the magic words "Hiram Abiff!" In this way, as well as providing excellent entertainment for the audience in general, he was able to let Masonic brethren know that he, too, was in the Craft.

Thurston finally passed his title to Harry August Jansen (1883–1955), stage name Dante the Magician. He appeared with another famous Masonic brother, Oliver Hardy, in the Laurel and Hardy films *A Haunting We Will Go* and *Bunco Squad*. Dante, in turn, gave the title to Lee Grabel in 1954, who subsequently passed it on to Lance Burton, the brilliant current holder. Burton generously maintains the highest standards of Masonic charity by raising funds for the Shriners' Hospital, children's charities, and animal welfare funds. He also helps to support the John F. Miller School and the Variety Special School for children who are physically or mentally challenged, or who have other learning difficulties.

As well as for its high ethical standards and benevolent, charitable behaviour, Freemasonry is famous for its gentle wit and kindly humour. Harry Keller, for example, demonstrated this remarkably well. He was on board a ship that went down in the Bay of Biscay, but a diving team later recovered the passengers' baggage. Among the items salvaged for him was a Masonic diploma that he greatly prized. On having it restored to him, Keller smiled broadly and said, "Grand Master Neptune has inspected it and kindly returned it!"

Masonic historians are well aware of the intriguing parallel between the closely guarded professional secrets of conjurors' fellowships and the secrets of the Craft itself. The great unanswered question that hangs perpetually over all first-class illusionists is: Are we really looking at a very gifted illusionist who is pretending to be a magician, or are we watching a person with genuine paranormal powers who is only pretending to be an illusionist? In contemporary society the man or woman gifted with *genuine* paranormal powers would quickly attract unwelcome attention from government security organizations. Disguising real magic as clever stage illusions would not only provide perfect camouflage for the magician, it would also provide a comfortable standard of living. There can be little doubt that whatever magicians such as Merlin or Paracelsus knew, their proto-Masonic contemporaries also knew.

Chapter 15

MEDIEVAL MASONRY AND THE CATHEDRAL BUILDERS

WORDS HAVE particular associations in the minds of writers, readers, speakers, and listeners, and those associations may not always coincide. *Gothic* is a case in point. The idea of Gothic horror conjures up visions of deserted burial grounds, shadowy mausoleums, skeletons chained in dungeons, vampires, werewolves, ghouls, and poltergeists. Gothic architecture, on the other hand, has connotations of daring spires, towering walls, and beautiful decorations exquisitely carved in stone by master craftsmen. The Goths, from whom the adjective was originally derived, were regarded with fear by their enemies. If a thing was Gothic, it was wild, untamed, fierce, and barbarian in nature.

But words change with time. *Disgusting* is a pretty strong form of criticism in the twenty-first century, yet it once meant no more than "not to my taste" in the way that a polite guest would turn down a ginger biscuit or a garlic pickle if he simply didn't care for the taste of ginger or garlic. *Naughty* in William Shakespeare's day was a term of the darkest and heaviest opprobrium. It meant "a thing of no value, worthless, useless." Today it is reserved for a mischievous toddler who has spread the jam from his bread all over himself and his nursery school neighbours. *Naughty* today is used as a gentle, smiling, very minor admonition. To call someone "a naughty man" in Elizabethan times was to run the risk of pistols at dawn or rapiers on the spot!

So *Gothic* ceased to mean "wild, fierce, and barbarian" and came to signify "beautiful, daring, attractive, and awesomely wonderful" in architectural terms. In more sober terms the dictionary definitions of Gothic architecture would use phrases such as "characterized by the pointed arch." But there was far more to the Gothic world than its outstanding architecture and characteristically pointed archways. There were Gothic bridges, furniture, ornaments, and styles of clothing.

W.R. Lethaby's scholarly and definitive works on medieval art and architecture imply that the term *Gothic* can include the beauties of early stained glass and medieval writings. Another expert on the period, Dr. Albert G. Mackey, maintains that Gothic architecture is synonymous with the architecture of Freemasonry — a very telling and accurate comment indeed!

The mysterious secrets of Como, guarded and preserved by the wise and valiant proto-Masons there after the fall of Rome, not only included all the architectural and structural wisdom that had been known to the earliest proto-Masonic fellowships, but held within it the secrets that would one day be liberated to evolve into the splendour of Gothic art and architecture. Some historians are inclined to argue that Gothic art and architecture simply *developed* in a natural sequence after the old Romanesque style fell out of favour. We prefer to suggest that the Gothic style was not so much discovered and developed as *revealed*.

There are Masonic philosophers and historians who see the whole Gothic architectural principle as a vast allegory in stone and glass. The older, traditional Romanesque buildings show their strength in their massiveness and squat shapes, their overall sturdiness that defied time as well as the military enemies of Rome. That is good. Allegorically, it reflects Masonic strength, resolution, and enduring purpose. The Gothic style is different. It is a system of supporting pillars, flying buttresses, and brilliantly designed archways. To an architectural eye, the huge, lofty, Gothic cathedral is now *two* distinct entities, not *one*. The first entity is the frame, or skeleton, on which everything else hangs. This architectural skeleton is the ingenious, versatile device on which the rest of the building is supported. Here are the pillars, the arches, and the flying buttresses. The rest of the structure is like the muscles, cardiovascular system, and organs of a living body that depends on its skeleton for support.

Here lies the great Masonic allegory through which Masonic architects teach ethical and moral truths to members of the Craft and to anyone else willing to listen. The human being is a twofold entity. There is a vital *framework* of mind and spirit, like the pillars and buttresses of the cathedral on which all else depends. There is then the *functional* entity of commercial life, social life, and the fellowship of the lodge and of loved ones, family, and friends. The deep truth behind this Gothic architectural allegory is that neither an individual nor the society of which he or she is a part can live happily and successfully unless the vital role of the supporting frame is recognized.

Commerce, trade, and industry degenerate into corruption and social decay unless they are suspended from a totally reliable and trustworthy ethical and moral frame. Human relationships that are based on greed and selfishness, exploitation and the manipulative abuse of other people, will bring nothing but disappointment, misery, suffering, and death. The control freaks who threaten society with their insufferable arrogance eventually destroy themselves as well as their hapless victims. The ethics and morals of Freemasonry teach the importance of this vital truth not only in words and deeds of honour and kindness, but via the mystery of Gothic cathedral architecture.

When a thing is universally recognized as good, beautiful, and awe-inspiring, there will be strident rival claims about its origins. The overwhelming wealth of evidence points to the vital proto-Masonic skill and wisdom that were preserved at Como as the true sources of later Gothic architecture.

There were, however, some understandable national rivalries. English claimants look to Durham Cathedral. French enthusiasts point to the superb structure of the Basilica of St. Denis in northern Paris. One of the greatest and most mysterious of all Gothic cathedrals, however, is the one found in Chartres, France. Its true distinction depends more on its many strange mysteries than on its undisputed architectural brilliance. One thoughtful writer, impressed by Chartres Cathedral's many enigmas, has described it as a crucible for the transmutation of humanity. He could well be right. It has also been proposed by thoughtful, mystical writers that Chartres Cathedral serves as a vast menhir or cromlech — like the cromlech of Rennes-les-Bains that was central to the mysteries that Father Boudet, Saunière's mentor, discovered there. These mysteries were in some enigmatic way related to the ancient Celtic language, perhaps involving its intricate codes, ciphers, and cryptograms.

Chartres was a spiritual centre before the present Christian building occupied the site. A favourite destination for both Celts and Gauls in those early days, Chartres most certainly contained proto-Masonic secrets that drew so many people so frequently. But what were they?

Some perceptive and sensitive researchers have suggested that the crypt below the cathedral can be compared to a dolmenic chamber. This idea is elaborated into the hypothesis that telluric currents exist within the Earth, an intriguing aspect of ley-line theories. The stone table type of dolmen, according to this theory, acts as an amplifier or a focal point for the telluric current in that area. Within the dolmenic chamber a searcher after truth was believed to receive enlightenment. It has been argued that long before Chartres Cathedral was erected on that ancient sacred site, the power of the dolmenic chamber beneath it was known to the wise and skilful proto-Masons of the area. Their knowledge was later shared with the Masonic architects and craftsmen who erected the magnificent building.

Proto-Masonic wisdom and knowledge are inseparable from mathematics and Pythagorean philosophy, as a swift survey of Chartres Cathedral's labyrinth will indicate. The labyrinth, which was completed at the end of the eleventh century (another significant date for numerologists), has eleven concentric circles. A curious thing about the number eleven (one of the primes) is the secret of its power as a divisor. To take any long number and test to see if it can be divided exactly by eleven, simply add every *other* digit and then find the difference between those two totals. If the difference is zero, or a multiple of eleven, then the large number will divide exactly by eleven. Consider this example 1928370655607. Add every other digit: 1+2+3+0+5+6+7=24. Add the remaining alternate digits: 9+8+7+6+5+0=35. Find the difference between these totals: 35–24=11. This means that 1928370655607 can be divided exactly by 11. The answer is: 175306423237.

The strange eleven-ringed labyrinth in Chartres Cathedral may well be a curious amalgam of Hindu, Muslim, and Christian numerology. There are Hindu shrines with eleven roofs, and the Sufis also regard the number eleven as highly significant. The Gnostics, who were centred at Chartres at one time, also regarded eleven as an important spiritual number.

In accord with secret proto-Masonic wisdom and its allegorical revelation of ethics and morality, each part of the Chartres labyrinth has a special meaning. Each segment represents part of the Way of Holiness. The cathedral is designed to bring worshippers up to the altar, from which the sacred bread and wine are administered during the Eucharist. The labyrinth is a mystical model of this same journey, representing in proto-Masonic allegory the journey that every human being must make in order to reach the summit of his or her own spirituality.

There are deeper and more complicated meanings to the labyrinth that require an extensive knowledge of the secrets of words and numbers, often referred to by researchers as gematria. This term can be defined broadly as a method of searching for concealed meanings inside groups of letters. In gematriac systems, individual letters have numerical values. These numbers are calculated and then a search is made for other words possessing the same numerical total.

Credit for establishing gematria is often given to Sargon II of Babylon more than 700 years before Christ. Sargon II was thought to have employed the technique while constructing the wall of Khorsabad in present-day Iraq. This wall was 16,283 cubits long, which was believed to have been the number corresponding to Sargon II's name. The ancient city was called Dur-Sharrukin, which translates as Fort Sargon. Two famous investigators responsible for much of the important archaeological work there were James Henry Breasted and Professor Edward Chiera of the University of Chicago.

The buildings they unearthed were of very advanced design in terms of their layout and architectural perfection, clearly indicating that their creators had access to proto-Masonic skills. The most important discovery, however, was a vast statue of a winged bull protecting the throne room of Sargon II. Protective spirits of this type were referred to as *lamassu* and were carved with human heads, the wings of a colossal bird, and the body of a bull. It has already been noted that bull imagery had major significance within proto-Masonry. A case can be made for suggesting that this important symbol survived, with minor variations, as a means of recognition among Craft members throughout the centuries.

The proto-Masons who worked for Sargon II in Dur-Sharrukin would have recognized the winged bull left by medieval European craftsmen in

This winged bull on the Babylonian pattern is carved in the Church of Walpole St. Peter in Norfolk, England. Were the secrets of the skilful Babylonian proto-Masons handed down to their English brethren?

Carving of St. Peter outside the mysterious St. Sulpice Church in Paris. Is his pointing hand indicative of heaven, or is it an important clue to an earthly hiding place? Notice in particular the book and key symbols. What secrets are guarded by this Masonic saint, the Rock?

the Church of Walpole St. Peter in England. The very dedication of the church to St. Peter is itself indicative of Masonic connections. We should recall that when Christ renamed Simon the fisherman as Peter, this new name (from the Greek word *petros*) meant "rock" or "stone." The disciple who bore such a name would have been a favourite among stonemasons.

Gematria was also employed by the Gnostics, who were intrigued by the names of various mystical beings such as Abraxas and Mithras because their names in gematria added up to 365, the number of days in the year. Gematria made its way into early Christianity because the word for *dove* in Greek is *peristera*, which adds up to 801. The first and last letters of the Greek alphabet A and Ω (alpha and omega, symbolizing the beginning and the end) also add up to 801. To Christians, Jesus is thought of as the Beginning and the End. The Cabalists in medieval times thought that their sacred books were written in a cipher devised by God, and they hoped that gematria would unravel this mystical code for them. They also used gematria to search for the names of God, which they believed held a power they could use.

Medieval Cabalists were further interested in the destiny of the Lost Ten Tribes and the legend of the Sambatyon River. After the Ten Tribes of Israel were exiled by the Assyrians nearly 2,700 years ago, they were said to have been separated from the Holy Land by the mysterious and awesome Sambatyon River. It was a raging flood and totally impassable on weekdays, but on the Sabbath it became calm and easily navigable. The Ten Tribes, however, felt that they would be breaking their Sabbath Law if they used boats on that Holy Day, so they never got home!

As outlined in chapter 10, the great medieval Jewish traveller was Benjamin of Tudela, a Spanish diocese taken from the Moors in 1115 by a formidable warrior called Alfonso el Batallador, meaning Alfonso the Fighter. Benjamin, son of Jonah, ventured out in 1165, a time when travel was extremely hazardous. He called on Jewish communities all around the Mediterranean shores and wrote a book about his adventures. When in Persia, he reported that he encountered a group of fierce Jewish warriors whose courageous independence Benjamin greatly admired. He was convinced that he had rediscovered at least four of the Lost Tribes there, and perhaps he had.

The Jewish community Benjamin had visited reportedly lived in a great city they had built among the mountains. What emerges from his account of them is that as well as their fighting prowess and independent spirit they had retained a very high level of building and architectural skills. If they were survivors and descendants of the Lost Ten Tribes, then the proto-Masonic wisdom of Hiram Abiff was still part of their heritage.

Another puzzle raised by the medieval cathedrals is the enigma of their gargoyles. Our modern word *gargoyle* is derived from the French *gargouille*, which originally meant "throat." An older Latin word, *gurgulio*, meant not only "throat" but also "a gurgling sound." To be technically correct, gargoyles carry water; strange-looking figures that don't are more accurately called grotesques.

A typical gargoyle from St. George's Church in Lisbon, Portugal.

The oldest of the gargoyle legends has a similar theme to that of St. Francis taming the wolf. One version of the legend says that during the Dark Ages the citizens of Rouen were terrorized by a hideous dragon called La Gargouille, which demanded human sacrifices. St. Romanis turned up and subdued and conquered the beast. The monster was then burnt in the Rouen marketplace, but its head and neck were impervious to heat because of the fire it had breathed when alive. The good folk of Rouen then built a church to please Romanis and set the dragon's head and neck upon it.

There may be more to this real-dragon theory from the Rouen folktale than meets the eye. Some researchers have suggested that when the fossilized remains of ancient dinosaurs were discovered during the Dark Ages and in later medieval times they became the inspiration for gargoyles.

Another thought is that Romanis may actually have been one of the surviving Roman masons from Como who was requested to help the church builders at Rouen when they were trying to carve the head and neck of a dragon to decorate and cover one of the water pipes that carried excess water away from the roof. The task was beyond the skill of the local builders, and a master mason was needed. Hence, allegorically, the Rouen people could not "conquer" their dragon-carving problem, but the highly skilled master mason from Como could do it easily. His name, Romanis, might simply have meant "the man from Rome."

Gargoyles date back several millennia to ancient buildings in Greece and Egypt. It might be possible that the important architectural secret of conveying water away from a building was part of the wisdom and skill of the master masons of those ancient days.

Another purpose of gargoyles was to drive away evil spirits, and here again there are proto-Masonic overtones. The morality and high ethical standards of the proto-Masonic craftsmen averted evil because every inch of their work was sound, strong, and sturdy. Nothing built by a true master mason would fall and cause injury or death.

A third important aspect of gargoyles on medieval cathedrals was the irrepressible Masonic sense of humour — one brother might well have carved a cartoon version of another. These cartoons might also have served a serious purpose by letting one brother know that a crafts-man who knew the secrets and belonged to the brotherhood was there with him or had recently been there. There is nothing to prevent a humorous code from being just as secure and secret as a serious one.

Having looked at some of the evidence for medieval Masonry in the cathedrals, we proceed in the next chapter to examine Gnosticism, Catharism, and Mediterranean Masonry.

Chapter 16

GNOSTICISM, CATHARISM, AND MEDITERRANEAN MASONRY

IT IS not possible fully to understand the origins and survival of real Masonic wisdom and knowledge without paying close attention to the Gnosticism that was a parallel thought system to that of the genuine proto-Masons for many centuries. Gnosticism can be defined in a single sentence as the doctrine of salvation by knowledge. There are other major religions that advocate salvation by faith, by adherence to divine law, by good deeds and worthy actions, or by the intervention of a benign deity. For the Gnostic, however, salvation is attained by *knowing* special, secret, sacred things. Once this concept of Gnosticism is clear and central, it is easy to understand how proto-Masonry and Gnosticism felt they had certain important elements in common.

Freemasonry emphasizes the importance of wisdom and knowledge, but not as a means of salvation. For the true Mason, wisdom and knowledge are instruments like the square, the compasses, the trowel, the mallet, and the chisel. They are not ends in themselves. Freemasonry *uses* wisdom and knowledge to improve life, to help and support those in need, to heal the sick, to shelter the homeless, and to care for widows and orphans, because its supreme and ultimate purpose is *goodness* rather than *knowledge*. Freemasonry also *uses* its wisdom and knowledge to improve the lives of those who share that wisdom and knowledge — to strengthen, develop, and improve the human personality, and in so doing, to create happiness inside the individual and inside the society of which that individual is a member.

Again, as with the origins of Freemasonry, the more deeply and carefully the roots of Gnosticism are studied the farther back we find ourselves delving into the remote past. There is no doubt that Gnosticism first appeared in a recognizable form long before the start of the Christian era. In the sixteenth century the Belgian genius Justus

Lipsius (1547–1606) regarded the beginnings of Gnosticism as being Syro-Phoenician. Centuries later respected academics such as the church historians Professor Johann Karl Ludwig Gieseler (1792–1854) and Professor Johann August Wilhelm Neander (1789–1850) traced Gnosticism all the way back to ancient India.

Gieseler has a particularly interesting and significant link with Freemasonry. It came about like this. The Reverend John T. Desaguliers was a Masonic grand master in 1719, and in 1737 he conferred Masonic degrees on Frederick, the Hanoverian Prince of Wales. Another, much later Hanoverian, King George IV, held the rank of grand master, and in 1837 he rewarded Gieseler with a knighthood in the Royal Guelphic Order.

It is significant that all these learned theories of Gnosticism's possible origins are paralleled by theories of proto-Masonic origins. It is almost as if there was a symbiotic relationship between proto-Masonry and Gnosticism, and it seems highly likely that they were closely associated in the popular mind because each was to a greater or lesser extent knowledge-based. It was their vastly different attitudes to secret knowledge and wisdom that distinguished them for those who really knew and understood.

Other scholars attempted to trace Gnosticism all the way back to Plato and the concept of a "real" world of perfect ideals as opposed to the very imperfect world of "unreal" and "inferior" physical reality that our senses *tell* us we are "experiencing" — whatever *experiencing* really means — hence Plato's allegory of the prisoners in the cave, detailed from another perspective in chapter 7. Here, too, the ancient wisdom of Greek proto-Masonry can be seen at work. Masonry teaches the mystical truth about everlasting life after death and the transcendent, absolute spiritual reality of moral and ethical standards in their own right — the eternal verities. Gnostics interpret Plato's cave one way; Freemasons understand it rather differently.

The powerful writings of Hermes Trismegistus, or Thoth — scribe to the Egyptian gods and keeper of their strange secrets — are also thought by some scholars to have contained the seeds of Gnosticism. There can be little doubt that the enigmatic Trismegistic writings contained much wisdom and knowledge that was also known to

Egyptian proto-Masons. Perhaps the most reasonable suggestion is that both Hermes and Plato were very important, high-ranking proto-Masons who also understood the Gnostic quest for knowledge in their own societies and in their own ways.

There was also a strange, shadowy, negative aspect to Gnosticism that did not seem to have come from any of the earlier religions with which Gnosticism co-existed in its earliest days. Their pessimistic view of creation was about as far from the happy, optimistic ideas of freedom-loving proto-Masonry as it was possible to get. The Gnostics thought that the entire physical universe was the work of an evil deity whom they referred to as the demiurge, and that the only way to achieve happiness was to escape from the evil material universe as soon as possible. That was what the Gnostics wanted their knowledge for — to escape from the misery of physical existence into the spiritual realm. For many of them the good, spiritual God was equally matched with the evil demiurge. For them goodness was not the supreme power; it was merely the desirable characteristic of that realm into which the Gnostics hoped to escape. It was merely a refuge, not an irresistible, all-conquering force. For the proto-Masons, however, with their high moral and ethical standards, goodness, freedom, and love were supreme, and evil, though a serious problem, could and would be conquered.

The Gnostics did not get their depressing ideas about the evil nature of this physical universe from the life-loving Greeks, to whom all that was good and beautiful in this world made life here worthwhile. The Egyptian religion to which Gnosticism was also exposed was a faith that concentrated on a glorious future life, but which nevertheless had plenty of room for enjoying all that was good and pleasant on Earth. To the ancient Egyptians, Thoth (alias Hermes Trismegistus) had designed a good, pleasant, and orderly universe that human beings could, and should, enjoy during their time within it. The Medes and Persians of those days saw Ahura-Mazda, their god of light and goodness, as vastly superior to the evil Ahriman. For them life on Earth was meant to be the Perfumed Garden of legend — a happy, pleasant, and positive physical experience, not a nightmare of evil physical matter from which they should seek to escape.

Brahminic teachers saw God in everything. Their faith was undeniably pantheistic. All that was, was God, and God was good. He not only dwelt *in* their universe, he *was* their universe. It was a place to enjoy, not a place from which to seek escape. The Palestinian and Canaanite religions, focused on Baal (the local lord) and Ashtoreth (the local lady), were very much terrestrially centred, and the fertility cult pleasures with which they attracted their worshippers were unashamedly physical. If there was an afterlife, they didn't pay much attention to it. Worshipping and placating their local gods to ensure good harvests and fertile flocks was about as far as their theology went. Buddhism was the only major religion that came anywhere near Gnosticism in its quest to leave what it saw as this imperfect world of trouble and desire, but Buddhists were moral and positive about it. Gnostics, on the other hand, were looking for strange, secret, hidden knowledge that would give them power over the physical universe, insofar as it enabled them to escape from it.

Gnosticism, then, although apparently following a broadly parallel course to proto-Masonry in its quest for ever deeper and more significant secret *knowledge*, had totally different goals as far as the uses of such knowledge were concerned. Gnostics sought for an emergency escape route; proto-Masons wanted to help and serve others, to reduce suffering, and to spread happiness, while enjoying it themselves as part of the process. The practical, working Mason built superb cathedrals that he and other worshippers could enjoy; the speculative Mason did his best to build ethical and moral structures to make the world a better and happier place for others, and for himself. In view of these major differences, how did Gnosticism come to permeate the Cathar religion?

The mysterious Languedoc area around Carcassonne and Albi, including Rennes-les-Bains and Rennes-le-Château, was the Cathar homeland. Their religion was undoubtedly a form of Gnosticism, but how had it reached them? The great travellers of those early days were the proto-Masons whose superb architectural and building skills were in high demand. If there was, as has been suspected, a symbiotic relationship between Gnosticism and proto-Masonry, some Gnostics might well have travelled with early Masonic craftsmen, perhaps as helpers or labourers, perhaps even as junior members of the Craft itself.

The earliest Christians in the first century seem to have followed three diverging paths. There were those who followed St. Paul's teachings and developed over the centuries into the Orthodox Church, the Roman Catholic Church, and the mainstream Protestant Churches. There was another strand that might best be described as Judeo-Christian and which was led by James, the brother of Jesus, in Jerusalem. The third branch was Gnostic Christianity, which associated itself with St. John, the gospel writer, and seems to have regarded his gospel as the most, if not the only, truly authoritative scripture available. Was it members of this third, Gnostic strand who travelled with the proto-Masonic craftsmen, first throughout the Roman Empire, and later, after the fall of the Western Empire, throughout Byzantium and beyond?

Catharism seems to contain traces not only of Christian Gnosticism but also of Eastern Zoroastrianism. Allegorically, if the proto-Masonic craftsmen were the powerful locomotives travelling all over the remains of the Western Empire, Byzantium, and the Mediterranean coasts, some of the passengers on those mighty locomotives may have been the pre-Cathar advocates of Gnosticism.

A key player in this elusive history of the arrival of Catharism in Languedoc was Bogomil, a priest who advocated Gnostic Dualism, and after whom a branch of it was termed Bogomilism. Modern Bulgaria was once part of the Byzantine Empire, and during the reign of Peter I, early in the tenth century, Bogomilism was rife there. Furthermore, it seems to have survived until the fall of Constantinople in 1453.

The Bogomils are thought to have been closely connected with, or even to have descended from, another Gnostic sect known as the Paulicians. They were mentioned as early as the sixth century and appear to have owed a number of their non-traditional doctrines to Marcion, or to Paul of Samosata. Theologically, they were Adoptionists (believing that Jesus was not pre-existently divine, but was *adopted* by God at his baptism in the Jordan) as well as Gnostics, and whereas the mainstream Gnostics preferred St. John's gospel, these Paulicians favoured St. Luke's writings.

In what ways were the Paulicians associated with the proto-Masonic craftsmen of the Dark Ages and medieval times? Just as the Gnostics and followers of Bogomil had been inclined to travel with traders, merchants, and proto-Masonic craftsmen, so did the Paulicians, and these travels took them as far as Armenia. There are records that suggest the Paulicians of Syria may have made their way to the Balkans (where they would have joined up with the Bogomils), almost certainly working alongside travelling proto-Masonic craftsmen. When the Paulician sect was at its zenith, it actually ruled a small state called Tephrike (currently named Divrigu, in modern Turkey), which was destroyed by the Byzantine emperor Basil I. Paulician survivors from Tephrike may well have subsequently sought refuge in Syria or Armenia.

Other theories suggest that the kind of Christian Dualism indicative of Paulicians, Bogomils, and Cathars began in Armenia during the seventh century and was led by a preacher known as Constantine of Mananalis. He taught that there were two gods: the good one who had created human souls, and an evil one who had spawned the whole of the physical universe, including human bodies.

Despite the varying and often confused theories of their actual origins, there is no doubt that the Cathars of Languedoc were a potent and influential force during the eleventh century. They would have known the proto-Masons of their time and place. They would have known the Knights Templar. They would have known the troubadours and minstrels. They would have been in an ideal situation to learn and to share the deepest and most important ancient knowledge and wisdom.

By the thirteenth century the Cathars, almost certainly strengthened by the wisdom and knowledge they had acquired from their friends among the Languedoc proto-Masons, whose craftsmanship enriched the citadel of Carcassonne, were so powerful that the Roman Catholic Church saw them as a grave threat. Cathars were at this time the majority religion in Languedoc, where they enjoyed the protection of local aristocrats and landowners, as well as the admiration of the ordinary citizens who had come to rely on their healing talents and generosity to the poor and hungry. The Cathars were also referred to as *les bonhommes*, meaning literally "the good men." This would seem to indicate that their association with the proto-Masons in the area had led to their acquiring many of the Masonic standards of ethics and morality.

From these hypothetical links between the wise and kindly proto-Masons and the dualistic Gnostics, Paulicians, Bogomils, and Languedoc Cathars, we go next to examine the intriguing and controversial theories concerning the early Freemasons, the Knights Templar, and the Priory of Sion.

Chapter 17

MASONS, TEMPLARS, AND THE PRIORY OF SION

THERE ARE a number of researchers who have put forward the theory that the Priory of Sion may once have existed briefly in the thirteenth century as a rather inconsequential and totally innocent clerical or monastic organization. They also suggest Pierre Plantard and a number of pranksters, forgers, and co-conspirators created a modern version of the priory in the 1950s that bore little or no resemblance to the original institution.

There is in all research plenty of room for frank and open discussion and disagreement without rancour, and there are oceans of difference between those investigators who take the Priory of Sion seriously and those who regard it as a cheap fraud. The *serious* possibilities relating to the priory are awesomely significant. Everything depends on which way the evidence that exists is read and what conclusions are drawn from it. It is like the story of the innocent observer from a remote and peaceful land who had never seen a military airplane before. He explained it to his friends by reporting that he had seen a great iron bird, then proved his point by indicating an unexploded bomb that the plane had dropped, saying, "It must have been an iron bird. See, there, it's laid a great iron egg!"

One of the strangest of the mysteries that tends to surround investigations into other mysteries is what can best be described as the "Now you see it now you don't now you see it again" syndrome. When Harry Price investigated Borley Rectory in Suffolk, England, it was described with some justification as "the most haunted house in England." Accompanied a few years later by a journalist, Harry was caught with a coat pocket full of pebbles and was accused of trying to produce "poltergeist phenomena" by flicking the stones around surreptitiously. His reputation and that of Borley Rectory were badly damaged. Not long afterwards, the rectory burnt down.

Modern houses now occupy the site, but Borley Church still stands, and various groups of serious, professional, scientific investigators have recorded strange events there. The place was reputedly haunted. Harry Price was seemingly caught cheating. Then, many years later, odd phenomena were again reported from the village of Borley. Where is the real truth hiding?

Similarly, it seemed that the so-called Croglin Grange Vampire in Cumbria, England, was some sort of hoax, or at best a misunderstanding in good faith. The authors' firsthand, onsite investigations showed that the building was wrong (it should have been single storey but wasn't), the weapons the boys used against the alleged "vampire" were anachronistic, and the Croglin church was in the wrong place and was far too modern. Our later investigations proved that the ancient building had once apparently been a single storey to which an upper floor had been added. There had once been a church with numerous vaults close to it that fitted the vampire legend, and the events hadn't taken place in 1875 — as Augustus Hare had indicated in *The Story of My Life* — but two centuries earlier. The outline of the story was originally intriguing, but it fell apart in three directions when we made our first onsite investigation. However, at least *part* of a genuine mystery was restored when we dug deeper, as open-minded professional investigators always try to do.

Another point to bear in mind when examining the evidence, as well as the sensationalized myths and legends that are associated with the so-called Priory of Sion, is that a genuinely ancient, secret, and powerful organization might well decide to encourage the debunkers, cynics, and skeptics to proclaim that it was either a fraud, or nonexistent. Is it possible that the loudest of the debunkers are actually members of the priory? Have they prudently decided that the best way to hide their great secret (that is perhaps being explored too closely for comfort) is simply to *pretend* the whole thing is a prank, or just a harmless hoax that somehow got out of hand? Are we in the same ball game here as the conjuror who has genuine paranormal powers but is *pretending* that his or her "magic" is only tricks, prestidigitation, and stage illusions?

If the Priory of Sion is genuine, it goes back millennia, not just centuries. And like the Templars, Freemasons, Illuminati, Rosicrucians, and other mysterious groups, it guards vital ancient wisdom and secret knowledge. If the evidence that has often been challenged as spurious is actually correct, then grand masters of the priory *may* have included Melchizedek, the mysterious priest-king of Salem who assisted Abraham. An extract from the Melchizedek Document was found among the other enigmatic Nag Hammadi library items. This collection consisted of thirteen very old codices dating back at least to the fourth century AD, which were found in Egypt in 1945. As well as the Melchizedek text, the Nag Hammadi collection includes the Gospels of Thomas and Philip, which are both inclined towards the Gnostic strand of early Christianity and which the orthodox church leaders apparently did their best to wipe out. Some lines from the Melchizedek extract are particularly interesting to historians of proto-Masonry: "The opposing spirits do not know him, neither do they know of their own impending destruction. I am here to teach you the Truth, which is known to the brethren."

We return to the original hypothesis that the superhuman guardians of our earliest ancestors were benign extraterrestrial aliens who were protecting us from similarly advanced but exploitative, malevolent, alien entities. These enemies can then be understood as the *opposing spirits* in the Melchizedek fragment. It also looks as if our proto-Masonic guardians had planned to wipe out these enemies of primitive humanity who did not *know of their own impending destruction*. The reference to teaching the Truth, *which is known to the brethren*, seems to be just about as proto-Masonic as the text can get.

One of the sources of information about the Priory of Sion is the *Dossiers Secrets* attributed to Henri Lobineau. His name is an anagram of "Hub or inane lie," which suggests there are two possibilities regarding the list of grand masters of the Priory of Sion that he included in the curious *Dossiers Secrets*. They are either the allegorical *hub*, or centre, of the real, powerful, and historical priory, or the whole thing is a meaningless fabrication — *an inane lie*. Some researchers believe that Lobineau itself was a *nom de plume*, largely because there is a Rue Lobineau in Paris, close to the mysterious old church of St. Sulpice associated with Bérenger Saunière and the Rennes treasure.

Theories about the real identity of Henri Lobineau include suggestions that he may have been an Austrian historian named Leo Schidlof who died in the mid-1960s. The anagrams for his name are "School if led" and "Hid cool self." Could they imply that following Schidlof's clues will "school" or educate those who are prepared to be led by him? Do they also make it plain to the code-breaker that his real identity is coolly hidden? Whether the list of grand masters of the real (or imaginary?) Priory of Sion is the work of a genuine but as yet unidentified Henri Lobineau, or the work of a well-camouflaged Austrian historian named Leo Schidlof, remains unanswered. Nevertheless, what may be described as the Lobineau List from medieval times to the present is an intriguing one. Here are some extracts from it:

- Jean de Gisors   1188–1220
- Edouard de Bar   1307–1336
- Jean de Saint-Clair   1351–1366
- Nicholas Flamel   1398–1418
- Leonardo da Vinci   1510–1519
- Robert Boyle   1654–1691
- Isaac Newton   1691–1727
- Victor Hugo   1844–1885
- Claude Debussy   1885–1918
- Jean Cocteau   1918–?

Nicholas Flamel was one of the most powerful, the most wealthy, and the most successful of the Masonic magicians of the Renaissance. Leonardo da Vinci was immortalized by his brilliant scholarship, his enigmatic paintings, especially *The Last Supper*, and by the profound questions that novelist Dan Brown raised in connection with the riddles wrapped in the so-called Da Vinci Code. Victor Hugo's famous historical novels, such as *The Hunchback of Notre Dame*, contain veiled references to the Craft, and we can say with confidence that whether or not Hugo was ever a grand master of the Priory of Sion, he was certainly a high-ranking Freemason. One of his most interesting works, *La Légende des Siècles*, is a very long epic poem, or rather a collection of historical poems, of which he himself said: "All these poems are … condensed historical reality or guesses at historical reality." In one of the poems he tells of a hidden treasure — a coded reference perhaps to the mysterious treasure of Rennes-le-Château, of which Hugo says: *"Un seul homme sait où est caché le trésor."* (Only one man knows where the treasure is hidden.) It is also interesting to note the connection between Hugo and the enigmatic old church of St. Sulpice. He was married there!

Leonardo da Vinci was allegedly the grand master of the Priory of Sion from 1510 to 1519.

If, however, the priory is, as some researchers suspect, a far older organization that simply changed its name more than once during the long millennia of its existence, then who were some of its leaders in the remote past? The Hebrew patriarchs are strong candidates, as are the mysterious Enoch, Hermes Trismegistus (alias Thoth), the prophet Ezekiel who described what sounded like a UFO, Nimrod, Melchizedek, Moses, Socrates, Plato, Euclid, Pythagoras, Thales, Alexander the Great, and Cyrus of Persia.

What were the connections between the Knights Templar and the shadowy Priory of Sion? It has often been conjectured that the Templars were the military arm of the medieval Priorists, who set them up for that specific purpose. It has also been speculated that the Priorists knew a great deal about what was hidden under the Dome of the Rock in Jerusalem and wanted the strong arms and fearless hearts of the gallant and noble Templars to retrieve it for them. Just as Boudet's intellect needed to be supported by Saunière's muscles in tackling the Rennes mystery, so the intellectuals in charge of the Priory of Sion required a band of warriors to overcome hazardous obstacles that would prove too difficult and dangerous for scholars and academics to surmount by themselves.

The secret wisdom and knowledge held by the Templars, Priorists, and proto-Masonic brethren of their time were likely to have been shared, at least in part, by members of all three organizations. It is also well within the bounds of possibility that some proto-Masons were Priorists and Templars. Membership of one great organization did not necessarily preclude inclusion in the other two.

Chapter 18

MASONIC SYMBOLS IN ROSLYN CHAPEL AND FARTHER AFIELD

FROM THE very earliest days of proto-Masonry, members of the Craft have left codes, ciphers, signs, and symbols that their brethren would recognize and understand. As well as indicating that other Masonic brethren had been, or were currently, in the area, these mysterious Masonic markings were believed to have carried additional messages in codes known to the brotherhood. The triangles resting with point on point as shown in the top left corner of the first illustration in this chapter could indicate that very fine and delicate work was required on the site, and that only master masons would be capable of producing work of that standard. It could also indicate that a worshipful master, two wardens, and two deacons were present. A further interpretation is that at least two lodges were represented on the site.

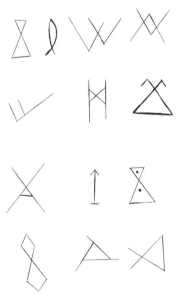

A selection of miscellaneous Masons' marks from the United Kingdom and Continental Europe.

The second figure from the left in the top row of the same illustration is closely related to the Christian fish symbol dating back two millennia. Some researchers argue that the device was originally a pagan fertility symbol. Sigmund Freud, for one, would probably have gone along with that idea! The widely accepted Christian interpretation, however, is based on a Greek acrostic. The Greek word for *fish* was *ichthys*, and the newly established Christian Church used it to represent *Iesous Christos Theou Yios Soter*, meaning "Jesus Christ Son of God and Saviour." This is Ιησους Χριστος Θεου Υιος Σωτηρ in the original Greek.

The arcs that constitute the sides of the "fish" can carry a totally different interpretation — simply as arcs. The square and compasses that constitute the best known of all Masonic symbols are important working tools for architects and builders. The compasses are used to inscribe arcs. When it is essential for a line to be perfectly vertical, and to be at exactly ninety degrees from its horizontal base, compasses can be used to ensure that it is. And the construction that bisects the line in the second illustration in this chapter looks very much like the fish symbol in the previous illustration of Masonic marks.

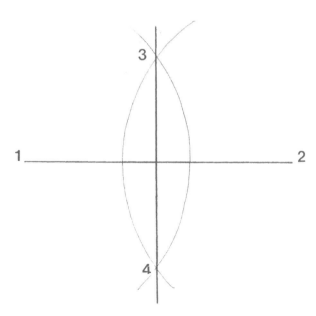

Was this geometrical technique the real meaning behind the second Masonic symbol in the top row?

The craftsman places the compass point on 1 and draws an arc from 3 to 4. Keeping the compasses the same distance apart, he places the point on 2 and draws a second arc from 3 to 4 so that it cuts the first one in two places. These intersections demarcate points 3 and 4. The craftsman then joins 3 and 4. This connecting line bisects the line from points 1 to 2 and is perpendicular to that line.

The third and fourth symbols to the right of the intersecting arcs also have more than one meaning. The third from the left can be said to represent the upper portion of the traditional Masonic square and compasses lifted off its base and laid alongside its base — in other words the compasses have been lifted from the set square and placed alongside it. This can indicate that there are vacancies in the local lodge — it is literally "open" just as the diagram is open, so that applications from prospective craftsmen of good character and high moral and ethical principles can be considered. It can also represent *movement* — the two overlapping V shapes may show that a craftsman, or a group of craftsmen, have moved to the next site.

Returning to the first illustration in this chapter, we see that the final sign in the top row is similar to a square and compasses that have been placed closer together. This sign may represent undue pressure of work and be a warning to a brother in the Craft that the demands made on the workmen here are unreasonable. A wise and knowing sojourner will, therefore, walk on, taking the hint that this site is not a good one. The compressed square and compasses may also suggest conflict or hostility. Perhaps rival craftsmen have spoiled the customary harmony of the lodge.

It is thought that the sign at the left-hand end of the second row from the top has the opposite meaning of the warning sign at the right-hand end of the top row. This is a sign of openness and welcome. The main slope, the incline from left to right, may be intended to represent the potential for progress. It could be saying that there is a hill to climb here, but it is the hill of opportunity, a place where hard work and professional skill will be rewarded with a good standard of living. The two shorter parallel lines at ninety degrees to the main incline show that craftsmen are treated as equals here. There is fairness, justice, and balance of the kind that meets with Masonic favour. It is a good place to work, and skilled, friendly brothers will be welcome.

The central sign in the second row is indicative of professional approval. It means that the design is good. Walls are sturdy and well braced, and there is good fellow feeling and harmony among the brethren who work here. Stone braces and supports stone; craftsman braces and supports craftsman. The third sign in this row, the one at the right-hand edge, is less reassuring. The workers have less confidence in the architects here. The down-turning upper portions of the diagram are like tiles sliding from a roof. They are also thought to represent the prying eyes of overzealous supervisors and inspectors. A good and honourable craftsman always prefers to be trusted and given his necessary autonomy to carry out the work with which he has been entrusted.

Co-author Lionel's father, Robert, who was born in 1880, was a high-ranking Freemason in Norfolk, England, for many years. As a young practising craftsman (a carpenter, not a stonemason) over a century ago, he worked on the internal timber roofing of Wymondham Abbey. It was a long way up for young carpenters like Robert on their perilous scaffolding, and the foreman never joined them there if he could possibly avoid the dangerous ascent. Instead he sat on the abbey floor a good fifty feet below his industrious young craftsmen and watched them through field glasses. More than once Robert and his colleagues wondered how the bright-eyed old foreman could see the joints so clearly that he would shout up to them when the timbers weren't tightly fitted together enough. Although never angry or bitter about their foreman's continual hawk-like supervision, young Robert and his colleagues never ceased to marvel how he could pick out the detail so scrupulously from that distance — but he could. The young carpenters would undoubtedly have enjoyed their work more without that constant supervision.

Going down to line three on the left-hand side of this chapter's first illustration, we see a figure that resembles a capital *A* combined with an *X* in such a manner that the crossbar of the *A* braces the base of the *X*. It has been suggested that this is a very ancient sign indeed, dating all the way back to the proto-Masonry of classical Greece. One suggestion is that the *A* was the initial letter of Αγγελος (meaning a "messenger" and often applied to angels as messengers of God) and the *X* was the initial letter of Χαρις (meaning "good and well favoured"). The Masonic logo consisting of *X* with an *A* inside it could well have indicated that a "good messenger," in other words, a brother in the Craft, had been in the area. The remaining marks also have a number of similar conjectural and allegorical meanings.

If ever "good messengers" in the Masonic sense left their marks behind them, they did it in Roslyn Chapel near Edinburgh. Spellings of Roslyn vary and include the *ss* version Rosslyn. Although the present building dates back only to 1446, the mysterious messages it contains are much older. Roslyn preserves in stone secrets that were known to select brethren long before the foundations of Roslyn Chapel were laid. Its builder was Sir William St. Clair (or Sinclair), a member of the old and noble family that had ruled the Kingdom of Orkney as its jarls or princes. He was a grand master to several of the important fifteenth-century craft guilds, who were, in turn closely associated with early Freemasonry in the Edinburgh area. Sir William was a great believer in the importance of knowledge and education, and it was his original plan to turn Roslyn into a collegiate centre where religion, ethics, morals, and wisdom would be studied side by side. His intentions here were strong indicators of his own Masonic sympathies.

A Mason's mark on the wall of Roslyn Chapel near Edinburgh.

Nearly forty years after starting his great project, Sir William died and still lies buried in the great chapel that he was unable to complete.

During those forty years, however, he was a generous and greatly revered employer. His workers were brought in from many distant centres of excellence and were given houses and land in the Roslyn area, as well as ample wages. This was typical of a good Masonic employer. Sadly, Sir William's son, Oliver, did not share his father's vision, and apart from making sure that Roslyn was well roofed so that none of his father's efforts were wasted by exposure to the elements, he did little or nothing to expand and develop the work.

However, the Masonic traditions of Roslyn were powerfully reinforced in 1736 when another William St. Clair was made "A brother of the Antient and Honourable Company of Free and Accepted Masons." In December of that year he was elected as the first grand master of the Grand Lodge of Scotland.

What Masonic mysteries then does Roslyn contain? It has been suggested that one of the oldest and most mysterious secrets known to the ancient proto-Masonic guardians in the dim dawn of history was that there were superhuman, extraterrestrial forces of good *and* evil. The proto-Masonic guardians did all they could to protect humanity's remote ancestors.

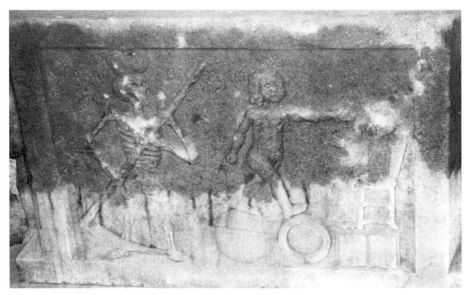

A curious old stone at Roslyn representing the King of Terrors pursuing a terrified mortal.

The mysteries of the Green Man carvings are very well-known. Roslyn has more than a hundred of them, which suggests that deeply symbolic stories such as Gawain and the Green Knight may be represented here. It would certainly be appropriate in Masonic terms because of the ethical and moral value of the story. Gawain is a good and honourable man: even though he expects it will lead to his death, he keeps his word to the mysterious Green Knight. His valour and honesty are rewarded, and he lives through the ordeal.

The story of the Roslyn apprentice pillar is also well-known. A master craftsman allegedly went overseas to study ways of making the pillar perfect and returned to find that his apprentice had done it superbly. Overwhelmed with jealousy, the enraged craftsman killed the boy. There are one or two queries, however. It was traditional for an apprentice not to let his beard grow until he had qualified as a master of his trade or profession. Close inspection has led some experts to suggest that the carving is not of a boy, but a bearded master craftsman. So if it wasn't an apprentice who was killed, is Roslyn Chapel retelling the moral allegory of Hiram Abiff from the time of King Solomon and Hiram of Tyre? Did the proto-Masonic teachings about Hiram Abiff reach Roslyn with the craftsmen?

The mysterious head in Roslyn Chapel: is it the murdered Hiram Abiff? Some experts have suggested that it is John the Baptist, beheaded on the orders of King Herod at the request of Salome.

Another of the strangely coded Masonic mysteries of Roslyn refers to music. The detail is such that these angelic orchestral carvings, some of which can be seen here, have more significance than simply to praise and commemorate the beauty of music as an aid to worship and to recognize the craftsmanship of the musicians who provide it. Each angel plays a different instrument. Percussion probably symbolizes the importance of rhythm and routine for a craftsman. The woodwind and brass wind instruments may refer respectively to the importance of harmony and proclamation of truth. All of these are Masonic virtues, and wrapping these ethical and moral truths inside the allegory of music would be a typically Masonic technique. It is also important to remember the strong connection between the stonemasons on one hand and the bands of troubadours and minstrels on the other.

Is this a musical angel, or is the heavenly creature clutching a scroll or a book?

Do we have an unusual percussion instrument here? Or is it an angelic craftsman mixing mortar?

What strange complex instrument is this angel playing? Is it a brass wind instrument with a sound box to amplify it? Does the carving symbolize the proclamation of Masonic ethical and moral truth far and wide?

An angelic musician, probably with a soft, sweet woodwind to symbolize
Masonic harmony and brotherhood.

Chapter 19

RENAISSANCE MASONRY AND
THE ARTISTS' SECRET CODES

IN THE previous chapter we looked carefully at the musical angels carved among the other mysterious signs and symbols in Roslyn Chapel. Music may have another significant Masonic link with the Renaissance, and with the massive contribution the Craft made to the re-emergence of vital knowledge and wisdom it had helped to safeguard through the Dark Ages.

As part of the meaningful, educational ritual that makes up what is known as the fellow craft degree in Freemasonry, the brother who is being admitted to this rank is told about the Seven Sciences and Liberal Arts. This sevenfold educational curriculum dates back to the proto-Masons of classical Greece and Rome, and consequently, it became the foundation stone of the universities of Western Europe during medieval times. For ancient Greek educators there were seven fields of study that deserved cultivation. These were arithmetic, astronomy, geometry, grammar, logic, music, and rhetoric. The Romans divided these into a *trivium* (three subjects) and a *quadrivium* (four subjects). Their *trivium* consisted of grammar, logic, and rhetoric. The *quadrivium*'s four parts were arithmetic, astronomy, geometry, and music. The great Greek thinker and proto-Mason Aristotle expressed the view that every freeman should study the seven liberal arts and sciences, and during the eighth and ninth centuries, Charlemagne, almost certainly another proto-Mason, changed history more effectively by his support for education in those classical categories than by his successes on the battlefield.

Looking again at the significance of the musical angels in Roslyn Chapel, we note that Masonic wisdom points to the close nexus between music and mathematics. Another great thinker with a proto-Masonic mind, Gottfried Wilhelm von Liebniz (1646–1716), said that music was the delight that the human mind experienced from using numbers without realizing that it was using numbers. Liebniz's deep psychological idea provides the clue to the connection between *musical* codes and *numerical* codes. Just as traditional gematria uses words and letters with numerical equivalents, so there may also be a gematria of music that links notes and musical phrases to numbers. Perhaps among the most advanced and secretive gematria there are *triple* codes that need words, music, *and* numbers to solve them. Are these what the mysterious angelic musicians of Roslyn Chapel are trying to tell us?

Could these strange decorations in the roof of Roslyn Chapel represent numbers, musical notes, and artistic symbolism?

The brilliant Scots composer Stuart Mitchell recently made a great contribution to understanding *one* of the musical mysteries in Roslyn Chapel. He carried out a particular study, concentrating on the strange roof decorations and some of the pillars, perhaps modelled themselves on the pillars of Solomon's Temple in Jerusalem.

Mitchell focused his perceptive musical gifts on some cubes that he found there and came up with an unusual set of musical cadences. To a talented composer like Mitchell, who also has a profound knowledge of musical history, the very *simplicity* of the Roslyn music dated it to the Middle Ages. Yet it remains to be seen whether the music that Mitchell has so far discovered is itself a clue to a more sophisticated and complex code.

Could this strange carving at the foot of one of the Roslyn pillars suggest that the strange aquatic creature is playing a musical instrument, something like a conch shell?

Just as it may be argued that it was the scholarly proto-Masons who helped so much to keep knowledge and wisdom alive during the Dark Ages and medieval times, so it may also be suggested that it was their dynamic input that contributed to the explosive flowering of art, music, drama, philosophy, and science during the Renaissance. If words, music, and mathematics are useful media for code and cipher makers, especially when they are combined, *art* is even more compliant. At the heart of one of the most significant and mystifying codes used by the artistic fraternity of the Renaissance and after, we find the enigmatic words *et in Arcadia ego*. Not surprisingly, there are elusive anagrams to be found in that arcane Latin phrase: "Age eradication," "Radiate coinage," "Create in adagio," "I aid a grace note," "And indicate go area."

The best-known example of the Latin phrase appears on the tomb in Nicolas Poussin's famous *Shepherds of Arcadia*, central to some of the theories associated with the Rennes-le-Château mystery, because the Tomb of Arques, which stood until recently at Pontils, was thought by some researchers to resemble the one in Poussin's painting. Poussin was born in 1594 and worked in Rome for most of his productive life. He died in 1665.

In 1656 the younger brother of Nicolas Fouquet, the French minister of finance, met Poussin in Rome and wrote an intriguing letter about him to his powerful and influential elder brother in France. An extract from it reads: "I have planned certain things of which in a little while I shall be able to inform you fully; things which will give you, through M. Poussin, advantages that kings would have great difficulty in obtaining from him and which, according to what he says, no one in the world will ever retrieve in the centuries to come …"

Was this amazing secret that Poussin claimed to possess connected in any way with the alchemical legend of the Elixir of Life? ("Eradicate age.") Was it some means of creating wealth? ("Radiate coinage.") Did it offer a solution to well-concealed musical codes like the one at Roslyn? ("Create in adagio," "I aid a grace note.") Or was it an indication that Poussin and other members of the artistic brotherhood knew the location of a hidden treasure cache?

Poussin studied the Greek and Roman classical myths and legends and frequently used them in his canvases. He also painted historical scenes. In that way he served as a bridge between the ancient "gods" (whoever they might really have been!) and the emperors, kings, princes, warlords, and generals who led the real world. If Poussin understood the deepest and oldest secrets of proto-Masonry, he may well have been party to the idea that the very first proto-Masonic guardians came from *beyond*. If he and a few other select members of the elite painters' brotherhood were actually in contact with them, then indeed Poussin held a truly great secret.

Leonardo da Vinci was born in 1452 and died in 1519, three-quarters of a century before Poussin was born. They were by no means contemporaries, but it needs to be remembered that da Vinci was listed among the grand masters of the Priory of Sion. If the priory was *genuinely* old and not a twentieth-century hoax, then the knowledge that da Vinci would have acquired as grand master would have been both profound and priceless. As a later member of the artists' brotherhood, and possibly a Priorist, as well, Poussin might have gained access to some of da Vinci's awesome secrets.

One of the most important mysteries in the whole of da Vinci's artistic work is the identity of the enigmatic disciple who sits on the right of Jesus in the Italian's *The Last Supper*. Da Vinci's painting is in the refectory of the convent of Santa Maria delle Grazie in Milan. It has been frequently cleaned and restored, and it suffered damage from the bombs that came close to the convent in World War II. While due allowance must be made for this destruction, and any modifications resulting from the subsequent cleaning and restoration, the face of the disciple sitting on Christ's right is both feminine and beautiful. Since this disciple and Jesus are leaning away from each other at angles of about forty-five degrees, it has been suggested by some researchers into the da Vinci mystery that the artist has deliberately created a letter *M* effect, meaning *Married*.

Da Vinci's use of colour is also important to prospective code-breakers who are working on the picture. Jesus and the mysterious disciple on his right are wearing reds and purples, the colours of royal robes. Is it possible that da Vinci is hinting at secret, proto-Masonic, Priorist knowledge that came his way as grand master of the Priory of Sion? Is he trying to tell those who study his famous painting in sufficient depth that Jesus and Mary Magdalene were partners in a *dynastic* marriage?

Various apocryphal religious writings were excluded from the canon of scripture by traditional, orthodox church fathers. These apocryphal documents included the Gospels of Philip, Thomas, and Mary Magdalene. With the contents of these apocryphal documents in mind, some researchers have contended that Mary Magdalene was actually a member of the Benjaminite dynasty and that the defamatory stories about her were circulated by the early church fathers with the sole intention of reducing her status as the wife of Jesus and a leading disciple. If that is true, and if da Vinci knew about Mary's royal Benjaminite ancestry, it would account for the regal red and purple robes that he painted for her and her husband in *The Last Supper*.

The well-worn speculations and heretical theories then recur. A Benjaminite princess marries a descendant of King David, and their children clearly have major claims to the throne of Israel. This does not suit the Herodians, Sadducees, or occupying Romans. After Mary's noble and fearless husband is crucified by these malicious and treacherous plotters, it is conjectured that she escapes to France with their children, who eventually marry into the Merovingian Dynasty. It is also a matter of speculation as to whether their secret descendants, still carrying the Ultimate Bloodline, are hidden in France even in the twenty-first century.

According to these theories, the great secret of that Unique Bloodline was known to proto-Masons, to the Priory of Sion, to some surviving Templar organizations, and to other secret societies that will be examined in the next chapter. According to these hypotheses, it was also known to Leonardo da Vinci, to Nicolas Poussin, and to other high-ranking members of the artists' brotherhood who concealed the knowledge in their paintings by the use of gentle hints, subtle symbols, and carefully placed clues.

The huge, and often angry, controversies that arise out of these theories are formidable, yet they need not be. Sound, traditional, academic theologians in all the major Christian denominations cannot accept that Jesus was any less than the uniquely divine Son of God. Understandably, it seems to them at first appraisal that if Jesus was Mary Magdalene's husband and the father of their children, his divinity is somehow compromised. To those church members who see celibacy as some sort of virtue, rather than the sadly misguided folly that it actually is, the idea of Jesus having a wife and children somehow diminishes him.

In our opinion such an idea doesn't diminish Christ whatsoever. In fact, it does exactly the opposite. For Jesus to be a perfect and complete man as well as the perfect and complete God, it seems essential to us that he should have experienced the roles of a loving husband and father during his earthly incarnation.

Traditionalists argue that Christ was celibate because of his unique mission as guide, leader, and saviour. The "married to Mary Magdalene and father of her children" school of thought argues that Jesus was merely an earthly king, a member of David and Solomon's royal lineage. These people contend that all the supernatural and religious elements that have accrued around Christ over the centuries are nothing more than myths, legends, and historical errors.

There is a *third* way, though. The real error lies in the assumption that the positions are irreconcilable, but they are not. Jesus the loving husband of Mary Magdalene and father of her children is *also* Jesus the Son of God and Saviour of the World. His passion, suffering, and cruel death become infinitely more poignant because by fulfilling his unique mission he is leaving the earthly family that he loves so deeply. Death is grim enough for a single man to face; it is infinitely worse for a loving husband and father. His adoring wife can cope with her grief only because after her experience in the garden on the morning of the resurrection, she has no doubt that they will all be reunited in the next world where life is abundant and eternal. With that absolute certainty inside her heart and mind, Mary takes the children to safety in France where they ultimately unite with the Merovingians.

We should consider the possibility that the secret known to proto-Masons, to the Priory of Sion, to Leonardo da Vinci and the artists' brotherhood could be simply that this third way was the true explanation. The great secret may be that there is no contentious either/or situation here. Both are true, and one enriches and reinforces the other. In our opinion there is a strong possibility that Jesus was indeed married to Mary Magdalene and was the father of her children, but he was also incontrovertibly the pre-existent Logos, the unique Son of God and Saviour of the World.

ILLUMINATI, ROSICRUCIANS, AND OTHER SECRET SOCIETIES

THE MYTHS and legends of a great cosmic tree can be found in more than one ancient culture. Genesis talks of the Trees of Knowledge and Life planted in Eden. Norse mythology centres on Yggdrasil. Slavic legends contain a sacred oak, while for some Hindu traditions the tree is a vast banyan. Mayans once believed in Wacah Chan, meaning the world tree connecting the Middleworld inhabited by humanity with Xibalba, meaning their Otherworld. The most elaborate form of the giant-tree allegory is in Norse mythology. Here Yggdrasil is also referred to as Mimameid and as Lerad. It connects all nine worlds of Scandinavian mythology and is sometimes thought of as an ash, although it has also been regarded as a yew because of its evergreen qualities. The trunk formed the world axis, and the roots were sustained by three wells, the most significant of these being Urd, guarded by the Normir, whose power exceeded even that of the gods. Does this allegory conceal the concept of beings from *elsewhere* who are more powerful than any terrestrial rulers?

The more deeply and widely researchers look into secret societies like the Rosicrucians and Illuminati, the more relevant the allegory of a tree becomes. There is one great central trunk of very ancient and intriguing mysteries. From it, over the millennia, many boughs and branches have grown. Some are in contact with one another; others acknowledge the existence of the main trunk but are reluctant to accept that the other groups share their particular knowledge. However, to extend the analogy, when the foliage is lost in winter, the shape of the tree and its branches is easier to discern. When some of the liturgy and ritual with which a number of these secret societies surround themselves is no longer in the way, the basic pattern emerges.

One possibility that seems to become apparent is that *somewhere, somehow*, a very long time ago, *someone* or *something* brought (or *sent*) scientific, technological, sociological, and philosophical information to Earth. Consequently, there was a great leap forward in all these areas. It looks as if there may well have been guides, guardians, helpers, educators, and inspired leaders who did their best to aid and protect our earliest ancestors, not only from themselves but from something powerful that was also hostile, negative, sinister, and malevolent. Myths of angels and demons, of pantheons of good and evil gods and demigods, pointed to this central outline of the allegorical tree and branches. Whether in science fiction terminology these were rival groups of extraterrestrials with powers far beyond those of our earliest ancestors, or whether in psychic terminology they were nonhuman entities like the demons in C.S. Lewis's brilliantly written *Screwtape Letters*, remains a matter of conjecture.

Myth, legend, and historic religious writings all point broadly in the same direction. We were not alone in those earliest times. Some of those who were *not us* were benign and protective while others were intent on control and exploitation. Secrecy and confidentiality became important weapons in the armoury of those who were intent on helping us. Whether we refer to them as proto-Templars, proto-Masons, Priorists, or simply as guides and guardians, a number of researchers and investigators believe that their ancient and vitally important secrets are known and carefully protected by the best and most ethical of the secret societies.

Another useful analogy can be found in Charles Spearman's two-factor theory of general intelligence. In essence, Spearman (1863–1945) believed that it was possible to make relatively accurate measurements of special abilities such as musical talent, memory, mathematical calculating power, and language skills. He also thought that these special abilities, which he labelled S factors, correlated to different degrees with general ability or general intelligence, measurement of which was a far less certain process.

If the deep, secret truths and primeval knowledge, wisdom, and skill that lie at the core of what the benign guardians brought to us in the beginning are the trunk of the Tree of Knowledge or Spearman's General Intelligence (G factor), then the S factors in our diagram represent the different ancient secret societies such as Cabalists, Templars, proto-Masons, Priorists, Rosicrucians, and Illuminati. As can be seen

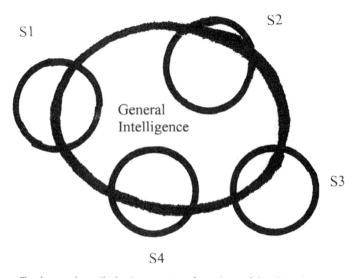

S1

S2

General
Intelligence

S3

S4

This diagram shows Charles Spearman's two-factor theory of the relationships
between special abilities and general intelligence.

from the Spearman diagram, these S factors — the circles around the edge — are correlated with General Intelligence to differing degrees. So it is with the various secret societies. In the Spearman diagram, S2 has penetrated deeply into the central area. For our analogy S2 would represent Freemasonry with its great wisdom and knowledge and high levels of morality and ethics.

What role did the Illuminati play in this mysterious history of secret societies? The name was first applied two millennia ago during the early years of Christianity simply to designate baptized Christians. It meant that they had seen the light, been illumined by spiritual truth, and were in consequence "the illuminated ones." Another seemingly harmless sect of mystical Christians, called the Alumbrados or Illuminati, worked in Spain during the sixteenth century. But the group that attracted the most attention and that fell under the greatest adverse scrutiny was the one led by a Bavarian intellectual named Adam Weishaupt, who taught at the University of Ingolstadt, where he became professor of canon law in 1773. He was the first secular holder of the post. In 1776, with the help of Baron Adolph von Knigge, Weishaupt started an organization called the Perfectibilists, who became the Illuminati shortly afterwards.

Opponents of Freemasonry and the Illuminati launched a massive barrage of propaganda against them at the time, accusing them of plotting to abolish royalty, governments, and the church. The monarchists and supporters of the wealthy and powerful aristocrats, landowners, and kings of commerce and industry more or less blamed the Illuminati and the irregular and only semi-formal Freemasons of their day for causing the French Revolution. Looked at objectively, some of the ultimate ideals of Weishaupt and his Illuminati were ethical, moral, and commendable, and the group advocated liberty, equality, and brotherhood. The Illuminati's opposition to the established churches of the time was stimulated largely by what the organization saw as the corruption, greed, and authoritarianism of church leaders who sought to control and dominate their members instead of loving and serving them. Weishaupt was banished in 1785 and supposedly died in 1811, though some researchers believe he may have survived until 1830. It doesn't seem likely that the S factor of Weishaupt's group of Illuminati penetrated very far into the zone of central secrets, if they even penetrated it at all.

Rosicrucianism is a great deal more mysterious and esoteric than the semi-political, semi-revolutionary Illuminati of Knigge and Weishaupt's making. Some Masonic descriptions of Rosicrucian origins give the credit to Mark, an early Christian disciple and possibly the same Mark who wrote the gospel that bears his name. In this tradition Rosicrucianism goes back to the middle of the first century when Ormus and his disciples, who were all Egyptian Gnostics, were converted to Christianity by Mark. This led to a fusion of early Christianity and Egyptian mysticism, a union that later grew into Rosicrucianism. According to Rosicrucian teaching, their founder was Christian Rosenkreuz, who lived from 1378 until 1484. If the two traditions can be combined, however, it would appear that Rosenkreuz was not the original founder of the movement but one of its most wise and celebrated grand masters. There are also Rosicrucian traditions concerning his studies of Egyptian and hermetic texts, and of his body being found in suspended animation many years after his supposed death. These notions parallel the strange legends of Sarah, the sister-wife of Abraham who discovered the body of Hermes Trismegistus in a secret cave.

The old Rosicrucian diagram on this page of the sun and what were then the known planets, plus the moon, indicates how deeply the Rosicrucians were involved with astrology. What is particularly intriguing is that their astrological diagram bears a curious resemblance to the Spearman two-factor theory illustration, and there are good reasons to believe that Spearman was a Freemason. Is it remotely possible that his knowledge of Rosicrucianism pointed him in the right direction for his work on the measurement of intelligence using special abilities as indicators of general abilities?

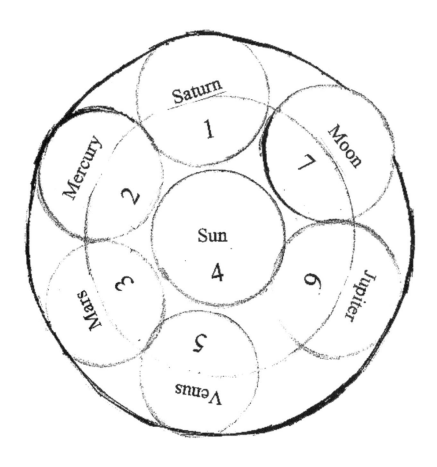

A Rosicrucian astrological diagram.

Were these mysterious watermark codes used by Francis and Anthony Bacon and their mysterious secret society also known to the Albigensians of Montségur who were skilled papermakers?

The Rosicrucians, whose knowledge was shared by their contemporary Freemasons, attached special meanings to the celestial bodies shown in the diagram reproduced on page 259. Mars represented the emotion of fear and the sensation of heat. Mercury was mobility. Saturn was the representation of harshness and severity, and a coldness that was the opposite of Martian heat. The sun was fire and life, the source of energy. The moon was thought of as a container or receptacle in which good and precious things were stored, in a sense representing memory and tradition. Jupiter stood for power and authority as well as for goodness, morality, and ethics in the Masonic sense. Venus, most important of all, signified love in all its aspects — physical, mental, and spiritual.

Certain interesting theories concerning the origins of Rosicrucianism conjecture that Christian Rosenkreuz was a pseudonym of none other than the brilliant Francis Bacon of Elizabethan times. One of the strangest and most mysterious secret societies of all time was the one that Francis Bacon ran with his younger brother, Anthony. Enigmas and riddles revolve around the Bacon brothers like planets circling their parent star. Well-informed researchers have put forward the theory that many of the deep secrets that were known to the Bacons were encrypted in the strange watermark codes they were believed to have used. These codes can also be traced to the surviving Cathar, or Albigensian, refugees, who were skilled papermakers. Were the ancient secrets, smuggled out of Montségur at such great cost in innocent human life when that Cathar stronghold finally fell in 1244, preserved in the Albigensian papermakers' watermark codes? And were these secrets later exchanged by the Bacon brothers and their hidden fraternity?

The Carbonari, another later group whose name relates to a brotherhood of Italian charcoal burners, was more political than philosophical and aimed to establish a constitutional monarchy or a republic. After the mid-nineteenth century, the movement virtually vanished. The group's highest moral principle was the abolition of all types of absolutism, which strongly accords with the Masonic love of freedom and respect for the individual. Although the Carbonari had something in common with Freemasonry, their S factor on the

Spearman-type diagram doesn't penetrate very deeply into the central area of mystery and ancient wisdom. The Carbonari became Europeanized when a French branch made its headquarters in Paris, where it was known as the Charbonnerie Démocratique.

Now that we have looked at various European secret societies of the past to see what similarities and differences they had in relation to the tenets of Masonry, it is time, in the next chapter, to examine in more detail the development of Freemasonry itself in Europe, particularly during the past few centuries.

Chapter 21

MASONRY IN EUROPE

THE HISTORY of European Freemasonry is contentious and difficult to follow in places. First it is necessary, but practically impossible, to draw firm demarcation lines between what may be defined as Masonry in the sense that a majority of contemporary Masonic historians would define it and what falls outside those parameters. The earliest evidence for the existence of what we have termed proto-Masonry during our researches dates back not just centuries but millennia. At what point in the history of European Masonry is it possible to say yes or no and to include or exclude any particular individual or any specific organization *definitively*?

When we consider eighteenth-century England, we see that the First Grand Lodge, known as the Grand Lodge of London and Westminster, came into being in 1717 when four lodges joined to create it. In 1719 the Reverend Brother John Desaguliers became grand master of what was then referred to as the Mother Grand Lodge of England. In that same year Dr. William Stukely, the antiquarian, became a Freemason and left an important reference to the organization in his diary.

In 1725 the Grand Lodge of Ireland was founded and the existence of the Paris lodge became known. These developments tie in with the intriguing and mysterious theories concerned with the Paris Meridian, which preceded the Greenwich Meridian and held sway from 1687 until 1884. Even after Greenwich superseded the old Paris Meridian, the French held on to it loyally until 1911.

Louis XIV, the powerful French Sun King, decided in 1666 that he wanted an observatory. Accordingly, the Paris Observatory was built in 1667 by a brilliant architect named Claude Perrault, who was also a doctor of medicine. Claude was the elder brother of Charles Perrault, who was a close friend of the French minister of finance, Jean-Baptiste

Colbert, the same Colbert who had destroyed his predecessor, Nicolas Fouquet. The Fouquets had been involved with the mysterious *et in Arcadia ego* enigma associated with Nicolas Poussin, the painter. After the fall of Fouquet, Charles Perrault remained a friend of Colbert, and Colbert, as Louis XIV's right-hand man, acquired for his king the services of Christiaan Huygens, one of the greatest scientists of the seventeenth century. Huygens, who lived from 1629 until 1695, was especially outstanding in the fields of mathematics and physics. He collaborated with Isaac Newton (1642–1727) whose name appeared on the controversial Priory of Sion documents as being its grand master from 1691 until his death in 1727.

Again, according to that somewhat suspect listing, Newton's predecessor as grand master had been Robert Boyle (1627–1691). Boyle in turn had been a great admirer of Paracelsus and Francis Bacon and had studied their work avidly. He had also investigated alchemical processes and believed that he had succeeded in turning gold into a baser metal. This achievement, of course, was the exact opposite of what the get-rich-quick school of alchemists was always attempting to do. Boyle, a highly moral and ethical seeker after knowledge, was far more interested in discovering scientific truth than in making money. So considering all these connections together, it begins to look as if the men associated with the mysterious Paris Meridian may all have been proto-Masons, and as such, parties to a great deal of ancient wisdom, skill, and knowledge.

The line these wise men created for Louis XIV included an ancient church at Dunkirk that was dedicated to a Merovingian bishop, who was associated with goldsmiths; a zone in the Pas-de-Calais referred to as Arques, just like the Arques near Rennes-le-Château with its sinister tomb riddle at Pontils; then on to Amiens with its proliferation of mysterious ancient burial sites. It was in Amiens that the enigmatic Mérovée, from whom the Merovingians derived their name, was crowned. It was also in Amiens that Jules Verne wrote his early science fiction stories, and it is in that same place that Verne lies in the graveyard of the Church of St. Mary Magdalene. Wes Penre includes Verne in his list of famous Freemasons on the website *www.illuminati-news.com/famous-freemasons.htm.*

The intriguing Meridian then proceeds south from Boves until it reaches Paris itself. Here it is marked by 135 bronze seals set into the ground and bearing the initials *N* and *S* for north and south, along with the name Arago. François Arago (1786–1853) was the director of the Paris Observatory and was almost certainly closely associated with French Freemasonry. The Meridian passes close to St. Sulpice — within 100 yards of it — but the lines marking a meridian *inside* St. Sulpice refer to a local meridian, not the main one. The proper Paris Meridian, however, passes very significantly under the Louvre with its inverted pyramid and controversial 666 panes of glass. Raphaël Aurillac's intriguing reference book *Le Guide du Paris Maconnique* suggests this is highly significant.

The Paris Meridian then goes down to Lussat, where the geometry becomes extraordinary. With the Masonic compasses centred on Lussat, it is possible to draw a large circle that takes in Rheims, Varennes, Toul, and Sion in the northeast; a different Sion due east of Lussat; Montségur, where the Cathars were massacred, and Rennes-le-Château; Sion-les-Mines and the large Rennes up in the northwest. It was very likely Masonic compasses that created that circle.

Farther south along the Paris Meridian at Conques, a Benedictine abbey houses a strange holy relic usually referred to as the "A of Charlemagne." It bears a strong resemblance to one of the Masonic marks listed and illustrated in chapter 18.

Does the mysterious "A of Charlemagne" in the Benedictine Abbey at Conques on the Paris Meridian resemble this Masonic mark and do both hint at the symbolism of the Masonic square and compasses?

There can be little doubt that the old Paris Meridian had mystical as well as mathematical and scientific significance and that the skill and knowledge that went into its creation was Masonic in origin. Some researchers refer to it as the Rose Line, a name with clear Rosicrucian connections. There were also very ancient meridian lines, such as the one that passed through Rhodes, where the mysterious Colossus once stood. That in itself poses another proto-Masonic riddle: some historians believe that the Colossus fell in an earthquake; others suggest that it was intended to be an extremely well-designed *weapon*, the massive bronze arm of which could be swung down to destroy enemy shipping attempting to get into the harbour of Rhodes. Differing theories include its use as a lighthouse. If it was a mechanical device with a weapon-arm, its construction would have needed the highest levels of proto-Masonic engineering skill and knowledge. Although the Paris Meridian has interesting connections with European Freemasonry and is well worth examining from end to end, there are other clues to European Freemasonry that need to be traced.

Pursuing the thread to Germany, we find lodges as early as the opening decades of the eighteenth century. Frederick II of Prussia (1712–1786) became a Freemason in 1738, and this popularized the Craft in Germany. Before the rise of Nazism and the onset of World War II, Freemasonry in Germany, as measured by its lodges and membership, was among the most successful in the world. The tragedy of the Nazi rise to power almost destroyed the excellent work for charity and society as a whole that was undertaken by German Freemasonry. Masonic buildings were confiscated and the Craft's registers were taken to Gestapo headquarters to be scrutinized. A great deal of useful and interesting additional information about the history of Masonry in Europe can be obtained from the Canonbury Masonic Research Centre (CMRC), whose website is *www.canonbury.ac.uk*.

Turning next to the complex history of Freemasonry in France, we find references to the English Civil War, the victory of Oliver Cromwell, and the decapitation of King Charles I. The king's widow, Henriette, was the daughter of Henri IV of France, and she took refuge in her homeland after Charles's execution. In her sanctuary at Saint-

Germain-en-Laye, she was joined by a number of Scots and Irish aristocrats with Masonic connections. The early eighteenth-century London Freemasons assisted their French brethren to establish their lodges.

The official date for the founding of the first regularized French lodge seems to have been 1726 when Lord Derwentwater launched a Paris lodge named Louis d'Argent. In 1731 the duke of Lorraine, the future emperor of Austria, was initiated into a lodge at La Haye. In 1743 Louis de Bourbon-Condé, count of Clermont and grandson of Louis XIV, was installed as grand master of the English Grand Lodge of France. In 1756 the word *English* was dropped from the title and it became simply the Grand Lodge of France. In 1771 the duke of Chartres became that lodge's grand master.

Napoleon Bonaparte, Emperor Napoleon I, was made a member of the Army Philadelphe Lodge in 1798, and his brothers Jerome, Joseph, Louis, and Lucian were also members of the Craft. Many of Napoleon's councillors were Freemasons, as were two-thirds of the French marshals. The case is often made against Napoleon that he was a bloodthirsty upstart who had ruthlessly slaughtered his way to power, destroying much of Europe because of his greed and ambition. Such behaviour would be totally un-Masonic and diametrically opposed to all that is good and worthwhile in Freemasonry. Yet the case can also be argued that Napoleon was not without honour, chivalry, and a sense of justice.

The supporters of Napoleon would aver that he was a good man as well as a great one, and that most of the criticisms levelled against him were merely propaganda spread by his political and military enemies. Napoleon's life and character create such an intriguing mystery that he deserves an entire volume to himself, but here we can look only at his links with Freemasonry. There may be some truth in the many negative criticisms of him and the serious accusations made against him, but two things are certain: he was a Freemason, and if he had not sometimes tried to live up to the ideals of Masonic ethics and morality, his evil deeds would have been more numerous and his virtues far fewer. Freemasonry may not be a perfect panacea for all of the world's troubles, nor for all of the defects in a flawed human character, but it *can* increase what is good and reduce what is wrong.

Chapter 22

CANADIAN AND AMERICAN MASONRY

TRADITION MAINTAINS that the first record of a Freemason in Canada was in 1634, even before the nation was known as Canada. Viscount Canada, Lord Alexander, was the son of the first earl of Stirling in Scotland. He was master of works for Britain's King Charles I and was responsible for leading a band of Scots who settled along the banks of the St. Lawrence River during the first half of the seventeenth century. Viscount Canada was recorded as being a member of Edinburgh Lodge Number 1, which met in St. Mary's Chapel in that city. It must be remembered in connection with this very old and honourable Scottish lodge that it was situated very close to Roslyn Chapel, which is filled with Masonic mysteries as we saw in chapter 18. This venerable Edinburgh lodge has records dating as far back as 1599, and there is some evidence that it existed more than a century before that.

Annapolis Royal in Nova Scotia was named after the British Queen Anne (1665–1714) and passed its historic name to Annapolis County in August 1759. In 1738 it had the distinction of being home to the first Canadian lodge.

On October 25, 1854, a very efficient and gallant Canadian soldier, Lieutenant Alexander Dunn, who was also a Freemason, took part in the Charge of the Light Brigade during the Crimean War. Dunn was responsible for saving the lives of two of his equally heroic companions and was awarded the Victoria Cross, which he richly deserved. He was the first Canadian to be recognized in that way. Four years after Dunn's unselfish gallantry at Balaclava, Amor de Cosmos, who was a newspaper proprietor in Victoria, British Columbia, advertised for interested local Freemasons to start a lodge there. He was a very good and capable man who demonstrated Masonic ethics and morals throughout his life and was destined to become the second premier of British Columbia. The following year was a sad one, but it nevertheless brought a landmark in Canadian Masonic history. Brother Samuel Hazeltine was a government inspector with special responsibility for steamboats. He died after an accident and was buried with full Masonic honours.

In 1860, just one year after Hazeltine's death, Victoria Lodge Number 1085 was formally constituted. Two years later Brother Thomas Harris was elected as the first mayor of Victoria. When the Dominion of Canada was formally established on July 1, 1867, Brother Sir John A. Macdonald became the country's first prime minister.

Canadian Freemasons have made tremendous contributions to their great nation over many years. Famous Canadian Freemasons include Brother Henry Josiah DeForest, the artist, and Brother Charles Mair (1838–1927), the poet and dramatist who wrote *Tecumseh*. This is a singularly interesting and significant work in which the magical tradition of the odd-looking, carnivorous fluted red pitcher plant is recalled — the pure-hearted who drink from it are said to find both forgetfulness and endless, enchanting dreams of love and romance. Brother Oscar Emmanuel Peterson, the outstanding jazz pianist who was born on August 15, 1925, in Montreal, Quebec, has been listed as a very distinguished member of the Craft in the annals of the Grand Lodge of British Columbia and the Yukon.

One of the world's most outstanding Freemasons was the great and good Canadian Joseph-François Perrault (1753–1844) who was known as the Father of Education. A member of the Lower Canada (Quebec) House of Assembly from 1796 until 1800, he abandoned politics and directed his energies towards education. He and his associates in the Canadian educational societies devoted themselves to providing education for the poor and went as far as providing free footwear for needy children so that they could walk to school in cold weather. Perrault launched schools for both boys and girls and inaugurated agricultural educational establishments as well as academic ones. Here, indeed, was a man to admire and follow, a brother who practised the highest standards of Masonic ethics, morality, and charity.

Among outstanding Masonic sportsmen were Brother Tim Horton, the hockey star and namesake of the coffee-and-doughnut franchise, and Brother Fred "Cyclone" Taylor (1884–1979) who played professional ice hockey for the Ottawa Senators, the Vancouver Millionaires, and the Vancouver Maroons.

Benign and honest leaders of business and commerce also make great contributions to society. They manufacture quality products at fair prices and provide worthwhile jobs at fair wages. Two such notable Masonic contributors were Brother Ezra Butler Eddy of the Eddy Match Company and Brother John Molson, the founder of Molson Breweries. As well as being outstanding captains of industry, Freemasons also serve as statesmen. Brother John G. Diefenbaker served with distinction as Conservative prime minister of Canada from 1957 to 1963.

Shifting focus from Canadian statesmen to the United States, we note that the Masonic life of George Washington leaps out of the pages of history. Born on February 22, 1732, Washington combined the roles of surveyor, planter, military leader, and politician, rising to become the greatly revered and deservedly admired first president of the United States. Born in Virginia, his family had Scottish and English blood. Serving with great gallantry and ability during early wars, Washington left the army to marry Martha Dandridge Parke-Curtis, a widow with two children. He became commander-in-chief of the Continental Army during the American Revolutionary War, which raged from 1775 to 1783, and first president of the United States from 1789 to 1797. He died on December 14, 1799.

Throughout every sphere of his life Washington demonstrated the highest Masonic ethics and morals. In 1752 he joined Fredericksburg Lodge Number 4 as an entered apprentice. In March of the following year he rose to the rank of fellow craft Freemason and became a master mason in August. In 1779 the Grand Lodge of Pennsylvania put him forward to be grand master of the United States. In 1782 there is documentary evidence that Brothers Cassoul and Watson from Nantes in France sent him a gift of a very beautiful Masonic apron made from silk. Another beautiful apron was made for him by Madame de Lafayette, wife of General Lafayette, who was also a high-ranking Freemason. In 1788 Washington was worshipful master of Alexandria Lodge Number 22 in Virginia. On December 18, 1799, four days after his death,

Washington was buried at Mount Vernon with full Masonic rites as well as the normal church ritual. Deservedly loved and venerated as the Father of his Country, George Washington was everything that a true and honourable Freemason should aspire to be.

On July 30, 1733, Henry Price, one of Freemasonry's founding fathers in what was to become the United States — after Washington played his part — organized the Provincial Grand Lodge of Massachusetts. By the following year Price's authority was recognized over all of North America, and the first American Masonic Temple was erected in Philadelphia. In 1735 a lodge was formed in North Carolina.

The influence of Freemasonry in the United States was very powerful indeed and entirely benign. Brother Patrick Henry was born in 1736 at Studley, Virginia, and became a member of Tappahannock Lodge there. In his rousing, patriotic speech of March 23, 1775, Brother Patrick used the unforgettable words: "I know not what course others may take, but as for me, give me liberty or give me death."

Of all that is good and worthwhile in Masonic philosophy, morality, and ethics over many millennia, it is this same recurring theme that Brother Patrick Henry declaimed so well: *Masons believe passionately in freedom and independence.* Potential control freaks, dictators, tyrants, obsessive bureaucrats, and their ilk will never destroy human freedom and independence while stout-hearted Masonic brethren hold the fortress of liberty against them. Does this Masonic insistence on the importance of individual freedom date back millennia to the very first proto-Masons from *elsewhere,* who came to protect our earliest ancestors from enslavers, exploiters, and abusers from *another elsewhere* and taught our ancestors the importance of freedom?

With the passage of the years and the growth of the United States, Freemasonry grew and flourished. In 1842 the Texan Orphans' Friends Lodge Number 17 set up a school with the special objectives of helping children who were in most need of help and education. In 1848 the Grand Lodge of Texas requested its grand master to appoint a superintendent of education. Luther Burbank, the renowned expert in horticulture, was a brother in Santa Rosa Lodge in California. So it can be demonstrated without difficulty that such diverse fields as statesmanship, education, and science were all improved and developed by able American Freemasons.

Masonic writers and humorists included greatly talented authors such as Mark Twain, who was made a Mason in Polar Star Lodge Number 79 in St. Louis, Missouri. Brother Samuel Langhorne Clemens (Twain's real name) was born in 1835 and lived until 1910. There are several coded allusions to Freemasonry in his many brilliant books and speeches. During an after-dinner speech at the New York City Lotus Club on November 10, 1900, Twain referred to "the grip and the word that lift a man up and make him glad to be alive …" He was, of course, talking about the discreet Masonic handshakes and passwords that brethren in the Lotus Club would instantly have understood. In *The Innocents Abroad*, published in 1869, Twain refers to God in chapter 22 with the Masonic phrase "Great Architect of the Universe." In *Tom Sawyer's Conspiracy*, which was written in 1897, a character is described as the "Inside Sentinel of the Masons, and Outside Sentinel of the Odd Fellows." In *A Tramp Abroad*, Twain not only refers to a character as being a Freemason, but also goes on to describe his Masonic ethical and moral principles in the dialect the character's son is using: "I think 't if a feller he'ps another feller when he's in trouble, and don't cuss, and don't do no mean things …" In standard English, Twain is summarizing the core of Masonic social teachings here, which is to give help to those in need, to speak to other people in a friendly and supportive way, to curse no one, and to do good, positive, and constructive things.

One of the deepest and most important insights into the role of Freemasonry in the history of the United States can be found in *America's Secret Destiny*. The author, Dr. Robert Hieronimus, is an outstanding philosopher and researcher into ancient, mysterious, and esoteric knowledge. The authors of this book had the pleasure and privilege of staying with Dr. Bob and Zoh Hieronimus when completing their own Dundurn book *The Oak Island Mystery*, and co-author Lionel was a guest on Dr. Bob's prestigious *21st Century Radio* show. The trigger for Dr. Bob's research that led ultimately to *America's Secret Destiny* was his close inspection of the pyramid side of a U.S. dollar bill.

Also an outstanding musician and artist, Dr. Bob has done fine work on the Egyptian Meditation Room at Ruscombe, which clearly reveals the importance of the effect on consciousness of two-dimensional forms. Dr. Bob has made a profound study of Pharaoh Akhenaton, as is revealed in the superb decor of the Egyptian Meditation Room. His writings, teachings, and paintings all reveal his deep awareness of the connection between ancient Egyptian wisdom and knowledge and the work of contemporary societies such as the Freemasons and Rosicrucians in the United States.

In this chapter we have looked at some outstanding Freemasons in Canada and the United States and their significant contributions to society. In the next chapter we make a survey of international Freemasonry and its vital importance throughout the entire world.

Chapter 23

MASONRY WORLDWIDE

IN ORDER to understand the work and importance of worldwide Masonry today, it is necessary to read the insightful results of the inspired and dedicated research carried out by Brother Dr. Robert Lomas and Brother Christopher Knight in *The Hiram Key*. An equally important volume is Lomas's brilliant work *The Invisible College*.

What Lomas has highlighted is that the Royal Society, founded in 1644 thanks to the tireless work of Brother Sir Robert Moray, succeeded in bringing together former Royalists and former parliamentarians after the bitterness and tragedy of the English Civil War. Seventeenth-century Freemasonry was the bridge that enabled the founders of the Royal Society to put the quest for scientific truth above personal grief and political differences.

In so doing, Freemasonry has made possible innumerable scientific advances of the type that are still being made exponentially in the twenty-first century. Scientific advances throughout the entire world at the present time owe more to Brother Sir Robert Moray's work in 1644 than is understood and realized today. One of the greatest Masonic secrets is Masonic modesty. The movement succeeds in doing so much that benefits society. The mystery is that so little of that good work is known and acknowledged. As an example of this, it is undoubtedly true that Lomas himself has been indirectly instrumental in saving a great many lives. His wide scientific skills include statistics and information systems, which have been placed at the disposal of the Fire Brigade in the United Kingdom to which he is a national consultant adviser. Lomas and his team at Bradford University created the first computer-based training simulators for firefighters. Practice on those simulators has fine-tuned the skills of many heroic firefighters.

As long ago as 1795, G. and T. Wilkie of Paternoster Row in London published a very interesting and informative Masonic book written by William Preston, a past master of the Lodge of Antiquity. The book was entitled *Illustrations of Masonry*, and yet again, Brother Robert Lomas has performed a great service by co-transcribing it with Geraint Lomas. In the introduction to *Illustrations of Masonry*, Preston quotes a definition of Freemasonry from *Arnold's Dutch Dictionary*. Arnold says that Freemasonry is a moral order created by virtuous men and was designed to remind us of sublime truths along with innocent social pleasures. Freemasonry, he says, is founded on liberality, brotherly love, and charity.

It is with that definition in mind that we survey Masonry worldwide. We have already looked at the Masonic situation in Canada, Europe, and the United States. Now let us turn to Africa. The Cape of Good Hope was opened up in the eighteenth century by the Dutch East India Company to provide fresh food for trading vessels making their way to the East Indies. Many skippers were Freemasons, and it was only natural that Brother Abraham van der Weijde should be appointed as deputy grand master abroad for Grand East of the Netherlands (GEN) with full authority to found lodges in Africa. On September 1, 1772, the Lodge de Goede Hoop was duly ratified, and is now Lodge Number 1 on the register of the Grand Lodge of South Africa. When Nazism almost destroyed the Craft in occupied Europe, it was the strength of the South African Grand Lodge that helped to revive GEN under whose aegis it had originally come into existence. Freemasonry flourishes in South Africa today and does much to aid society there. On April 22, 1961, the Grand Lodge of Southern Africa was formed with Colonel Colin Graham Botha as its first grand master.

An examination of Freemasonry in Argentina highlights the work of Brother General José Francisco de San Martín (1778–1850). Regarded as one of the prime liberators of Spanish South America, San Martín was a national hero of Argentina. His father was a Spanish official in Yapeyú in the province of Corrientes, then one of Spain's colonies. San Martín was trained as a soldier in the Military Academy of Madrid and was commissioned in 1793. By 1808 he had risen to the rank of lieutenant colonel. In 1812 he left the Spanish army and returned to Argentina to fight for the revolutionaries who wanted freedom from Spanish rule. He was massively successful, and it can be argued that he was one of the most significant liberators of modern South America. His love of liberty, independence, and freedom was typically Masonic, and he was an honest and honourable man as well as an outstandingly able one.

There is a very real sense in which Freemasonry enabled South American liberator Simón Bolívar to cope with the tragedies that shrouded his short life. Born in 1783, he died of tuberculosis in 1830 when he was only forty-seven. His parents died when young Bolívar was only nine years old, and the maternal grandfather who took care of him also died shortly afterwards. An uncle then took care of him in Madrid, where Bolívar met and married the lovely Maria Teresa Rodríguez in 1802. He returned with her to Venezuela, where she died of yellow fever in 1803. Bolívar became a Freemason in Cádiz and joined the Scottish Rite in 1807. He later founded the Order and Liberty Lodge Number 2 in Peru. After Bolívar's victories in the Wars of Liberation, Bolivia was named after him. The lives of San Martín and Bolívar clearly indicate the significant role of Freemasonry in major world events.

Contemporary Indian Freemasonry can be traced back to the work of the Grand Lodge of Scotland, which appointed Brother Dr. James Burnes as provincial grand master for Western India. This development took effect in 1836 in Bombay, which is now known as Mumbai and is located in the Indian state of Maharashtra. The modern city of Mumbai has an estimated population of close to thirteen million. Burnes's Masonic jurisdiction was extended to the whole of India in 1846. Despite the wide religious differences, and occasionally the antagonism among the different major faiths of India, Indian Freemasonry attracted members who were Hindus, Muslims, Sikhs, and Parsees. Because of this phenomenon there were sometimes as many as five distinct volumes of the Sacred Law in an Indian lodge: the Koran, the *Bhagavad-Gita*, the *Granth Sahib* (also known as the *Adi Granth*, the holy book that is venerated by Sikhs), the *Zend Avesta* of Zoroastrianism, and a Christian Bible.

In 1885 the Lodge of Hope and Perseverance Number 782 in Lahore in Punjab needed a secretary. The man they appointed was the assistant editor of a local paper and the son of the curator of the Lahore Museum. He was also a Freemason and a very talented artist. That young lodge secretary was the incomparable writer Rudyard Kipling (1865–1936). One of his deeply thoughtful and perceptive Masonic poems is called "The Mother-Lodge," and it expresses so much that is a great credit to Freemasonry in India. The following extract expresses the truth about real Masonic fraternity, which ignores race, creed, and colour:

> Outside — "Sergeant! Sir! Salute! Salaam!"
> Inside — "Brother," an' it doesn't do no 'arm.
> We met upon the Level an' we parted on the Square,
> An' I was Junior Deacon in my Mother-Lodge out there!

Throughout the poem Kipling refers to his brothers in that lodge who were Jewish, Muslim, Sikh, and Christian — men of all faiths and all races brought together in harmony by the sublime ethics and morality of Freemasonry. That is one of the Craft's greatest powers as well as one of its most precious secrets.

Worldwide Freemasonry exercises its benign influence from the sun-drenched lodges of India to the unforgettable geothermal marvels of Iceland. The first recorded Icelandic Freemason was Thordur Skulason Thorlacius, who was initiated in the Zorobabel and Frederic Lodge in Copenhagen in 1817. Next was Brother Dr. Grimur Thorgrimsson Thomsen who joined in 1858. The brother known as the Father of Icelandic Freemasonry, however, was Ludvig Emil Kaaber, who became a member of the Craft in 1906. The Icelandic Lodge Edda Number 1 was instituted on January 6, 1919, and the Freemasons Order of Iceland was set up in 1951. There are eleven lodges there today.

Freemasonry is established almost literally from pole to pole and from the utmost east to the utmost west where it does more good and prevents more evil than is dreamt of by those outside the Craft. Sadly, the greatest obstacles to the innumerable benign works and acts of charity that worldwide Freemasonry carries out so generously and so willingly are the totally unwarranted, groundless, and irrational attacks made on the Craft by critics who know little or nothing about the immense good that worldwide Freemasonry does.

In the next chapter we look into the real facts behind one such attack centring on the mysterious death of Roberto Calvi, the Vatican Bank, and the organization called P2.

Chapter 24

THE VATICAN BANK, P2, AND THE ENIGMATIC DEATH OF ROBERTO CALVI

THROUGHOUT THIS book we have endeavoured to show our belief that real, true, and genuine Freemasonry is totally ethical, moral, and positive. We also consider it to be a vital power for good in a difficult and dangerous world, a world where we all need to live by those benign Masonic principles that have stood the test of time and improved human life in the past.

It cannot be denied, however, that there also seem to be a number of negative and secretive organizations that unfortunately carry quasi-Masonic labels in the public mind. There are hints and rumours of mysterious, clandestine groups that are suspected of conspiracy on an international scale. There are whispered allegations concerning powerful, hidden societies that plot and plan for their own ends against the best interests of the rest of us.

Masonic wisdom over the ages has given ample warning of them. The old Latin proverb *corruptio optimi pessima* is as true today as it was 2,000 years ago. *The corruption of the best becomes the worst.* George Bernard Shaw (1856–1950), the great Irish playwright, said: "Power does not corrupt men. Fools, however, if they get into a position of power, corrupt power." Brilliant and challenging twenty-first-century science fiction author and real-life scientist David Brin writes: "It is said that power corrupts, but actually it's more true that power attracts the corruptible. The sane are usually attracted by other things than power." In our context of real and quasi-Masonry, we would argue that the banner of potential power flutters temptingly above certain secretive, quasi-Masonic institutions where, in Brin's wise words, it attracts the corruptible. The sane seek the knowledge, truth, honesty, love, and fellowship that are the hallmarks of genuine Freemasonry.

Charles Caleb Colton (1780–1832), an expert on art, wine, and deeply meaningful aphorisms, combined the roles of clergyman, sportsman, and eccentric genius. He said that corruption was like a ball of snow: once set rolling, it inevitably increased. He also said: "Nothing so completely baffles one who is full of trick and duplicity himself than straightforward and simple integrity in another." And that is where Colton makes such a profound contribution to the debate. Genuine Freemasonry provides a fathomless reservoir of that straightforward and simple integrity that is the best possible defence against trickery and duplicity.

Propaganda Due, Italian for Propaganda Two, was founded innocently enough in 1877 as a lodge catering to Freemasons who were prevented by business travel from attending their mother lodges. Almost a century later it was quietly ticking over with fewer than twenty regular members. Then, it is reported, Licio Gelli came on the scene in the 1960s. Born in Pistoia, Italy, on April 21, 1919, Gelli became grand master of P2 and was also said to have been a prominent member of the Knights of Malta. In 1976, P2 was expelled from worldwide genuine Freemasonry, but the mud associated with P2's alleged activities has continued to stick undeservedly to genuine Freemasonry. Further appraisal of Gelli's character may be made by considering his association with the Black Shirt Brigade that Benito Mussolini sent to Spain in the late 1930s to assist Francisco Franco. Gelli, it was said, then went on to become a liaison officer with Adolf Hitler's Nazi Germany, where he met Hermann Göring in the course of his duties.

Gelli also maintained that he was a personal friend of Juan Perón, president of Argentina from 1946 to 1955 and again from 1973 to 1974. One of the strangest and seemingly most conspiratorial events connected with Perón and his hypothetical links with Gelli (and Gelli's ultimate command and alleged gross misuse of P2) was the Huemul Project for nuclear fusion. An Austro-German scientist named Ronald Richter was in charge of this atomic project taking place in Argentina with Perón's encouragement and lavish financial backing. Able, orthodox nuclear physicists saw through it and derided it, but Richter and Perón were convinced for a while that they had mastered an advanced power technology.

On March 24, 1951, Perón said "the Argentine scientist Richter ... has achieved the controlled release of nuclear fusion energy." As an interesting side note to Perón's assertion of Richter's Argentine nationality, Richter could not speak Spanish! There were also allegations that with the encouragement and help of Gelli, numerous Nazi war criminals found refuge in Argentina with Perón's tacit approval.

Perón died on July 1, 1974, and was buried in La Chacarita Cemetery in Buenos Aires, but in 1987 his tomb was desecrated and the hands were cut from his corpse. Was this the work of a weird secret society that believed in evil and sinister necromantic magical practices involving power transfers via the hands of those who had once held power?

Apart from Gelli's alleged connections with Perón and Argentina, it was also said that he was linked to the CIA. A turning point came in 1981 when the police raided Gelli's villa in Arezzo, Italy, and found a list of distinguished industrialists, financiers, journalists, and politicians, including Silvio Berlusconi. The name of Vittorio Emanuele, the Savoy dynasty claimant to the Italian throne, was also on the list. It must always be remembered that *anyone's* name could have been placed there with or without that individual's knowledge or approval. It is all too easy to *allege* that someone is a member of something with negative connotations. Political career destroyers do it all the time, and as noted earlier, when enough mud is thrown some of it tends to stick. With that caveat in mind, the *alleged* list was *said* to have included Roberto Calvi (banker), Michele Sindona (banker), Maurizio Costanzo (television personality), Massimo Donelli (television director), Angelo de Carolis (politician), Pierluigi Accornero (businessman), Alberto Vignes (Argentine minister), Guido Ruta (United States), and Randolph K. Stone (United States). And there were many more, making a total of 900 names altogether!

Gelli fled to Switzerland and was arrested attempting to withdraw millions of dollars in Geneva, but escaped and made his way to South America. He gave himself up in 1987. In 1994 he was sentenced to twelve years in jail in connection with a fraud involving the Banco Ambrosiano from which more than a billion dollars had mysteriously drained away.

There are also some very serious allegations centring on the puzzling, sudden death of Pope John Paul I, who died on September 28, 1978, after only thirty-three days of his pontificate. *Allegedly*, John Paul died of a myocardial infarction, a heart attack of the type where part of the heart muscle dies. John Paul I's real name was Albino Luciani, and he was born in Belluno, Italy, on October 17, 1912. He was ordained in 1935, consecrated as a bishop in 1958, and promoted to be patriarch of Venice in 1969. Made a cardinal in 1973, this gentle, friendly, affectionate, and characteristically smiling man was a modernist, a liberal theologian, an ecumenist, and a quietly determined church reformer. Within those first few vital days of his pontificate, it may well have become clear to those around him in the Vatican hierarchy that, from their point of view, he was an intolerable *threat*. He had sensible, liberal views on contraception, he wanted to reduce church wealth in order to help the poor, he intended to investigate and reform the Vatican Bank, and it was probably suspected by those around him who felt themselves threatened that he was going to get rid of any cardinals and archbishops who were connected with, or sympathetic to, P2.

Among supporters of the conspiracy and papal-murder theories, it was suggested that Luciani had been elected pope because he was thought (wrongly!) to be such a weak and gentle man that the P2 cardinals and other alleged Vatican officers could easily either ignore him or control him. It was further theorized that when they found to their dismay that they could *not* control him, they had recourse to murdering him instead.

Thorough, painstaking, and fearless — a credit to his profession — English investigative author David Yallop has produced an outstanding book on the mystery of Luciani's sudden, unaccountable death. Entitled *In God's Name*, it goes through every stage of what Yallop sees as a sequence of cunning lies and sinister cover-ups. He asks a number of searching and unanswerable questions. Why was there such a mad rush to get John Paul I embalmed? It is apparent that a Vatican car was dispatched *immediately* to fetch the embalmers. Why was Sister Vincenza, who found the pope's corpse, apparently instructed to *say* she found the pope dead in bed when in another version she allegedly found his body in the bathroom? Why had his spectacles and slippers vanished? Why was Dr. Buzzonati called in to pronounce the cause of death instead of Professor Fontana, who was head of the Vatican Medical Services? It may also be pertinent to ask *why* members of Luciani's family reported that he was in good health, and *how*, if he had been frail and liable to die of natural causes, he had satisfactorily passed a Vatican medical examination just a few days before his sudden death.

The murder-conspiracy theorists suggest that it was Cardinal Villot who gave Luciani the fatal dose of digitalis. Sister Vincenza was told to say nothing about the pope's body being found in the bathroom in case it looked as though whatever had killed him had taken effect soon after his drink with Cardinal Villot.

From the very suspicious-looking death of Pope John Paul I and its possible connections with P2, the trail moves to the indisputable murder of Roberto Calvi, who was almost certainly associated with P2. On June 11, 1982, Roberto Calvi, chairman of Banco Ambrosiano and one of the powerful, influential people listed as members of P2, left Italy with a mysterious black briefcase. On the morning of June 18 the London River Police cut down his body from the scaffolding below Blackfriars Bridge. This location was significant. Black friars had special connotations with members of P2. Calvi's pockets and the front of his trousers were stuffed with bricks and several thousand pounds in cash. His feet were above the water as he hung there suspended on an orange rope. An autopsy revealed no river water in his lungs, and his neck wasn't damaged the way it would have been if he had jumped. Almost unbelievably the first inquest on him, held in July, came up with a verdict of *suicide*! The cash and his expensive watch, still on his wrist when he was found, clearly indicated that robbery wasn't the motive for his bizarre murder.

Carlo Calvi, the dead man's only son, was determined to do everything possible to find out the truth about what had happened to his father. He hired the Kroll detective agency to do everything they could, and part of their very thorough investigation involved a re-enactment of the movements along the route to the scaffolding from which Calvi's body had been suspended. A stand-in of Calvi's height and weight repeated the trip many times, each time picking up paint traces from the scaffolding on the soles of his shoes. *There had been no such traces on Calvi's shoes*. After much long and careful investigation, Kroll considered that the most likely scenario was that the killers had strangled Calvi elsewhere and brought his body to Blackfriars Bridge in a small boat. They had then fastened him to the scaffolding and weighted him with bricks to keep the body vertical when the tide rose and fell.

The story is far from over. On October 5, 2005, in an Italian court, a group of suspects was charged with Calvi's murder.

What then of the Vatican Bank, the name often given to IOR, which stands for *Instituto per le Opere di Religione*, translating as the Institute for Religious Works? It is the central bank for the Roman Catholic Church and has its headquarters inside Vatican City. Some of the charges and accusations levelled against it have included collusion with the Nazi governments in Germany and Croatia before the fall of Adolf Hitler. Was it Pope John Paul I's decision to investigate and clean up IOR that contributed to the alleged conspiratorial decision to murder him? IOR was certainly involved, seemingly as a financial victim, in the monetary disasters of Banco Ambrosiano that Calvi had once led.

In concluding this chapter it needs to be made very clear indeed that although P2 may have had its innocent origins among orthodox Freemasonry, the dark rumours and legends surrounding it are about as far from true Freemasonry as it is possible to get. Consider this allegory. A good, generous, law-abiding citizen named Tom Smith is accused of various unpleasant crimes of which he is entirely innocent *because a cunning, unprincipled criminal has stolen his identity*. Because a dishonest, dangerous, conspiratorial group furthers its devious criminal plots by calling itself the South Wales Anti-Litter Society or the Chicago Street-Cleaning Volunteers, it most certainly does *not* mean that public-spirited volunteers who give their time and effort to make our streets cleaner and more hygienic are criminals. There is no finer or more honourable name than that of a true and genuine Freemason. Groups like P2 should never be associated with real Masonry, whatever such groups call themselves.

Chapter 25

MASONRY TODAY

FREEMASONRY TODAY is partly reflected in the power and prestige of its outstanding members past and present. An exceptionally good website, *www.durham.net/~cedar/famous.html*, contains an extensive and well-researched list. The following very short A to Z summary, however, makes the point sufficiently clearly. It includes outstanding Masonic brethren from all walks of life whose personalities and successes are typical of members of the Craft:

- Buzz Aldrin, astronaut, Montclair Lodge Number 144, New Jersey
- Louis Armstrong, musician, Lodge of Montgomery Number 18, New York
- Kemal Mustapha Ataturk, president of Turkey, 1923 to 1938, Macedonia Resorta e Veritas Lodge
- Gene Autry, western film star, Catoosa Lodge Number 185, Oklahoma
- Irving Berlin, songwriter, Munn Lodge Number 190, New York
- Ernest Borgnine, actor and film star, Abingdon Lodge Number 48, Virginia
- Robert Burns, Scottish poet, St. David's Lodge Number 174, Tarbolton, Ayrshire, Scotland
- William F. Cody, better known as Buffalo Bill, Platte Valley Lodge Number 32, Nebraska
- Edward VII, king of Britain, grand master of the United Grand Lodge of England, also provincial grand master for Lower Canada

- Edward VIII, king of Britain, Household Brigade Lodge Number 2614, grand master of the United Grand Lodge of England
- George VI, king of Britain, past grand master, initiated into Naval Lodge Number 2612
- William S. Gilbert, co-composer of the Gilbert and Sullivan operettas, St. Michar Lodge Number 54, Scotland
- Douglas MacArthur, Nile Shrine Temple, Seattle, Washington
- Derwyn T. Owen, archbishop of Toronto and primate of Canada, Ionic Lodge Number 25, Toronto, Ontario
- Roy Rogers, western film star, Hollywood Lodge Number 355, California
- Franklin D. Roosevelt, U.S. president, Holland Lodge Number 8, New York
- Robert Falcon Scott, polar explorer, Drury Lane Lodge Number 2127, London, United Kingdom
- Richard "Red" Skelton, film and television star, Vincennes Lodge Number 1, Vincennes, Indiana
- William B. Travis, Alamo hero, Alabama Lodge Number 3, Claiborne, Alabama
- Harry S. Truman, U.S. president, Belton Lodge Number 450, Belton, Missouri
- John Wayne, film star, Marion McDaniel Lodge Number 56, Tucson, Arizona
- Matthew Webb, English Channel swimmer, Neptune Lodge Number 22
- Steve Wozniak, co-founder of Apple Computers, Charity Lodge Number 362, California
- Florenz Ziegfeld, show business producer, Accordia Lodge Number 277, Chicago, Illinois

Throughout our research we have contended that the earliest dawn of Freemasonry was full of very curious mysteries, possibly stranger than we can imagine. J.B.S. Haldane (1892–1964) said: "The universe is not only queerer than we suppose, but queerer than we are *able* to suppose." Albert Einstein once said: "There are only two ways to live your life: one is as though *nothing* is a miracle; the other is as though *every-thing* is a miracle." He also said: "Imagination is more important than knowledge. Knowledge is limited. Imagination encircles the world."

We would argue that any real understanding of the beginning of Freemasonry has to combine the wisdom of Haldane and Einstein. It needs an awareness that there may well be mysteries that transcend human comprehension and that imagination may carry us farther than our present level of knowledge can.

Freemasonry, we would contend, is an essential instrument for improving and protecting humanity, for safeguarding our freedom, and for storing and using skill and knowledge, some of which may well have been brought to this planet from *elsewhere* long ago. We would also speculate, as we did in our previous Dundurn book, *Mysteries and Secrets of the Templars*, that there are five great universal enigmas wrapped in the kind of allegories that Freemasonry loves.

The first is the mysterious Ark of the Covenant. It seems to have been both a power source and a means of communication to *some-where outside*. Did the earliest proto-Masons create it and leave it in Egypt? Did they instruct Moses to take it with him when he led his people to freedom?

The second mystery is the so-called Spear of Destiny, taken over by Christian tradition as the Spear of Longinus, a Roman soldier present at the crucifixion. But a magical spear-like weapon features in ancient myths and legends that predate the Christian era by millennia. Sometimes it is referred to as a sword rather than a spear: it can pierce the scales of dragons and slice through chains binding hostages to the rocks where they await sacrifice.

The third mystery is the cornucopia, the source of plenty, an artifact that seems able to change energy into matter so that it can provide whatever is requested. It has links with Aladdin's genie in the ancient stories — the providing mystery. It also has connections with some versions of the Holy Grail legends.

The fourth mystery is something frequently described as a magical cloak. It has the power of flight and of invisibility. The fifth mystery concerns the Emerald Tablets of Hermes Trismegistus, precious stones that contained vast quantities of wisdom and knowledge and were also believed to hold the power of glimpsing the future. Did they also feature as the *urim* and *thummim*, the enigmatic stones that enabled the Hebrew high priests to foresee what was to come?

If, for the sake of argument, we look for the *allegorical* sense of each of these mysteries, we may find highly moral and ethical Masonic secrets revealed there, as well. Freemasonry teaches that good, clear, and adequate *communication* is one of the world's greatest needs. So many problems arise simply because we do not fully understand one another. Freemasonry is permanently at war with greed, corruption, oppression, and exploitation wherever and whenever they are found.

The *weapon* that destroys evil and sets prisoners free is more often a metaphorical one than a physical one today. This *weapon* is the honest and fearless Freemason's willingness to stand up and be counted and to speak out and take action against whatever is wrong, unfair, and unjust in the world. The *cloak* represents swift movement and invisibility. There are times when wrongs have to be righted by moving swiftly and secretly to put matters right. The *cornucopia* provides food and drink for the hungry and thirsty. It is metaphorical generosity and charity. This is another great strength of Freemasonry — it supplies money and help to the needy. It is a very charitable organization. The *precious stones*, perhaps in their later guise as *urim* and *thummim*, look to the future. So does Freemasonry. The environment, the dangers of global warming, the need for education and provision for scientific research, especially in medicine, are all part of the "futurology" of Freemasonry. It is part of Masonic morality and ethics today to plan for a better world tomorrow.

BIBLIOGRAPHY

Andrews, William. *Antiquities and Curiosities of the Church*. London: William Andrews & Company, 1897.

_____. *The Church Treasury*. London: William Andrews & Company, 1898.

_____. *Curiosities of the Church*. London: Methuen & Co., 1890.

_____. *Curious Church Customs*. London: Simpkin, Marshall, Hamilton, Kent, 1895.

_____. *Old Church Life*. London: William Andrews & Company, 1900.

_____. *Old Church Lore*. London: Simpkin, Marshall, Hamilton, Kent, 1891.

Bartlett, W.B. *God Wills It! An Illustrated History of the Crusades*. London: Sutton Publishing, 1999.

Boudet, Henri. *La Vraie Langue Celtique et le Cromleck de Rennes-les-Bains*. Nice, France: Belisane, 1984 reprint.

Brooke, Christopher. *Europe in the Central Middle Ages 962–1154*. London: Pearson Education, 2000.

Buren, Elizabeth Van. *The Dragon of Rennes-le-Château*. Vogels, France: 1998.

Burstein, Dan, ed. *Secrets of the Code*. London: Orion Books, 2005.

Cavendish, Richard, ed. *Encyclopaedia of the Unexplained*. London: Routledge & Kegan Paul, 1974.

Clapp, Nicholas. *Sheba: Through the Desert in Search of the Legendary Queen*. Boston: Houghton Mifflin, 2001.

Clark, Jerome. *Unexplained! 347 Strange Sightings, Incredible Occurrences, and Puzzling Phenomena*. Detroit: Invisible Ink, 1993.

Cruz, Joan Carroll. *Relics*. Huntington, IN: Our Sunday Visitor, 1983.

Dunford, Barry. *The Holy Land of Scotland*. Scotland: Brigadoon Books, 1996.

Duren van Bander, Peter. *Orders of Knighthood and of Merit*. Gerrards Cross, Eng.: Colin Smythe, 1995.

Edgington, Susan B., and Sarah Lambert, eds. *Gendering the Crusades*. Cardiff, Wales: University of Wales Press, 2001.

Encyclopaedia Britannica. Britannica Online: *www.eb.com*.

Evans, Joan. *Life in Medieval France*. London: Phaidon, 1957.

Eysenck, H.J., and Carl Sargent. *Explaining the Unexplained*. London: BCA, 1993.

Fanthorpe, Lionel, and Patricia Fanthorpe. *Mysteries of the Bible*. Toronto: Dundurn, 1999.

____. *Mysteries and Secrets of the Templars*. Toronto: Dundurn, 2005.

____. *Mysteries of Templar Treasure and the Holy Grail*. Boston: Red Wheel/Samuel Weiser, 2004.

_____. *The Oak Island Mystery*. Toronto: Dundurn, 1995.

_____. *Secrets of Rennes-le-Château*. Boston: Samuel Weiser, 1992.

_____. *Unsolved Mysteries of the Sea*. Toronto: Dundurn, 2004.

_____. *The World's Greatest Unsolved Mysteries*. Toronto: Dundurn, 1997.

_____. *The World's Most Mysterious Castles*. Toronto: Dundurn, 2005.

_____. *The World's Most Mysterious Murders*. Toronto. Dundurn, 2003.

_____. *The World's Most Mysterious Objects*. Toronto: Dundurn, 2002.

_____. *The World's Most Mysterious People*. Toronto: Dundurn, 1998.

_____. *The World's Most Mysterious Places*. Toronto: Dundurn, 1999.

Fanthorpe, Patricia, and Lionel Fanthorpe. *The Holy Grail Revealed*. Hollywood, CA: Newcastle Publishing, 1982.

Frayling, Christopher. *Strange Landscape: A Journey Through the Middle Ages*. London: BBC Books, 1995.

Friedlander, Noam. *What Is Opus Dei?* London: Collins and Brown, 2005.

Godart, Louis. *The Phaistos Disc*. Itanos Publications, 1995.

Green, Jim. *Holy Ways of Wales*. Talybont, Ceredigion, Wales: Y Lolfa Cyf., 2000.

Guerber, H.A. *Myths and Legends of the Middle Ages*. London: Studio Editions, 1994.

Guirdham, Arthur. *The Cathars and Reincarnation*. Wheaton, IL: Theosophical Publishing House, 1978.

____. *The Lake and the Castle*. London: Cygnus Books, 1992.

____. *We Are One Another*. London: Cygnus Books, 1992.

Hieronimus, Dr. Robert. *American's Secret Destiny*. Rochester, VT: Destiny Books, 1989.

Higenbottam, Frank. *Codes and Ciphers*. London: English Universities Press, 1973.

Jackson, Keith B. *Beyond the Craft*. London: Lewis Masonic, 1991.

Knight, Christopher, and Robert Lomas. *The Hiram Key*. London: Century, 1996.

Lomas, Robert. *The Invisible College*. London: Headline Book Publishing, 2002.

Mack, Lorrie, et al, eds. *The Unexplained*. London: Orbis, 1984.

Massingham, Hugh, and Pauline Massingham. *The London Anthology*. London: Phoenix House, 1950.

Matthews, Caitlin. *Sophia, Goddess of Wisdom: The Divine Feminine from Black Goddess to World-Soul*. London: HarperCollins, 1991.

Neil, William. *The Bible as History*. London: Lion/SPCK Book, 1991.

Nicholas, M. *The World's Greatest Psychics and Mystics*. London: Hamlyn Publishing Group, 1994.

Page, R.I. *Reading the Runes*. London: Trustees of the British Museum, 1987.

Playfair, G.L. *The Unknown Power*. London: Granada Publishing, 1977.

Potts, Mrs. Henry. *Francis Bacon and His Secret Society*. London: Sampson, Low, Marston, 1891.

Reader's Digest Book. *Folklore, Myths and Legends of Britain*. London: The Reader's Digest Association, 1973.

_____. *Strange Stories, Amazing Facts*. London: The Reader's Digest Association, 1975.

Riley-Smith, Jonathan, ed. *The Oxford Illustrated History of the Crusades*. Oxford: Oxford University Press, 1995.

Rolleston, T.W. *Celtic Myths and Legends*. London: Studio Editions, 1994.

Runciman, Steven. *The First Crusade*. Cambridge: Cambridge University Press, 1980.

Russell, Eric Frank. *Great World Mysteries*. London: Mayflower, 1967.

Saltzman, Pauline. *The Strange and the Supernormal*. New York: Paperback Library, 1968.

Sharper Knowlson, T. *The Origins of Popular Superstitions and Customs*. London: Studio Editions, 1995.

Sinclair, Andrew. *The Sword and the Grail*. London: Century, 1993.

Singh, Simon. *The Cracking Codebook*. London: HarperCollins, 2001.

Smail, R.C. *The Crusaders in Syria and the Holy Land*. London: Thames and Hudson, 1973.

Spencer, John, and Anne Spencer. *The Encyclopaedia of the World's Greatest Unsolved Mysteries*. London: Headline Book Publishing, 1995.

Target, George. *Holy Ground*. London: Bishopsgate Press, 1986.

Truman, Margaret. *Harry S. Truman*. London: Hamish Hamilton, 1973.

Tyack, Reverend George S. *Lore and Legend of the English Church*. London: William Andrews & Company, 1899.

Whalen, William J. *Christianity and American Freemasonry*. Milwaukee, WI: Bruce Publishing Company, 1958.

Wilmshurst, W.L. *The Meaning of Masonry*. New York: Gramercy Books, 1980.

Yallop, David. *In God's Name*. London: Corgi, 1987.

Young, George. *Ancient Peoples and Modern Ghosts*. Queensland, Nova Scotia: George Young, 1991.

How to
WIN IN A VOLATILE STOCK MARKET

How to
WIN IN A VOLATILE STOCK MARKET

The Definitive Guide to Investment Bargain Hunting

ALEXANDER DAVIDSON

**KOGAN
PAGE**

For Natasha and Ilia
With all my love

First published 2000

Kogan Page Limited
120 Pentonville Road
London N1 9JN

British Library Cataloguing in Publication Data

A CIP record for this book is available from the British Library.

ISBN 0 7494 3360 4

Typeset by Jean Cussons Typesetting, Diss, Norfolk
Printed and bound in Great Britain by Clays Ltd, St Ives plc